The Philosophy of
Merleau-Ponty

Continental European Philosophy

This series provides accessible and stimulating introductions to the ideas of continental thinkers who have shaped the fundamentals of European philosophical thought. Powerful and radical, the ideas of these philosophers have often been contested, but they remain key to understanding current philosophical thinking as well as the current direction of disciplines such as political science, literary theory, comparative literature, art history, and cultural studies. Each book seeks to combine clarity with depth, introducing fresh insights and wider perspectives while also providing a comprehensive survey of each thinker's philosophical ideas.

Forthcoming titles include

The Philosophy of Deleuze
Peter Sedgwick

The Philosophy of Derrida
Mark Dooley

The Philosophy of Gadamer
Jean Grondin

The Philosophy of Habermas
Andrew Edgar

The Philosophy of Husserl
Burt Hopkins

The Philosophy of Kant
Jim O'Shea

The Philosophy of Nietzsche
Rex Welshon

The Philosophy of Sartre
Anthony Hatzimoysis

The Philosophy of Merleau-Ponty

Eric Matthews

McGill-Queen's University Press
Montreal & Kingston • Ithaca

For Philip and Stephen

ISBN 0-7735-2383-9 (hardcover)
ISBN 0-7735-2384-7 (paperback)

Legal deposit second quarter 2002
Bibliothèque nationale du Québec

Published simultaneously outside North America
by Acumen Publishing Limited

McGill-Queen's University Press acknowledges the financial support of
the Government of Canada through the Book Publishing Development
Program (BPIDP) for its activities.

National Library of Canada Cataloguing in Publication Data

Matthews, Eric, 1936-
    The philosophy of Merleau-Ponty

(Continental European philosophy)
Includes bibliographical references and index.
ISBN 0-7735-2383-9 (bound).—ISBN 0-7735-2384-7 (pbk.)

1. Merleau-Ponty, Maurice, 1908-1961. I. Title. II. Series.

B2430.M3764M374 2002   194   C2002-900724-0

Designed and typeset by Kate Williams, Abergavenny.
Printed and bound by Biddles Ltd., Guildford and King's Lynn.

Contents

Acknowledgements

I have been an enthusiast for Merleau-Ponty's philosophy almost since I have been interested in philosophy at all, and have benefited from discussions of his thought with too many colleagues and students to mention individually. I do wish, however, to express my particular gratitude to a current doctoral student, Martin Wylie, who has read most of this book in draft form and helped me greatly by his acute comments on it. I am grateful also to the two publisher's readers for their constructive comments on the first draft of the book.

Thanks should also be expressed to Northwestern University Press for kind permission to quote from the following works to which they hold the rights: Merleau-Ponty, *Adventures of the Dialectic*, J. Bien (trans.); J. Stewart (ed.), *The Debate between Sartre and Merleau-Ponty*; Merleau-Ponty, *In Praise of Philosophy and Other Essays*, J. Wild, J. Edie and J. O'Neill (trans.); J. Edie (ed.), Merleau-Ponty, *The Primacy of Perception and Other Essays*; Merleau-Ponty, *The Prose of the World*, J. O'Neill (trans.); Merleau-Ponty, *Sense and Non-Sense*, H. L. Dreyfus and P. A. Dreyfus (trans.); Merleau-Ponty, *Signs*, R. C. McCleary (trans.); Merleau-Ponty, *The Visible and the Invisible*, A. Lingis (trans.). I am also grateful to Routledge for permission to quote from the following works published by them: Merleau-Ponty, *Phenomenology of Perception*, Colin Smith (trans.), with revisions by Forrest Williams and David Gurrière; J.-P. Sartre, *Being and Nothingness*, Hazel Barnes (trans.).

Full publishing details of all the works listed above are given in the Bibliography at the end of the book.

CHAPTER ONE

Merleau-Ponty in Context

I

Why should we still read Merleau-Ponty? He died, after all, in 1961, at a time when the social and cultural situation and the preoccupations of philosophers were very different from those of the end of the twentieth century and the beginning of a new millennium. Is he not simply a representative of a now outmoded "humanism", a philosophy of the "subject" and of the phenomenology of consciousness? That he was a humanist in some sense of that rather vague word is undeniable; he was certainly concerned to affirm human values and believed that there are such values to affirm. But he was not, as I shall try to show in the course of the book, a "humanist" in the sense in which that term is often used pejoratively by some of his "posthumanist" successors, such as Foucault and Althusser. That is, although he stressed the importance of the subject, he was not a defender of the Enlightenment conception of a human subjectivity that is independent of the physical, social and historical situation of the human being concerned. "Humanism" in this sense is sometimes associated by its critics with phenomenology and, clearly, Merleau-Ponty was a phenomenologist. But his "existential" interpretation of what that means, as again I shall try to show, was far from identifying it with a philosophy of the transcendental subject and a description of that subject's inner consciousness.

Merleau-Ponty certainly learned from other philosophers, from Hegel, from Bergson, from Marcel, from Heidegger, from Sartre and, above all, from Husserl. But he combined elements from different thinkers (in ways that went beyond mere eclecticism) and added new elements, such as his study of Gestalt psychology, contemporary neurophysiology and Freudian psychoanalysis and ideas derived from his political commitment to a humanistic Marxism, to make from this material something that was entirely his own. The result was something that often seems to belong more to our time than to the time when he was writing. His discussion of the relation between the neurophysiology of the brain and human mental life, for example, despite the necessarily out-of-date science on which it is based, has a clear relevance to recent debates between thinkers in the analytic tradition, such as Searle, Putnam, Dennett and the Churchlands; at appropriate places in this book I shall try to demonstrate how it is relevant. In a different direction, I shall suggest that his questioning of the sharp distinction between "subject" and "object" of experience points forwards to the "decentring of the subject" in more recent French philosophy.

In short, this book is an attempt to present Merleau-Ponty not as a mere figure from the history of philosophy, but as a participant in continuing debates about what it means to be human, about the relations between individual human beings and between individuals and society, about language, art and expression, about the relation between science, common experience and philosophy, about the nature of time and history, and about the possibilities for human progress. Any discussion of his thought can therefore succeed only if it takes him as such a participant. It is not sufficient (although it is necessary) to explain what he says in terms of his influences; he must also be subjected to the kind of critical analysis that he would have to face if he were literally here among us, engaging in the contemporary arguments. Before we begin this analysis, however, it will be useful to place him in his own historical context and to exhibit the general interconnections between his ideas; this outline will then make it easier to follow the more detailed discussions of the succeeding chapters.

II

Maurice Merleau-Ponty was born in 1908, in Rochefort sur Mer, in the *département* of Charente-Maritime, in the far west of France. He was one of three children of an artillery officer who died in 1913; thus he, together with his brother and sister, was brought up by his widowed mother alone. Nevertheless, as Jean-Paul Sartre relates in his memoir "Merleau-Ponty *vivant*", in 1947 Merleau-Ponty described his childhood as "incomparable", and said indeed that "he had never recovered from" it.[1] He went to school in Paris, at the Lycée Janson-de-Sailly and the Lycée Louis-le-Grand, and entered the École Normale Supérieure to study philosophy in 1926. It was at the École Normale that he first met Sartre and Simone de Beauvoir; Sartre says of their relationship at that time, "we knew each other without being friends".[2] (Later, during the Occupation, they were to become much closer to each other, with significant effects on Merleau-Ponty's life and thought.) During that time, too, he attended Georges Gurvitch's lectures on the phenomenology of Husserl, Scheler and Heidegger, and the lectures that Husserl himself gave in Paris in 1929.

After graduating with the *agrégation en philosophie* (the qualification desirable to teach philosophy in French schools) in 1930, and completing his year of compulsory military service, Merleau-Ponty taught philosophy in *lycées* (secondary schools) for the next few years, apart from taking a year out to do research in perception. In 1935, he returned to the École Normale as a tutor and remained there until the outbreak of the Second World War. Until this time he seems to have been a Left-wing Catholic (Simone de Beauvoir remembers that he still attended Mass while a student at the École Normale), but he left the Church in the late 1930s in disgust at the attitudes of many in the Catholic hierarchy to Left-wing activity. Thereafter, he was always positioned somewhere to the left of centre politically, although he could never bring himself to the point of joining the French Communist Party, as some other leftist French intellectuals did at the time. He did, however, develop an increasing interest in Marxism, marked, for example, by his attendance at the lectures on Hegel given by Alexandre Kojève in Paris in the late 1930s, in which Kojève presented what was effectively a Hegelianized or humanistic Marxism. This was to have a profound effect on Merleau-Ponty's own thinking, not only about political theory, but also about the wider questions of the historicity of human existence.

But the most important intellectual development at that time was Merleau-Ponty's discovery of the later thought of Husserl. He had already heard from Husserl's own lips, as well as from Gurvitch's lectures, about the earlier version of phenomenology. Having read about Husserl's later development in a journal article, Merleau-Ponty went to the Husserl Archive in Louvain in Belgium to read and study the later works of Husserl, which were then unpublished; much of this work was published after Husserl's death, most notably as the second part of the work often referred to as the "*Crisis*-volume", the *Crisis of European Sciences and Transcendental Phenomenology*.[3] This reading convinced Merleau-Ponty that, in his later doctrine of the "life-world", Husserl's conception of philosophy had taken a decisive new turn; it was this later version that was to shape Merleau-Ponty's own conception of phenomenology, as we shall see in Chapter 2.

Hegel, filtered through the young Marx (or, what amounts to the same, a younger Marx seen through Hegelian spectacles), and a certain reading of the later Husserl were two of the most important influences on

Merleau-Ponty's own thinking. What other influences helped to shape him intellectually? One, inevitably, was the French Cartesian tradition, with which Husserl had sought to connect his own phenomenology in the Paris lectures (which were published under the title *Cartesian Meditations*), but Merleau-Ponty was influenced by this only in the negative sense that he reacted against it. Another was the prevailing Kantianism of his teachers at the École Normale (and of others in the contemporary French philosophical establishment); his principal teacher there was the idealist Léon Brunschvicg, whose own thought was strongly influenced by Kant. Here again, however, the relevance of this tradition to Merleau-Ponty's thinking was largely negative, as we shall see in Chapter 3.

Another philosopher who influenced him, Henri Bergson, was still alive and publishing when Merleau-Ponty was a young tutor in the 1930s. Merleau-Ponty was later to be elected, as Bergson had been, to a chair at the Collège de France, and makes appropriately respectful comments on his philosophy in his inaugural lecture there (published in book form as *In Praise of Philosophy*[4]). For all this, all that Merleau-Ponty seems to have taken from Bergson (important though it is) is the insistence on starting from immediate experience rather than from theoretical explanations of it, which reinforced the lessons derived from his reading of Husserl's phenomenology. (In his inaugural lecture, Merleau-Ponty speaks approvingly of Bergson's view that philosophy "cannot be a judgment given from on high on life, the world, history…".[5]) Merleau-Ponty rejected the Bergsonian idea of a deep "inner self" which is the "real me", and criticized rather unfairly Bergson's views on "duration", the temporality of inner experience. Another French philosopher who was more of a contemporary was Gabriel Marcel; indeed, one of Merleau-Ponty's first published works was a review of Marcel's *Being and Having* in the Catholic journal *La Vie intellectuelle*. It was in Marcel that Merleau-Ponty found what was to be one of his own key ideas – that our subjectivity is essentially *embodied* or *incarnate*. He also shared Marcel's Bergsonian conception of philosophy as "concrete". But Marcel's presentation of these ideas, as of his philosophy generally, was much more literary and discursive than Merleau-Ponty's, and correspondingly much less analytic and related to contemporary science.

Heidegger had featured in Gurvitch's lectures on recent German philosophy, and in this sense must have entered Merleau-Ponty's philosophical consciousness. But there are not many explicit references to him, at any rate in Merleau-Ponty's earlier writings; we can infer an influence mainly from circumstantial evidence, such as the use of the central Heideggerian term "being-in-the-world" as a similarly central concept in Merleau-Ponty's thought, and the discussions of Being and recognition of the need for an ontology as well as a phenomenology in the posthumously published late works such as *The Visible and the Invisible*. (Similarities to and differences from a Heideggerian treatment of these themes will be considered below in the relevant chapters.)

And then there was the mass of scientific literature, in physiology, psychology and psychiatry, which Merleau-Ponty had worked through in his researches on perception, for instance, and to whose findings he gave his own interpretation based on his philosophical perspective. All this work features prominently in Merleau-Ponty's first book, *The Structure of Behaviour*, which was in effect his doctoral thesis, completed in 1938 but published in book form only in 1942. The purpose of this book, as he declares in the Introduction, is "to understand the relations of consciousness and nature: organic, psychological or even social".[6] By nature, as Merleau-Ponty goes on to explain, he means "a multiplicity of events external to each other and bound together by relations of causality". The work is essentially a critique, not of scientific psychology as such, but of a certain misguided *philosophical* conception of what a "scientific" psychology has to be like. The philosophy of psychology that Merleau-Ponty opposes is a dualistic conception that opposes "the mental" and "the physiological" as two orders of reality that are external to each other and so can be only causally related.

Given that conception, there seem to be only three possible ways to make psychology scientific. One is to follow the way of classical materialism: to make the "mind" another kind of object in the world, in effect identified with the brain, and thus to treat psychology as identical with the study of brain processes and the causal relations between them and between what happens in the brain and what happens in the rest of the body. Another, which Merleau-Ponty describes as "critical thought", is to distinguish between "analytic psychology", the study of the conscious judgements that we make, and the study of bodily mechanisms. The third is the way of Watsonian behaviourism or Pavlovian reflex theory, the identification of "the mental", at least as an object of scientific study, with the external behaviour that manifests our thoughts and feelings, and the interpretation of that behaviour as simply equivalent to physiological movements, so that it could be studied and understood in purely causal terms. The last-mentioned approach is explicitly non-dualist, since it does not appear to recognize "the mental" as a separate objective domain from "the physiological". Nevertheless, it shares the dualist assumption that the term "mind" can have an independent reference only if it denotes an entity separate from anything physiological, where an entity is something that can stand in causal relations to other entities. Since behaviourists can identify no such separate entity, they identify the mental with physiological movements.

The assumption that is common to all three approaches is what Merleau-Ponty calls "realistic analysis and causal thinking": the belief that consciousness, or the mental, can be taken seriously as a reality only if it can be considered an object in the world, separate from other objects, such as the body, and standing in causal relations to them. This is the assumption that his critique seeks to challenge. His method is to analyse the fundamental notion of "behaviour" itself, to show that it cannot be equated with purely physiological movements that might be explained in a straightforwardly causal fashion. The very facts cited by psychologists themselves, he argues, require for their explanation notions of "form", "structure" and "intention", which do not fit with such a mechanistic conception of behaviour. These established findings of psychology are described in abundance and analysed in intricate detail. His reliance in this early work is on the concepts of Gestalt psychology, which emphasizes such notions of form or structure. The word "phenomenology" hardly appears at all, but there are hints of the phenomenological approach of the later works, for instance, in starting from our actual experience of our own behaviour, which seems to require for its description and understanding notions of intention and meaning.

III

By the time *The Structure of Behaviour* finally appeared in print, the Second World War had broken out, Merleau-Ponty had been mobilized as an infantry officer and France had fallen and had been partially occupied by the German forces; Merleau-Ponty had thereupon been demobilized and had returned to teaching philosophy in the Lycée Carnot in Paris. Later in the war, in 1944, he moved to the Lycée Condorcet, where he succeeded Sartre. He had renewed his acquaintance with Sartre in 1941, when Merleau-Ponty had joined a small Resistance group called *Socialisme et Liberté* (Socialism and Liberty), to which Sartre already belonged. It was, as Sartre admitted, a group of *petit bourgeois* intellectuals, enthusiastic but not terribly effective, which "caught a fever and died a year later, of not knowing what to do".[7] But it did have the effect, as Sartre also says, of bringing the two men closer together than they had been before, and from then on they had a close, if sometimes stormy, relationship, both philosophical and political. Philosophically, Sartre says,

The key words were spoken: phenomenology, existence. We discovered our real concern. Too individualist to ever pool our research, we became reciprocal while remaining separate. Alone, each of us was too easily persuaded of having understood the idea of phenomenology. Together, we were, for each other, the incarnation of its ambiguity.[8]

This wryly humorous and affectionate characterization of their philosophical relationship, and of the similarities and differences between them in their interpretations of existential phenomenology, is also accurate.

Merleau-Ponty's developing interest in Husserlian phenomenology, and in particular the thought of Husserl's late period, which had really begun in the late 1930s, continued throughout this wartime period, and was no doubt stimulated further by his discussions and disagreements with Sartre. He applied it, above all, to thinking about perception – work that was embodied in his principal doctoral thesis, entitled *Phenomenology of Perception*, published in book form in 1945 and generally agreed to be his masterpiece. In later chapters we shall return, as relevant, to the details of Merleau-Ponty's argument in this work, but here, by way of introduction, we can try to offer a general view of some of its main themes.

Phenomenology of Perception is philosophically a much richer and more wide-ranging work than *The Structure of Behaviour*. In the first few chapters, Merleau-Ponty argues for a broad, phenomenologically based, concept of perception that equates it, not with a detached awareness of objects, but with our active involvement with our world, and against those concepts that are based, not on a phenomenological account of what our experience is actually like, but on assumptions about what it *must* be like. In particular, he focuses on two views that are opposed to each other in their conclusions but share certain common assumptions.

On the one hand, there is a realist empiricism, which assumes that the perceiving subject is one object among others in the world, causally acted upon by those other objects in ways that are covered by the laws of natural science. Perceptual experience is then described, not as we actually find it, but as science tells us it must be: it consists of discrete "sensations", each corresponding to a quality in the object that causes it, and each without meaning of any kind or necessary connection with any other sensation. Empiricism in this sense clearly fails to account for the unity and connectedness of our experience, and it is this that motivates the opposing view, which Merleau-Ponty calls "intellectualism". Intellectualism is an idealist view, which Merleau-Ponty sees instantiated in such thinkers as Descartes and Kant. For the intellectualist, the structures that give unity to our experience are imposed on it by our own minds. In effect, perception is equated with *thought about* perception; the units of experience are not, as they are for the empiricist, meaningless sensations, but the judgements that we make about those sensations, in which the sensations provide the "matter" that is given "form" by the structure of the judgement. But both empiricist and intellectualist share the common assumption that experience cannot contain its structure or form *in itself*, that it can have such structure only if our minds impose it upon a formless matter of sensation.

As we shall see in Chapter 2, a phenomenological approach to perception, according to Merleau-Ponty's interpretation, requires us to start by describing perception as we actually experience it, before we begin to theorize. Both empiricism and intellectualism, in their different ways, start from the wrong end, from the scientific theories that we devise in order to *explain* that pre-theoretical experience. A phenomenological description of perceptual experience, by contrast, will show it to be, in Merleau-Ponty's words, "that vital communication with the world which makes it present as a familiar setting of our life".[9] On this view, the world of objects is not something apart from us as subjects, acting upon us causally, but the place we as subjects *inhabit*. Its unity and meaning for us come from the fact that we live and act and move about in it; and in turn our being is, in the Heideggerian phrase that Merleau-Ponty adopted, "being-in-the-world". So the account of perception that Merleau-Ponty defends implies a view about the inseparability of subject and world.

A subject that is essentially "in-the-world" is necessarily *embodied*, for only a subject that is inseparable from a particular body can have a place in the world, in space and in time. A body-subject, as it were, "looks out on" the world from a particular perspective, from a "here'" and a "now". Such a subject cannot be identified with a pure reason or a pure consciousness, able to take in the whole of reality at once and make sense of it as a whole. The real world stretches out beyond what we can perceive of it, and is, to use one of Merleau-Ponty's words, "inexhaustible". Even to say that, however, is to imply an endless commitment to try to "exhaust" it, that is, to make rational sense of it, to examine the world from different perspectives and to seek to connect one perspective to others. Our experience of the world is necessarily "ambiguous", never capable of being fully spelled out in rational terms.

Our experience of ourselves, as this implies, is also not dualistic in the Cartesian sense; our subjectivity is not separable from our embodiment, or vice versa. Our inner life as conscious persons necessarily develops out of the impersonal physiological life of a certain kind of organism: a human being. And conversely the intentionality that the Austrian philosopher Franz Brentano, followed to this extent by Husserl in his phenomenology, had confined to consciousness is seen by Merleau-Ponty as at least capable of being a feature of physiological movements also. It is this that makes our

8

way of being in the world as body-*subjects* different from that in which bodies that are mere objects are "in the world". An inanimate object like a stone, for instance, is "in the world" in the sense that it has a position in space and is acted upon by other objects; but an embodied subject is "in the world" not only in these ways but also in the sense of being actively involved with the world about it. To explore our being-in-the-world is to explore our ways of being involved with the world, the purposes we have in relation to surrounding objects and the meanings that we give to them (neither of which are necessarily part of our explicit consciousness). This concept of an intentionality that is not necessarily conscious enables Merleau-Ponty to give an account of Freudian psychoanalysis, and of mental disorder generally, that avoids any hint of mechanistic or reductionist modes of thought.

As body-subjects, Merleau-Ponty goes on to argue, we are not isolated from other subjects in the way that Cartesian dualism seems inevitably to imply; our being-in-the-world is being in the *social* and *cultural* world as well as in the world of physical nature. (Indeed, being the kinds of creatures we are, we cannot ultimately separate our inherence in nature from our inherence in society.) We communicate with other subjects through language; but we also live in a world of streets and houses and cultural institutions that we share with them and that also necessarily have a meaning for us. Our individual experience is thus lived out against the background of a certain social reality, and cannot be understood except by taking account of that social reality. Social and political involvement is in this way for Merleau-Ponty not an optional addition to individual life, but a necessary part of our being-in-the-world; his political theory is likewise an integral part of his philosophy as a whole.

Experience, whether individual or collective, is essentially temporal: it has a direction, from the past, through the present to the future. Our actions in the present spring from what we have been in the past and help to shape our future. This, along with the conditions of our embodiment, inevitably sets limits to our freedom. Merleau-Ponty takes seriously (in a way that is not always true of Sartre himself) Sartre's insistence that freedom is always *in a situation*, or Marx's dictum that men make their own history, but under circumstances that were not chosen by themselves, but "directly encountered, given and transmitted from the past".[10] As individuals, our past (including our past choices as well as circumstances that were not chosen) constrains what we can choose, without determining us to choose one course of action rather than another. Similarly, as societies, we are constrained by history, without any particular historical development's being "inevitable". Merleau-Ponty's humanistic version of Marxism accords with Marx's rejection of talk of abstractions like

"History", and his insistence that human beings still have to make choices, and in particular to choose whether they are going to be on the side of human emancipation or of the continuation of oppression.

IV

The publication of *Phenomenology of Perception* established Merleau-Ponty as someone to be reckoned with in French intellectual life, and its overall themes, in particular its political implications, perfectly fitted the mood in Paris after the Liberation and the end of the war. It was seen (to some extent correctly) as having affinities with Sartre's existentialism, which dominated philosophical and cultural life at that time, although, as I shall suggest shortly, there were also significant differences between the two men's thinking and the implications of their respective philosophies. Eventually, these were to lead to a rift between them, at least on the intellectual plane, but for the time being their general views and especially their approach to political issues seemed sufficiently similar to enable them to work closely together. The most important fruit of this collaboration was their joint founding of the review *Les Temps modernes* in 1945, thus realizing a project that they had first conceived during the Occupation. Sartre and Merleau-Ponty were to be joint editors and directors of the journal, with Merleau-Ponty writing most of the editorials (anonymously) and being responsible for its political content; not only did he not sign his editorials, but, for reasons which he never explained to Sartre's satisfaction, he refused to allow himself to be identified on the front cover as one of the two directors of the review.[11] (Other articles by Merleau-Ponty in *Les Temps modernes* were signed.)

The aim of the journal was to publish articles on politics, philosophy and literature. In politics, its values were those typical of most intellectuals throughout western Europe in the aftermath of the Second World War and the defeat of Nazism: a general desire to make a break with the injustices of the past and to create a more human society. To some extent, Communism and the Soviet Union were still bathed in the afterglow of their role during the war, and to many on the Left it seemed that what they saw as American imperialism constituted as much of a threat to the creation of a decent human society in Europe as Communism. On the other hand, anxieties were felt about the Stalinist show trials in the Soviet Union, and details were beginning to filter through about the Soviet labour camps. For the first few years after the war, Merleau-Ponty retained a broad sympathy with Communism, although he was also beginning to feel some reservations about it. These mixed attitudes were expressed in a number of his articles for *Les Temps modernes*, which were collected in the book *Humanism and Terror*, published in 1947. In 1948, Merleau-Ponty and Sartre helped to found a short-lived new Left-wing political party, the Rassemblement Démocratique Révolutionnaire, which, as its name suggests, was intended to create the conditions for a European socialist revolution that would, in Sartre's view, establish Europe as a "third force" between the Soviet Union and the USA.

As evidence grew over the next few years of the extent and full horror of the Soviet labour camps, however, Merleau-Ponty's initially favourable attitudes towards the Soviet Union began to weaken. It is true that in his 1950 article "The USSR and the Camps",[12] while attacking the degeneration of Soviet Communism as manifested in the evils of the camps, Merleau-Ponty refused to equate Communism and Fascism, and affirmed that his own values still had more in common with those of his Soviet than of his American friends. Nevertheless, his admission of injustice on the Soviet side led to serious criticism from the French Communist Party (PCF), and indicates how Merleau-Ponty was moving away from the more fellow-travelling position of the immediate post-war years.

The outbreak of the Korean War in 1950 was crucial for Merleau-Ponty. He saw the Soviet Union unequivocally as an imperialist aggressor in that conflict, and that proved to be a turning point in his attitude to Communism generally. As Sartre put it, "The Soviet Union had simply lost, in his [Merleau-Ponty's] eyes, any privileged status. It was nothing more nor less than the other powers of prey."[13] The Soviet Union, as Merleau-Ponty saw it, had passed into the "Bonapartist" phase of its revolution, in which the initial revolutionary impetus had been taken over by dictatorship and nationalistic expansionism. But if the Soviet Union could not be identified as the home of "actually existing socialism", then the real possibility of achieving a socialist society anywhere, for the time being at least, might be called into question, and with it the whole *raison d'être* of a review such as *Les Temps modernes*. Merleau-Ponty consequently resigned as political editor of the review, although he remained for a few years more as editor-in-chief.

Sartre responded to these events differently. Although concerned about Soviet involvement in Korea, he saw the war as much more the result of American attempts to maintain their sphere of influence; indeed, the events in Korea made him *more* sympathetic to the Soviet side than before. While not becoming a Communist, he increasingly saw anti-Communism as a device of the despised bourgeoisie to keep in check the oppressed – the workers in France and other capitalist countries and the colonized peoples in other parts of the world. ("An anticommunist", he says in "Merleau-

Ponty *vivant*", "is a rat."[14]) Merleau-Ponty did not become an anti-Communist; he merely ceased to be pro-Communist, he "refused complicity", as Sartre put it, with either side. But this neutrality was already beginning to create difficulties in the relationship between the two men as co-editors of *Les Temps modernes*.

At first, the problem could be evaded by playing down the political content of the journal. But readers became more and more discontented over this, and the tide of angry, critical letters swelled. Sartre became more and more frustrated with Merleau-Ponty's "silence" – his refusal to become politically involved. But, Sartre says, "The truth was that he felt our growing discord and it hurt him."[15] Matters finally came to a head in 1953 over an article about the contradictions of capitalism written by a Marxist friend of Sartre's, with which Sartre himself was broadly in sympathy. Merleau-Ponty, as editor-in-chief, however, was unhappy about the tone of the article and agreed to publish it only if it was accompanied by a preface, written by himself, in which he apologized to readers for its content and criticized the author for failing also to discuss the contradictions of socialism. Sartre was absent from Paris when this decision was made. When he returned and learned about it, he was offended and insisted on removing Merleau-Ponty's preface and printing the article as it stood. Merleau-Ponty knew nothing of this decision until he saw the proofs of the relevant issue. He telephoned Sartre immediately and tendered his resignation from the editorial board of the journal. This was the beginning of an estrangement between the two men that was to last for around three years; indeed, the relationship between them could never be quite the same again, even though they were somewhat reconciled to each other after 1956.

V

As is clear from what has just been said, the quarrel between Sartre and Merleau-Ponty was primarily over politics. Sartre came to be increasingly close to the PCF and to lend his support to pro-Soviet policies and attitudes; Merleau-Ponty distanced himself more and more from the Communists and from sympathy for the Soviet Union. Sartre expressed his views in his series of articles published as *The Communists and Peace* in 1954. Merleau-Ponty responded with his book *The Adventures of the Dialectic*, published in 1955.[16] The content of *The Adventures of the Dialectic* will be discussed in considerably more detail in Chapter 6; here it will be sufficient to say that it is a critical account of different interpretations of the Hegelian–Marxist notion of the "dialectic" as a way of understanding the movement of history, and of the political implications of these different interpretations. Merleau-Ponty starts by examining Max Weber's theory of "understanding" sociology, and in particular the account that Weber gives of the relation between the Protestant ethic and the spirit of capitalism. Weber demonstrates, Merleau-Ponty says, "under what conditions a historical dialectic is serious".[17] The best Marxists, he argues, understood this, and "developed a rigorous and consistent Marxism which, like Weber's approach, was a theory of historical comprehension, of *Vielseitigkeit* ["many-sidedness"], and of creative choice, and was a philosophy that questioned history".[18]

In the light of that conception, Merleau-Ponty goes on to discuss the "western Marxism" associated with the Hungarian philosopher Georg Lukács, Lenin and his Soviet followers, Trotsky and, finally, Sartre and what Merleau-Ponty calls "ultra-Bolshevism". It is this chapter on Sartre (significantly, by far the longest single chapter in the whole work) that is most relevant in the present context. The chapter as a whole is an extended critical discussion of Sartre's essays on "The Communists and Peace", mentioned above, the great interest of which, from Merleau-Ponty's point of view, is that they in effect abandon dialectic and attempt to "understand'" present-day Communist action in itself and without regard to its history. This understanding is completely undialectical because it tries to make Communist action intelligible as simply the "immediate result of [human] volitions".[19] To the mechanistic objectivism of Soviet Marxism, Sartre opposes a purely subjectivist voluntarism "which, out of nothing, creates the proletariat as the subject of history".[20] But both extreme objectivism and extreme subjectivism are, in Merleau-Ponty's eyes, equally "terroristic".

What Merleau-Ponty seems to mean by this is that both, in their different ways, make it impossible to engage in any kind of evaluation of Communist actions: objectivism because it assimilates social and historical development to amoral natural change, and subjectivism because it makes that development the result of arbitrary acts of will. By the term "ultra-Bolshevism" in the title of the chapter, Merleau-Ponty means the "new phase . . . in which communism no longer justifies itself by truth, the philosophy of history, and the dialectic but by their negation".[21] Communism is thus removed from all possibility of rational discussion, and Sartre ends up by accepting the PCF, and the Stalinist policies that it supported, simply on the grounds that it was *de facto* accepted by the majority of the French working class as its representative. The arbitrariness of this choice is connected by Merleau-Ponty with Sartre's philosophical conception of human freedom, which Merleau-Ponty regarded as

13

fundamentally mistaken. This is, indeed, one of the main reasons why this dispute between the two men over a political situation that has long since passed into history is still of a wider philosophical importance.

Sartre's conception of consciousness and its relationship to its world, and his corresponding conception of freedom, were, in Merleau-Ponty's view, entirely unhistorical, even anti-historical. Consciousness, for Sartre, was a pure "negation"; it was defined in the paradoxical formula, "human reality . . . is what it is not, and . . . is not what it is".[22] Freedom was the power to negate the situation in which one found oneself. Although Sartre also held that freedom was always "in a situation",[23] that restriction seems necessarily to be ignored if it is always possible for agents to "negate" their situation, to act as if they were not in those situations. The choices open to Sartre in the France of the years immediately after the end of the Second World War cannot be significantly different from those facing someone in, say, America of the end of the nineteenth century or in Indochina in the 1960s, if all three choosers express their choice by "negating" the time and place in which they find themselves. The Sartrean doctrine of consciousness and choice, in short, effectively denies the importance of history, of the time and place in which one has to make one's choices. As Merleau-Ponty says, "the notion of consciousness as a pure power of signifying, as a centrifugal movement without opacity or inertia . . . casts history and the social outside, into the signified".[24] But such a rejection of the idea of history as a necessary setting for one's choices is, in Merleau-Ponty's view, completely undialectical and so un-Marxist. Plainly, Merleau-Ponty's own view of human freedom is implicitly asserted in this criticism of Sartre to be *more* dialectical, *more* historically rooted, and we shall see in more detail what this amounts to later on, in Chapters 5 and 6.

VI

Meanwhile, Merleau-Ponty's academic career and reputation continued to advance. In 1945, he had moved on from being a teacher of philosophy in *lycées* to a university post, being appointed a professor at the University of Lyon (in that same year, Sartre had given up teaching altogether and had become a full-time writer, as he was to remain until the end of his life). Merleau-Ponty remained at Lyon until 1949, when he moved to the Chair of Psychology and Pedagogy at the Sorbonne. In 1952, he moved again, this time to take up what is probably one of the most distinguished academic posts in France, a chair at the Collège de France, where, as has already been mentioned, Henri Bergson had also held a chair earlier in the century. His inaugural lecture at the Collège de France was published in the following year in his book *In Praise of Philosophy*.[25]

Throughout this time he had been publishing (often in *Les Temps modernes*) a number of short essays on a variety of topics, many of which were collected together in the two volumes *Sense and Non-Sense* (1948) and *Signs* (1960).[26] In the Author's Preface to the earlier collection, Merleau-Ponty speaks of the twentieth century's "revolt against reason" and argues that "we are born into reason as into language". Nevertheless, he accepts that we cannot simply ignore the lessons learned from this revolt; we need to develop a new idea of reason, out of our experience of art, of morality and of politics. In any of these fields, we may not know in advance where our activities are leading us, but to be deterred by that would be to accept that no solution is possible. Just as an artist like Cézanne did not know when he started out on a work whether it would have any meaning or be understood, so human beings in general simply have to follow the flow of "the spontaneous movement which binds us to others for good or ill, out of selfishness or generosity".[27] And just as in the end Cézanne managed to extract meaning out of contingency, so humanity can create a new idea of reason if we are willing to take the risks.

This "humanistic" message runs through the essays, which cover the arts (including painting, literature and film), philosophical ideas (including the relation between Hegel and existentialism, an essentially favourable view of Sartre, and Marxism and philosophy) and discussions of the current political situation in France and the world in the years immediately after the Second World War. Many of these essays will be discussed in more detail later, in the appropriate places, so we do not need to dwell further on them at this point.

Signs has a rather different character. For one thing, it is a product of a later stage of Merleau-Ponty's life, when he had moved on in many ways, personally, philosophically and politically. It belongs to the time after the quarrel with Sartre and the resignation from the editorial board of *Les Temps modernes*, during which Merleau-Ponty, while remaining broadly on the Left in his political thinking, had retreated from his fellow-travelling views of the early post-war years. In philosophy, too, (as evidenced, among other things, by his lectures at the Collège de France[28] and by his posthumously published works) he was beginning to have doubts about whether he had gone far enough in *Phenomenology of Perception*, and becoming more interested in language and the newly fashionable "structuralist" concerns of people like his friend the anthropologist Claude Lévi-Strauss. The book's contents are divided into two main sections, one on philosophical themes, and one of (mainly shorter) pieces on contemporary politics.

Merleau-Ponty himself, in his Introduction, comments on the difference between the two sections in a way that hints at his conception of the nature of philosophy. "The philosopher's road may be hard", he says, "but we can at least be sure that each step points a way for those to come. In politics, one has the oppressive sensation of blazing a trail which must be endlessly reopened."[29] For this reason, the purely political pieces in the collection are, in Merleau-Ponty's own phrase, "ad hoc"; to us now, they are primarily of historical interest, except in so far as they incidentally contain material that sheds light on his philosophical thought. The philosophical papers, on the other hand, are much more substantial and provide valuable further evidence of the new concerns that he was developing in the last years of his life, and which have been mentioned in the previous paragraph. Many of the papers show the increasing concern with language, with structural linguistics and structuralist thinking more generally, and their relationship to philosophy and phenomenology; others are devoted to reflections on the thought of Husserl, Bergson, Einstein and Montaigne, or to the nature of philosophy as such and its relationship to, for example, sociology. Once again, some of these themes will be considered in more detail in appropriate places in the rest of this book.

VII

Merleau-Ponty died suddenly of a heart attack on 3 May 1961. He was only 53, and at the height of his powers. In *Les Temps modernes*, Sartre wrote the long and generous tribute, "Merleau-Ponty *vivant*" ("Merleau-Ponty alive"), which has already been quoted several times in this chapter. This article provides a long and detailed account of the relationship between the two men, from their first encounter at the École Normale Supérieure onwards, including their post-war quarrel. It is honest about their differences, both of temperament and opinion, and the frictions that those differences led to, but at the same time reveals Sartre's genuine affection for the man he describes as a "friend" and an "equal", if not a "brother". There is also much useful material about Merleau-Ponty's philosophical development, as seen through Sartre's critical eyes.

After Merleau-Ponty's death, the manuscripts of two unfinished works were discovered among his papers. One, *The Prose of the World*, appears to have been abandoned by Merleau-Ponty himself; according to the editor who prepared it for posthumous publication, Claude Lefort, "There is good reason to believe . . . that, had he lived, he would not have completed it, at least in the form outlined."[30] The text as it was found consisted of

170 typewritten pages, with many corrections, divided into six chapters. Neither the whole work nor the individual chapters had been given titles by Merleau-Ponty himself.

The book is almost certainly the one referred to by Merleau-Ponty in the prospectus of his work submitted to Martial Gueroult as part of his candidacy for the chair at the Collège de France.[31] There Merleau-Ponty speaks of "a partially written book dealing with literary language", which he proposed to entitle *Introduction to the Prose of the World*.[32] Along with another work on *The Origin of Truth*, it was intended to elaborate the philosophical foundations of the views on truth and intersubjectivity, which he had adumbrated in his essays "Cézanne's Doubt" and "Metaphysics of the Novel" (both included in *Sense and Non-Sense*) and of the philosophy of history presented in *Humanism and Terror*. A chapter extracted from the unfinished draft was published, in revised form, as a two-part article in *Les Temps modernes* for 1952, under the title "Indirect Language and the Voices of Silence" (later reprinted in *Signs*).[33]

In the prospectus, he describes the central purpose of *The Prose of the World* as that of showing that language is not a mere outward expression of a pre-existing thought. "The writer's thought does not control his language from without; the writer is himself a kind of new idiom, constructing itself, inventing ways of expression, and diversifying itself according to its own meaning."[34] The development of this thought was meant to take us beyond the restoration of the world of perception attempted in *Phenomenology of Perception* and "to show how communication with others, and thought, take up and go beyond the realm of perception which initiated us to the truth".[35] On the basis of the conception of the subject as essentially *embodied* or "incarnated", he aimed to exhibit the mind as a domain of *expression*. His work on language thus marks a development of, rather than a turning away from, his earlier phenomenological studies.

Part of Merleau-Ponty's close friendship with Claude Lévi-Strauss, already mentioned, was a shared interest in the structural linguistics of Ferdinand de Saussure and its possible applications outside the narrowly linguistic sphere. He refers approvingly to Saussure's central doctrine that (as Merleau-Ponty expresses it) "A language is less a sum of signs . . . than a methodical means of differentiating signs from one another and thereby constructing a linguistic universe";[36] that is, signs have meaning, not by independently denoting some object in the world, but in virtue of their *differences* from other signs within a system. It was this doctrine that was to play such an important role in later structuralist and post-structuralist philosophies of "difference". But Merleau-Ponty was still too much of a humanist at this point to move on from that, as they did, to a position that played down the importance of human subjectivity in the creation of language. Indeed, he says later in the work that "Language is not like a prison into which we are locked or a guide whose directions we must follow blindly";[37] the very relation between signs in the whole linguistic system makes us verify "the power that speaking subjects have of going beyond signs towards their meaning – of which what we call language is, after all, only the visible result and record".[38] And he was too much of a historicist to accept the timeless universal structures of thought proposed by the full-blown structuralist thinkers.

The Prose of the World was, as was said earlier, abandoned by Merleau-Ponty himself, probably in 1951–52, for reasons that are still the subject of discussion among commentators. The other posthumously published work, The Visible and the Invisible, however, is unfinished because death intervened before it could be completed, so there is every reason to think that Merleau-Ponty would have continued to work on it if fate had allowed him to do so. The manuscript shows considerable signs of working and re-working, and the existence of dated "Working Notes" (included in the published edition) also indicates clearly that this was a project that Merleau-Ponty proposed to pursue to completion and publication. The significance of the work as evidence of the way Merleau-Ponty's thinking was developing in the last years of his life is thus much greater than that of The Prose of the World. Nevertheless, we cannot ignore the fact that what we have is unfinished, that it is work in progress; the manuscript that Merleau-Ponty left behind at his death is, in effect, the introduction to a larger work. Much in it is opaque without the further continuation, and in particular we do not have sufficient material to be sure of how the hints about the argument of the later part of the work would in fact have been filled out.

What does seem reasonably clear is that Merleau-Ponty does not reject the aims of his earlier writings but has come to feel that he had not done full justice to them. It was right to question the sharp distinction of traditional philosophy between subject and object, to affirm that human being is being-in-the-world and is therefore "ambiguous", to deny that philosophy could achieve absolute truth, for which philosophers would have to be God-like beings outside time, space and history. What was wrong was that framing these questions, affirmations and denials in the context of a phenomenological philosophy of consciousness weakened their radicalism. The phenomenological approach inevitably emphasized the role of the subject of experience, so moving away from that primitive level of experience in which our being was not sharply distinguished from being as a whole. The thrust of this last work is thus away from transcendental phenomenology towards ontology, the description of being as such rather than our experience of being as the necessary preliminary for understanding the relation of more refined domains of experience such as science to that primitive ground. Even to express things in this way is inevitably reminiscent of Heidegger rather than Husserl (even the later Husserl); and there are even echoes of Heidegger's rejection of "humanism", for instance in this quotation from the "Working Notes":

> My plan: I The visible
> II Nature
> III Logos
>
> March, 1961
>
> must be presented without any compromise with *humanism*, nor moreover with *naturalism*, nor finally with *theology*.[39]

Suspicion of "humanism" in this sense, as a view of the centrality of human subjectivity, is characteristic not only of Heidegger, but of much of the dominant mood in the French philosophers who came to prominence in the 1960s and afterwards and who were influenced by Heidegger and Nietzsche. Expressions of such suspicion by Merleau-Ponty in his last work could thus be taken as an indication that he was moving in a similar direction himself, and might have moved further if he had lived longer. Speculative "might have beens" of this kind are, however, of limited interest in a study such as this. What is more important is that, even if Merleau-Ponty was beginning to move away from transcendental phenomenology and "humanism", the motivation for that move was ultimately the same as that for his original attraction to phenomenology: a desire for a philosophy rooted in description of the experience of beings who were "in the world" rather than in attempts at general "theories" or "systems". This desire is the common thread that binds together the whole of Merleau-Ponty's thought, from his earliest writings to his posthumously published works, and that makes them "humanistic" in a wider sense than that rejected by his French successors.

VIII

In this chapter, I have tried to present a broad overview of Merleau-Ponty's philosophy, to provide a framework into which the more detailed discussions of the later chapters can be fitted. The course of his intellectual development has been traced through summary accounts of his principal writings and related to the events of his life and his involvement with the wider cultural and political currents in the France of his time. The main emphasis in this story has been on the elements of continuity in his development: the recurrent themes that serve to identify what is distinctive about his thought. And over and above that, some attempt has been made to place Merleau-Ponty's philosophy in relation to earlier and later thinkers in France and elsewhere – to show him as a contributor to the development of a broad tradition in terms of which his own ideas can be better understood (as he himself would certainly have acknowledged).

Before moving on, it would be helpful briefly to identify those central themes. First, as with all truly great philosophers, there is a conception of the nature and purpose of philosophy itself. For Merleau-Ponty, philosophy is essentially humanity's radical reflection on its own situation, our attempt as human beings to get beneath the theoretical pictures that we create out of our need to explain the world for various purposes to the "unreflective experience" that necessarily underlies those theoretical constructions and gives them meaning; in so doing, we understand better what their meaning *is*. To adapt one of his own images, it is like going for a walk in the countryside to see the actual forests, prairies and rivers that give meaning to the geographical theories we have been studying.[40]

Expressed in this way, the activity of philosophizing may seem to be of limited interest and value. But Merleau-Ponty argues that radical reflection of this kind reveals some fundamental and important truths about the nature of our situation and the roots of human rationality. It undermines, for example, the whole view that has dominated much of Western philosophy at least since Descartes, and to some extent since Plato: the view that has already been referred to as "humanism", in which human subjects are seen as confronting an objective world from which they are essentially separated, as disembodied reason. Human being is revealed in radical reflection as "being-in-the-world", human perception therefore as active engagement with a world of which we are part, rather than as detached contemplation. Such a subject is necessarily *embodied*; if our being is in-the-world, then our consciousness of the world must be mediated by bodily sense organs, a brain and nervous system, and, indeed, by our capacities for bodily movement. The experience of such a "body-subject" must always be from a particular *perspective* within the world, and so limited by the constraints of space and time. Because we are active within the world, that world must present itself to us as meaningful; but because we are also finite and within the world, those meanings must always also be *ambiguous* and the world must transcend our capacity to know and understand it. Reality is "inexhaustible", and there can be no possibility of the philosopher, or any other human being, arriving at a final "system" that will make ultimate sense of it all.

Like Sartre, Merleau-Ponty argues that the human power to become conscious of our situation entails that human action is not mechanistically determined, but his conception of human being as being-in-the-world, more consistently developed than Sartre's, leads him to recognize that human freedom can never be absolute, that it must be constrained by the nature of the situation in which we find ourselves, including the limitations imposed by our own pasts. This applies not only to the freedom of individuals to shape their own lives, but to the capacity of society as a whole to take a new direction. For being-in-the-world is, in part, being-in-the-social-world; our perspective is determined not only by space and time, but by history and culture. An individual human being engages with the world not only in pursuit of individual biological goals but as a member of a society. The meanings that we find in reality are in part social or cultural meanings, and the world we inhabit is in part a social or shared world, in which we join with others in common activities. Solipsism is theoretically always a possibility, but in practice it can mean only a wilful refusal to accept the humanity that we share with others. What applies to individual freedom thus applies also to the freedom of society as a whole. As a social progressive, Merleau-Ponty rejects both mechanistic interpretations of Marxism that treat social change as proceeding according to inexorable laws and purely voluntarist conceptions that treat it as dependent only on human decision.

Our social being is inseparable from the existence of institutions that embody our shared life, above all, from the existence of means of communication, both language in the narrow verbal sense and other means of expressing experience – gesture, the arts, and so on. In line with his doctrine of embodiment and the consequent ambiguity of human experience, Merleau-Ponty presents such expression as not essentially governed by explicit rules that give it a clear meaning, but as developing from pre-reflective gestural communication and as still embodying the diffuseness of meaning which that has even in most of its more refined forms (except in the case of scientific language, where for a specific purpose the modes of expression are more regularized).

All in all, then, Merleau-Ponty offers a comprehensive and yet unified account of the human situation, covering individual experience, mind–body relations, freedom, relations between self and others, society, history, politics and the arts. Many of his themes are recognizable in the work of other twentieth-century philosophers – notably Heidegger, but also Sartre, Marcel, and Bergson. What is distinctive and original about Merleau-

Ponty is the particular way in which he combines these themes, the style in which he develops them, and the implications that he derives from them. Together, these justify another distinguished contemporary French thinker, Paul Ricoeur, in describing Merleau-Ponty as one of the outstanding philosophers of the twentieth century.[41]

CHAPTER TWO

Phenomenology

I

Many philosophers influenced the direction of Merleau-Ponty's thinking, as was shown in Chapter 1, but the single most significant influence was that of Edmund Husserl (1859–1938) and the "phenomenological" school that he founded. If we are to understand Merleau-Ponty properly, we have to see him above all in relation to phenomenology. At least in his major works, he certainly saw himself as a phenomenologist, and even the other influences on his thought were filtered through his conception of phenomenology. And, clearly, if we are to understand Merleau-Ponty's relationship to Husserlian phenomenology, we must first say something about Husserl's own thought. As stated in Chapter 1, Merleau-Ponty first discovered Husserl's philosophy while still a student at the École Normale Supérieure, where he attended Georges Gurvitch's lectures on contemporary German philosophy and also the lectures given by Husserl himself at the Sorbonne in 1929, later published as *Cartesian Meditations*. But the version of phenomenology that had most influence on his own work was not that of this earlier phase of Husserl's life, but that on which Husserl was working in the last years of his life. An article about these developments in the *Revue internationale de philosophie* in 1939 aroused Merleau-Ponty's interest and inspired him to go to the newly established Husserl Archive at the University of Louvain in Belgium and to read avidly in the Husserl papers that were kept there (he was, in fact, one of the very first visitors to the archive).

Commentators disagree about the extent of the difference between the earlier and the later thought of Husserl, but that there is a significant change at least in the atmosphere and tone of Husserl's last writings seems beyond doubt. The phenomenology of the earlier period was, in effect, an a priori science of subjectivity, a study of human consciousness in its relation to its objects that had been freed of "psychologism", the doctrine that consciousness could be adequately studied by the methods of empirical introspective psychology. In his early work, the *Logical Investigations*, Husserl had rejected the psychologism of his previous writings, which Frege had criticized. On the basis of that rejection he had developed the view that logical principles were not descriptions of the workings of empirically detectable mental processes ("laws of thought"), as supporters of psychologism contended, but "ideal objects", entities that really, objectively, existed but in a non-material form. The realm of ideal objects was then extended to include meanings or "essences", the general characteristics by which things are identified as instances of a kind, referred to by a common expression. These meanings were taken to be both *objective*, in that they really existed independently of any particular person's awareness of them (as shown by the fact that different individuals can mean the same thing by a given expression), and *subjective*, in that a "meaning" is necessarily a meaning *for* some subject or subjects.

How then can we study "meanings" or "essences"? Husserl took over from the Austrian philosopher Franz Brentano the medieval concept of "intentionality", which the latter had reintroduced into philosophy. "Intentionality" means "directedness" towards an object (the "intentional object"), which need not actually exist, and it was taken to be a necessary feature of consciousness and its acts. For example, one mode in which we can be conscious is to be afraid; fear is essentially "directed to an object" in that to be afraid is necessarily to be afraid *of something*, but what we are afraid of is not necessarily something that actually exists in the physical world – we can be afraid of ghosts, for instance, whether or not there actually are such things. In a somewhat different way, we can think about numbers, say, even though numbers are not physical objects that we can observe with our senses. Intentionality thus becomes a relation between consciousness and an ideal realm, rather than a relation to the natural world of ordinary observation.

This suggests a method by which we can study meanings and their relation to each other: we can approach them simply as the intentional objects of our consciousness, that is, from the "subjective" end. But the "subjectivity" in question will not be that of the contingent empirical contents of our mind, in the manner of introspective psychology; it will be the *transcendental* subjectivity of the necessary relation by which consciousness as such (the "transcendental ego") "intends" objects of the relevant kinds. We will start from the "natural attitude", the assumptions underlying our ordinary awareness of the world around us – the assumptions that there are objects of certain kinds that we can observe with our senses, that these objects stand in certain spatial and causal relations to each other and to ourselves, and so on. We will then "put these assumptions in parentheses" or "bracket them" – that is, we shall set aside all questions of the real existence of the objects we are conscious of and regard them *simply* as "phenomena" or "appearances", in effect simply as the intentional objects of consciousness – in order that we can more readily identify their "essences" and the ways in which those essences are related to our mode of consciousness of them. This "bracketing" is what Husserl often refers to as the "phenomenological *epoché*", from the Greek word that means "holding off from" or "suspending judgement' (interestingly, it is the word that the ancient Greek sceptics used for the operation that Descartes was later to call "doubt"), or the "phenomeno-logical reduction", and the further step of moving from the instances to their essences is called "eidetic (essential) reduction". The study of essences and their interrelations by this method is "transcendental phenomenology". But the relations between essences, as ideal rather than empirical objects, are supposed to be *necessary*, not the merely contingent relations expressed in the laws of empirical science.

The very term "transcendental" irresistibly suggests Kant; transcen-dental phenomenology was clearly seen as a development of the Kantian inquiry into the fundamental a priori structures of experience. And, like Kant, Husserl was attempting, at this stage in his career, to put philosophy on the sure road of a science – as indicated by the fact that one of his works of this period bears the title *Philosophy as a Rigorous Science*. One way to understand Husserl's project, indeed, is to see it in the context of a culture in which a vaguely defined notion of "science" had taken over the prestige that had previously belonged to (an equally undefined notion of) "philosophy". In such a context, it is natural to think that philosophy needs to find a new role for itself, one that will show philosophy to have all the rigour of science, while applying that rigour to its own special domain, which is distinct from that of the empirical or special sciences, but which, like the empirical sciences, proceeds in a rigorous way, according to a *method*. A similar project was that of the Vienna Circle, who redefined the role of philosophy to make it "the logic of science", the investigation of the logical relations between the concepts and propositions of science. (More will be said about the Vienna Circle and its relation to Merleau-Ponty's version of phenomenology later on in the chapter.)

Husserl's "rigorous science" of phenomenology was not therefore to be an empirical science, like psychology or sociology, or even a science combining empirical and mathematical elements, like physics or chemistry. It aimed to establish, not contingent laws of nature, after all, but necessary relations between essences. It was consequently to be a purely a priori science, whose purpose was methodically to investigate the essential foundations on which the work of empirical science must rest. Before we can effectively study the physical world through sensory observation, for instance, we need to have a clear grasp of *what it is essentially* to "perceive a physical object", and that clear grasp is achievable, in Husserl's view, only by using the methods of phenomenology. In this way, phenomenology had a domain of its own, which was in addition more *fundamental* than that of the empirical sciences, but which it could study by methods at least as rigorous as those used in the natural sciences. As we shall see below, Husserl's later account of phenomenology, like that of Heidegger and Merleau-Ponty, is less easily described in these "scientific" terms.

We can also find antecedents for Husserlian phenomenology further back in the history of philosophy, in the project of Descartes to reconstruct human knowledge on a sounder rational basis by pursuing a method of doubt (cf. what was said above about the history of the term *epoché*). Descartes sought to arrive at an "Archimedean point" on which human knowledge could be securely balanced by first doubting everything that could possibly be doubted, including the very existence of a world at all, and came, as a result, to have confidence only in his own existence as a thinking thing and in the world only as something thought about. In similar fashion, in the phenomenological reduction, Husserl aimed to prepare the ground for an account of the essential structures of human experience by "bracketing" or "putting in parentheses" the objective existence of the world and the things in it in order to focus on it simply as an appearance to a pure consciousness or "transcendental ego". The title given to his Paris lectures, *Cartesian Meditations*, is in part a polite gesture to his French hosts and their philosophical traditions, but, much more importantly, it is a homage to Descartes himself and a recognition of the parallels between the Cartesian and Husserlian projects.

II

By far the most distinguished and original of Husserl's pupils was Martin Heidegger (1889–1976), but the relation of Heidegger's thought to that of his teacher was always complex and ambiguous. After his famous *Kehre* or "turn", indeed, Heidegger moved away from anything that could readily be identified as "phenomenology" towards "ontology", reflection on Being as such rather than on our consciousness of Being. In the work that most regard as his masterpiece, *Sein und Zeit* (*Being and Time*), however, Heidegger still presented himself as a phenomenologist. It was published in 1927, not only as a separate book, but also in Husserl's *Yearbook for*

Philosophy and Phenomenological Research. But the "phenomenology" of which Heidegger speaks in that volume seems very different from the "rigorous science" that Husserl himself was advocating at that time. Starting, as he often did, from the etymological history of a term, Heidegger seeks to define "phenomenology" by reference to the two Greek words from which it is composed: "phainomenon" and "logos". "Phainomenon" in Greek, Heidegger argues, really means, not "appearance" (as it is usually translated) but "that which shows itself". "Logos" means not, as the conventional translation has it, "account of" or "study of", but "making something manifest". On this basis, he declares that "phenomenology" means "making manifest that which shows itself", or, more fully, letting "that which shows itself be seen from itself in the very way in which it shows itself from itself".[1]

So understood, phenomenology does not sound like the name for a particular *method* of doing philosophy, in which the objects of experience are considered without reference to their existence or non-existence, simply as "appearances" to a subject, in order that we may intuit their essences. It is not, in that sense, a "science", or even a "super-science". Rather it is simply a battle against falsehood and the failure to recognize what is manifest. Conversely, the subject who engages in phenomenology is not a pure consciousness, contemplating that which "appears" to it, but a being who is actually part of the reality whose nature he or she seeks to grasp, a being who is "in the world", an "existing" being. Heidegger marks this by replacing the term "subject" with the German word *Dasein*, which literally means simply "existence" or, even more literally, "being there". Dasein's Being is "in-the-world", but not in the way an object is: it is actively involved with its own world, so that the objects it deals with are necessarily endowed with meaning. Its Being is *existence*, which reaches out into Being in general, so that analysis of the Being of Dasein (existential analysis) is at the same time analysis of Being as such. Effectively, what Heidegger means by phenomenology is just this kind of existential analysis, the making manifest of the ways in which we engage with Being in order to make manifest the character of Being itself. The very nature of the Being of Dasein, such that it necessarily calls itself in question, ensures that to analyse Dasein is also to reveal the essence of Being. This move of Heidegger's allows the possibility for phenomenology to become *existential* phenomenology, reflection on the world in which we have our being (although Heidegger himself was later to repudiate any association of his own thinking with "existentialism").

In his "Translator's Introduction" to the English translation of Husserl's *The Crisis of European Sciences and Transcendental Phenomenology*,[2] David Carr suggests that a principal motive for the changes in Husserl's thinking in his later years was his bitterness at the increasing philosophical influence of Heidegger's version of phenomenology at the expense of his own. Husserl certainly seems to have moved to a more "existential" interpretation of phenomenology in his last writings, and to have made use of much Heideggerian terminology in expounding it. As Carr also suggests, apart from any bitterness he may have felt, there also seems to have been a recognition that Heidegger (and other "existence-philosophers", such as Jaspers) were addressing a real problem in European culture and values to which Husserl's own earlier phenomenology had little relevance (indeed the earlier phenomenology could even be regarded as a part of the problem). The writings of Husserl's last years, the *Crisis of European Sciences* volume, above all, seek to go some way towards addressing the problem without departing too far from the essentials of phenomenological method and its concepts.

Central to this later version of Husserlian phenomenology was the notion of the *Lebenswelt* or "life-world". The life-world is the "pregiven" or "everyday" world that is the basis for all our theoretical constructions in the sciences and philosophy. Husserl describes it as the real world, the one that we actually perceive. It is the world in which we actually *live*, in which we must live before we can begin to theorize or try to explain it. The crisis that faces modern European culture, according to Husserl, is (to put it in its simplest possible terms) the result of substituting the abstract theoretical constructions for their basis, of taking the scientific account of the world and ourselves for the "real reality" rather than the underlying human experience that gives that account such meaning as it has.

Placing the concept of the life-world at the centre in this way implies significant changes in the significance and role of the phenomenological reduction, and so in the whole conception of phenomenology. In the earlier version, what had to be "put in parentheses" in the reduction was the "natural attitude", the set of assumptions that underlie not only scientific descriptions of the world but our ordinary experience. Nothing could be taken for granted, not even the life-world. The aim was to arrive at an understanding of reality that was deeper than that of ordinary experience. As we have already seen, and as Husserl himself recognized, this had parallels with the Cartesian project of methodological doubt, in which everything, up to and including the assumption that there was an "external world" at all, had to be called in question before a basis for absolute certainty could be achieved in the existence of consciousness and its contents. And, as in the case of Descartes, this implied that consciousness and its contents could be considered independently of questions about the existence of anything outside consciousness. Consciousness may be essentially "intentional", directed towards objects, but, as was argued above, these objects do not necessarily exist in a material world.

If, however, the fundamental layer of reality is not a detached consciousness and its purely intentional objects, but a pregiven life-world, our ordinary experience of a world that is always already there before we experience it, then the phenomenological reduction cannot "bracket" such a life-world. Rather, what it must put into brackets is the theoretical constructions of science and metaphysics (and any other discipline that is meant to *explain* experience), leaving us with the pure *description* of the life-world, which gives meaning to those constructions. The aim of phenomenology thus becomes, not the achievement of rational insight into the "essences" or necessary structures of experience, but a deeper understanding of the meaning of our theoretical activities through grasping their roots in ordinary lived experience. It moves from the realm of "rigorous science" to that of "radical reflection". Correspondingly, the human subject becomes, not a detached Cartesian "ego", but human beings who are part of the world that they experience, and who experience it, not in the form of pure contemplation, but in the course of active involvement with it.

Thus, Husserl criticizes previous philosophers who have attempted to reflect on the meaning of scientific work on the grounds that they were not radical enough; they did not carry their reflections as far as to consider the *purpose* of science, as the pursuit of certain human goals that were themselves based in the life-world.[3] And he criticizes Descartes for identifying the "ego" that is arrived at as a result of his "*epoché*" with the "soul" or disembodied intellect, rather than with the *whole* person, as naturally engaged with the world.[4] In this, Husserl argues, Descartes was again being insufficiently radical in rejecting all mere assumptions, for he failed to recognize that the "soul" in this sense was not something whose existence became apparent in the *epoché*, but an abstraction based on the requirements of a scientific way of looking at the world.[5] (Husserl's own earlier conception of the "transcendental ego" was, of course, open to much the same criticism that he now directed at Descartes.)

In other words, it is not possible to conceive of oneself as a disembodied soul while adopting the stance of the life-world, since our ordinary experience of ourselves is of a body–mind unity actively engaged with the world around us. We can arrive at Descartes's conception only by starting from unquestioned acceptance of a scientific construction of the world (including our own bodies) as an array of purely physical objects without any element of thought or consciousness. Once that is done, we are bound to think of our own conscious experience as belonging to *something else*, an entirely non-material "mental substance" that is detached from anything material, even our own body. But a genuinely radical "reduction" would make us aware of the priority of our ordinary lived experience over any theoretical construction of science whose purpose is only to enable us to explain and predict the phenomena of ordinary experience.

III

This, then, very briefly stated, was the version of phenomenology that so excited Merleau-Ponty in the late 1930s and inspired him to go to Louvain to study the Husserl Archive there. And this was the version that had such a profound influence on his own mature philosophy. Much of the time, the tone of Merleau-Ponty's language in his account of phenomenology suggests that Husserl's later version is definitive. For instance, he corrects Jean Wahl, a leading French commentator on Husserl, when he claims that Husserl separated essences from existence.[6] He even goes so far as to claim that it is wrong to make a distinction between Heidegger's and Husserl's versions of phenomenology, and that:

> the whole of *Sein und Zeit* springs from an indication given by Husserl and amounts to no more than an explicit account of the 'natürlicher Weltbegriff' or the 'Lebenswelt' which Husserl, towards the end of his life, identified as the central theme of phenomenology . . .

It should be clear from the earlier part of this chapter that the notion that Heidegger did little more than make explicit what was implied by Husserl's earlier phenomenology, as Husserl himself was later to do in his last writings, bears little relation to reality. It is certainly true, as I hope to show, that Merleau-Ponty's own conception of phenomenology is more closely related to that of the later Husserl, but it is also true that he developed that conception in new directions of his own.

The best place to examine Merleau-Ponty's view of the nature and significance of Husserl's later phenomenology is in the preface to *Phenomenology of Perception*. Merleau-Ponty begins there by asking what phenomenology is. The first answer that he gives is the conventional enough one that phenomenology conceives of philosophy as the attempt to find definitions of essences,[7] but he immediately goes on to qualify this answer, which would apply to Husserlian phenomenology at any stage in its development, by one which more specifically applies to the later version that we have just been considering. Phenomenology, he says, seeks to put these essences "*back into existence*" (my italics), and to understand human beings and their world solely on the basis of their "facticity": the way in which they actually exist.

The phenomenological reduction, from this point of view, involves accepting the world of our experience as already there, before reflection, and of our experience as of "factitious" or contingently existing beings: it is not a rejection of the assumptions of our natural attitude, but simply puts them temporarily out of action so that we can study them in a more detached way. What phenomenology seeks to do, Merleau-Ponty goes on to say, is "to give a direct description of our experience as it is, without taking account of its psychological origin and the causal explanations which the scientist, the historian or the sociologist may be able to provide". This is the view of the central theme of phenomenology, as an explicit account of the life-world, which Husserl adopted towards the end of his life. But it is clearly fundamentally different from Husserl's own earlier talk of phenomenology as a "rigorous science".

Such apparent contradictions in the statements of what phenomenology is may, Merleau-Ponty admits, lead some people to reject it out of hand, as a mere fad or fashion. But Merleau-Ponty contends that the apparent contradictions can be resolved if we take phenomenology not so much as a doctrine but as a particular style of thinking.[8] This style of thinking can be found, he says, not only in Husserl and Heidegger, but also in Hegel, Kierkegaard, Marx, Nietzsche and Freud: what matters, however, is not to approach it through a purely historical study of such texts, but to determine and express a "phenomenology for ourselves". As this clearly indicates, Merleau-Ponty's presentation of what phenomenology is really about is not based on mere piety to past philosophers, but on a desire to extract from their work whatever can be of most use to his own philosophical purposes. The historical accuracy of his interpretation of Husserl is thus of less importance than the light that what has been said about Husserl's concepts can shed on Merleau-Ponty's own philosophical project. As we shall see, Merleau-Ponty has, like Heidegger, effectively abandoned the idea of phenomenology as a "rigorous science" in favour of a pure description of our "being-in-the-world". Merleau-Ponty differs from Heidegger, however, at least in those works published in his lifetime, in his purpose for engaging in this description: this is not, as in Heidegger's case, to serve as a prolegomenon to a general "ontology" or theory of Being as such, but, perhaps more modestly, to illuminate our understanding of ourselves and our existence in relation to the physical, social and historical dimensions of our experience, and to understand *science* itself better. One of the crucial differences of *tone*, indeed, between Merleau-Ponty and Heidegger can be seen in the former's detailed discussions of contemporary scientific psychology and psychiatry, which play an essential part in his philosophical argument in a way that would be simply unthinkable in Heidegger.

Let us return to what was said in the last paragraph about the similarities between Merleau-Ponty and Heidegger. Both believe, as was said there, that phenomenology is concerned with *description* of the life-world, not with scientific or quasi-scientific *explanation* of our ordinary experience. The phenomenological "reduction" thus becomes a matter of setting aside the structures of scientific explanation and theorizing. In a certain sense, as Merleau-Ponty says in the Preface to *Phenomenology of Perception* (p. viii), this amounts to a "foreswearing [*désaveu*] of science". The first English translation of this work rendered *désaveu* as "rejection", but that word has all the wrong implications: it suggests that Merleau-Ponty was hostile to science, a suggestion that none of his writings supports. He was not opposed to science or to scientific explanation, but wanted only to distinguish between the roles of science and of phenomenology as he conceived it, and to use phenomenology as a means to explore the proper scope and limits of scientific explanation.

Science, for Merleau-Ponty, is perfectly in order when it is performing its proper role of enabling us to explain and predict our experience. But, he would argue, even to understand that role, we need to "*foreswear*" science, that is, to put aside the structures of scientific theorizing, in order to get back to the roots of such theorizing in ordinary human experience. Science is, after all, a human activity, the product of human beings pursuing one kind of human interest. It is thus getting things the wrong way round to *start* from the scientific account of human beings and their experience. From a scientific point of view, human beings are simply one kind of object in the world, and their experience is the result of the causal interactions between this kind of object and others. When I see an orange, for instance, a scientific account would be concerned to explain this experience in terms of the causal effect of light reflected from the orange on my retina and optic nerve and ultimately on my brain. But this scientific account has itself been developed by human beings on the basis of their experience, and the concepts used ("light-waves", "causation", "retina", "optic nerve", etc.) get their meaning from this relation to human experience. Science cannot be seen as *replacing* human experience, since its whole aim is to explain how that experience comes about. If we seek philosophical understanding, therefore, we need to return to a point *before* science, to a pure description of this lived experience on which science ultimately depends.

When we do that, we cannot regard ourselves as simply an object in the world like any other, with merely causal relations to other objects. From the point of view of pre-scientific experience, I cannot regard myself as simply an object to be studied by science, an object in the world like any other, to be understood in terms of the interactions of a number of causal laws. Rather, I am in the middle of my own world; the world of actual lived experience is, for each of us, "my" world, not in the sense that I created it, but in the sense that the things and relationships in it get their meaning for me through their relationship to my purposes, activities and needs. The desk that I am sitting at now is my familiar desk in my study at home, the one where I have written papers, letters and so on in the past; and I am working on a computer, whose meaning is determined by its use for precisely this kind of work. This is what Merleau-Ponty means by describing the human being as "the absolute source"; I am not the product of my social and physical circumstances, but rather that by which they exist as such.[9]

To repeat, this is not an *anti*-scientific statement, a "rejection" of science, but a claim that science must always be secondary, as an account of reality, to that ordinary experience that gives science itself its meaning. Husserl's slogan was "Back to the things themselves", and it was this return to the things themselves, to underlying realities, that was supposed to be the purpose of the phenomenological reduction. Merleau-Ponty is here saying that returning to things themselves is going back to the way in which we experience the world *before* we begin to theorize about it, as we do in the various sciences; the theories of science are abstract ways of describing that world of pre-theoretical experience, which we adopt for various reasons. Nor, as he goes on to say, is this to advocate any form of idealism, any reduction of the real world to the contents of consciousness. The world that precedes knowledge does not consist of any merely subjective "representations"; it is the world itself, the world in which we exist and act before we start to construct theories about it in order to explain our experience and the forms it takes.

Merleau-Ponty, indeed, criticizes Husserl's account of the phenomenological reduction as tending towards a form of idealism, because it is conceived of too much on the Cartesian model. As Descartes used his method of doubt to, as it were, strip away successive layers of external reality until only the *cogito*, the "I think", was left, so Husserl, according to Merleau-Ponty, talks as if the phenomenological reduction were a matter of setting aside the "external world" and its existence in order to get to the certainty of an inner realm of pure consciousness. (Whether this is a fair account of Husserl's position, at least in his later writings, is, of course, open to doubt.) By contrast, Merleau-Ponty wants to argue that there *is* no such "inner realm" of pure subjectivity or consciousness; a *cogito*, an "I" or "self" can exist only in relation to a situation, involving both a world of things and of other people. I can think only if I have something to think *about*, a world to relate my thoughts to; and I can conceive myself as an "I", a "subject", only if I am aware of other subjects, other "Is", from whom I can distinguish myself. "Incarnation" in a world and the existence of intersubjectivity go together, as Husserl himself acknowledges in the *Crisis of European Sciences* volume.[10] But to recognize this is the opposite of idealism, since it makes it clear that human being is "being-in-the-world".[11]

This has a bearing on the meaning of the *epoché* or "bracketing", which, as was stated earlier, forms an essential part of the phenomenological reduction. We do indeed, as phenomenologists, have to suspend our ordinary active involvement with the world before we can engage in reflection about our experience – to the extent that what we normally take for granted as "common sense" comes to appear to us as strange and paradoxical. But this loosening of our normal ties with the world can never amount to completely "putting the world in parentheses", since radical reflection itself depends on the unreflective life from which it emerges and from which it derives its "material". Phenomenological philosophers do not cease to be human beings, involved in the flux of experience within the world, when they begin to engage in reflection; the "suspension" takes the form rather of seeking to get back to the position of a "perpetual beginner", like a child who has learned nothing, can take nothing for granted, and so confronts the world of experience directly and naively, in wonder. But it is clear that we can never fully recreate that naive position in ourselves: "The most important lesson which the reduction teaches us is the impossibility of a complete reduction."[12] To see the idea of a complete reduction in this way, however, as an ideal limit towards which reflection may aspire without ever being able to achieve it, is very far from conceiving of phenomenology as anything like a "science".

Interpreted in this way, the phenomenological reduction, paradoxically perhaps, leads not to any form of idealistic distinction between "inner self" and "external world", but to a deepened awareness of our inescapable involvement with the world, of the impossibility of marking out a privileged domain of "inner experience", for by loosening our normal ties with the world and so coming to *wonder* at our relation to the world, we become more conscious both of the world's independence of ourselves, its simply "being there", and of the dependence of our own existence as conscious beings on our situation within the world. In this sense, Merleau-Ponty argues, phenomenology leads rather to existential philosophy: "Heidegger's 'being-in-the-world' appears only against the background of the phenomenological reduction"[13] (although this can only be said, of course, once we have radically reinterpreted the phenomenological reduction in the way just described, which may be said to have originated with Heidegger).

IV

Continuing in this vein of re-interpreting the central concepts of phenomenology (or, as he himself puts it, of correcting "misunderstandings" about Husserl's concepts), Merleau-Ponty then moves on to the concept of "essence". The phenomenological reduction in Husserl was also, as he says, intended to be an "eidetic" reduction, that is, to reveal the "essence" or "nature" of the world. For, he argues, to engage in the phenomenological reduction is to move from a practical engagement with the world, in which we view things in relation to our specific interests of the moment, to a more universal and disinterested standpoint in which we can consider things as they essentially are in themselves. But these "essences" that we discover in this way are not to be thought of in a Platonic way, as some kind of objects detached from all contact with the world of ordinary experience and accessible only to "reason". As was said in the previous section, the reduction, our disengagement from the life-world, can never be complete. The phenomenologist's concern with essences, as Merleau-Ponty interprets it, is part of the attempt to get more closely to grips intellectually with the life-world. Paradoxically, it is only by standing back a little from our ordinary engagement with the world that we can hope to understand that engagement better, much as we can only read a book properly if we hold it a little way away from our eyes. This is the point of the remark quoted earlier, that phenomenology does indeed study essences, but attempts to put them back into existence.

The study of essences for Merleau-Ponty (and, he would claim, for Husserl too, at least in his later thought) is only a *means* to the real end of phenomenology, which is to understand man and the world and the relation between them. To understand them necessarily involves the formation of general concepts, but these concepts and their analysis are not the central concern; rather, it is the relation to the world that gives meaning to these concepts that is the primary interest of the phenomenologist. Merleau-Ponty criticizes the logical positivism of the Vienna Circle, which he describes as "the antithesis of Husserl's thought".[14] The positivists, as mentioned earlier in this chapter, saw the remaining role of philosophy as being "the logic of the sciences", that is, the logical analysis of the relations between the statements and concepts of the empirical sciences, which were the only source of reliable factual knowledge.

But this "conceptual analysis" implied a radical distinction between "conceptual" and "factual" questions: questions about our thoughts and questions about the world. "Concepts", however, are the meanings of general words, so that this distinction in turn implied another one, between "language" and "fact"; "conceptual" or "linguistic" analysis came to be thought of as something that could be carried on without consideration of any factual issues. Indeed, one of the ways in which the "revolution in philosophy" initiated by the Vienna Circle developed, once the preoccupation with science and questions of "verifiability" had been abandoned, was the "linguistic analysis" characteristic of philosophy in Oxford in the years immediately following the Second World War, in which the terms of ordinary language (mostly) were studied in a purely detached and formal fashion, typified by the use of the *Oxford English Dictionary* as a major methodological tool. It may well have been this kind of linguistic analysis that Merleau-Ponty had in mind rather than the Vienna Circle itself.

To attempt to study concepts or word-meanings in isolation in this way is anyway, he argues, a mistake. Language may *look* like a self-contained system that can be studied in its own right, but this is an illusion. What words mean rests, Merleau-Ponty argues, on "the ante-predicative life of consciousness", in which can be seen appearing "not only what words mean, but what things mean: the core of primary meaning around which the acts of naming and expression take shape".[15] We cannot analyse concepts or word-meanings, in other words, without relating them to the experiences of the world on which they are based. He illustrates his point by taking the key concept of "consciousness". To attempt to analyse the *word* or *concept* "consciousness" by itself, as the philosophers referred to in the last paragraph did, is implicitly to ignore the fact that what the word means cannot be understood apart from our experience of ourselves and the ways in which we have thought about that experience. The word "consciousness" is, as Merleau-Ponty says, a relatively new one, in whose meaning have come together various strands in our reflection on what we are. In that sense, what we have to understand is not so much the *word* "consciousness", but the "thing" that it designates, the experience of ourselves, or rather we have to understand the word in its relation to that experience, and in so doing understand the experience itself better. "Husserl's essences", Merleau-Ponty says, "are destined to bring back all the living relationships of experience, as the fisherman's net draws up from the depths of the ocean quivering fish and sea-weed".[16] (Again, we may wonder here whether Merleau-Ponty is really talking about *Husserl's* essences or his own reinterpretation of the Husserlian concept.)

There are interesting echoes here of some aspects of Wittgenstein's later thought (although there are also important differences). Wittgenstein, too, came to reject his earlier view (expressed in his *Tractatus Logico-Philosophicus*) of "language" as something that could be considered in isolation from its use, and that stood to the "world" it referred to in the purely external relationship of "picturing". Instead, he came to see language as a part of human activity, such that questions of meaning could not be considered in isolation from the *use* of language in the course of human dealings with the world. In this sense, Wittgenstein is not a "linguistic" philosopher, any more than Merleau-Ponty is: in his later thought, he sees language as the source of philosophical problems, something that the philosopher needs to get away from, back to its roots in human activity. Merleau-Ponty's conception of philosophy, nevertheless, was certainly not identical with Wittgenstein's. Wittgenstein was suspicious of the notion of "essence", and would therefore not have used the term in describing the philosophical activity of reminding us of such uses of language; and he saw the philosophical point of that activity more negatively, as freeing us from certain typical philosophical misunderstandings. But to remove misunderstandings can also be seen more positively, as increasing our understanding, and this positive interpretation comes close to Merleau-Ponty's conception of the point of phenomenology. By first disengaging as far as we can from our ordinary involvement with the life-world, we can, in Merleau-Ponty's view, understand that involvement better, and so see better how our abstract, theoretical understanding of ourselves, our world and the relation between them gets whatever meaning it has from its roots in our existence in the world.

It is only against this background, Merleau-Ponty goes on, that we can fully appreciate the significance of that other central concept of phenomenology, "intentionality". As was remarked earlier in this chapter, Husserl took over from Brentano the revived medieval doctrine that all consciousness is "intentional" or directed towards an object, that consciousness is always consciousness *of some object* (its "intentional object"). But intentionality, Merleau-Ponty argues, can be understood only in the light of what has been said about the reduction. If we see consciousness, not in Cartesian fashion as a detached point of view, contemplating the world from a position outside it, but as "a project of the world",[17] then intentionality, the relation between our consciousness and its world, must be regarded, not as a relation to ideal objects, but as our active involvement with real things outside ourselves. As we have seen earlier, the "intentional object" of consciousness may be something that does not actually exist in the real world, as when, to use the previous example, we are afraid of non-existing things. This might seem to contradict Merleau-Ponty's account of intentionality, but he could avoid this contradiction by interpreting such modes of consciousness as particular *ways of relating* to the actual world, rather than as a relation to some kind of ideal object.

Once again, there is no room for any variety of idealism: our world is not to be identified with our thoughts about the world, but with the world itself that we inhabit and which those thoughts concern. It is "our" world only in the sense that it is *the* world as we relate to it. And we ourselves, as Merleau-Ponty argues, following Kant, come into being as consciousnesses only by virtue of our relationship to a world: the "inner world" of our own experiences cannot exist independently of our consciousness of the "outer world" of the objects of those experiences. Merleau-Ponty thus argues for a form of realism that is nevertheless different from objectivism; the reality that we experience, for example in perception, is distinct from that experience, but yet is not "objective" in the sense of being what it is in total independence of how we or anyone else experience it. It is a world of "phenomena", or "appearances", not in the sense that it is made up of purely subjective or mental entities of that name, but in the sense that it becomes a *world*, a collection of connected phenomena, only when it is conceptualized in a certain way in relation to the purposes of a particular perceiver or perceivers. We do not, for Merleau-Ponty, impose meaning on the phenomena of "our world"; rather, the world comes into being as "meaningful", and we come into being as "subjects" standing in meaning-ful relations to it, in the same interchange between ourselves as beings in the world and the world in which we have our being.

The phenomenological *epoché*, so understood, could never be confused with Cartesian or sceptical doubt, which is supposed to involve complete detachment from the world (such that the world as we experience it might even be a "grand illusion" created for us by an evil demon or a mad scientist). The notion of such universal doubt, Merleau-Ponty argues, is even incoherent since we can identify something as an illusion only by contrast with some other perception that is clearly *not* illusory. Once again, we can reaffirm that the phenomenological reduction is not a retreat into a pure subjectivity, a pure *cogito*, but a relative "putting out of play" of the kinds of theoretical and practical interests that normally involve us so closely with our world that we cannot see that relationship clearly. It is essentially a *humanizing* activity, but yet not a form of subjectivism or idealism. That is, it places the human subject at the heart of the world, seeing even the project of objective scientific understanding as the pursuit of a certain kind of human significance; but it does not *reduce* the world to human thoughts about it. The world, as Merleau-Ponty puts it, is not an object of thought, but where we live.[18]

V

One important consequence of this is that our relation to our world is not purely intellectual or cognitive, not simply a matter of having true thoughts about it, but also active, a matter of moving about the world and doing things in it. Intentionality is thus not just a feature of our thoughts, but of our desires, our evaluations, our actions, and in this wider sense is an essential aspect of what is meant by saying that the mode of being of human subjects is "being-in-the-world". The human subject is not seen as a disembodied pure consciousness, but equated with a real living human being who exists in a particular place, in a particular social and cultural setting, and at a particular time in history. In short, giving this account of phenomenology implies fully accepting the historical and social nature of human beings. If what I am cannot be understood except in terms of my manifold relationships, practical and emotional as well as purely intellectual, with the world that I inhabit, then the phenomenological description of my experience cannot be achieved without reference to my social and historical situation. The understanding aimed at by phenomenology cannot be regarded as a merely intellectual apprehension of relations between pure essences, but must rather be seen as what Merleau-Ponty calls "comprehension", so that phenomenology can become a "phenomenology of origins" (or, as he calls it elsewhere, a "genetic phenomenology").

What he seems to mean by this is that phenomenology can move back beyond Husserl to Hegel; that is, that phenomenological understanding can be distinguished from what philosophers of science call "deductive-nomological explanation", the causal explanation of particular events or states of affairs by deducing (a statement of) the event from general laws together with statements of specific initial conditions. Instead, phenomenological understanding would consist in "finding the idea in the Hegelian sense";[19] that is, finding an *intelligible pattern* in some variety of human behaviour or response to the world.

The terms in which Merleau-Ponty differentiates phenomenology here correspond to those used by several nineteenth- and early twentieth-century German philosophers of history, who distinguished between causal "explanation" of the kind found in the natural sciences and "empathetic understanding" (*Verstehen*, to use the German term) which they claimed to be characteristic of the "human studies" (history, the social sciences, literary studies and so on). "Empathetic understanding" was held to involve reliving the experiences of the human beings who were being studied in the mind of the historian or social scientist, as a way of grasping their unique significance for the human being in question. This tradition in philosophy is often referred to as "hermeneutics", from the Greek word *hermeneuein*, which means "to interpret". In other words, Merleau-Ponty here seems to be presenting phenomenology as a variety of hermeneutics: a method of understanding, not the concepts or "essences" in terms of which human beings order their experience, but the actual existence of human beings themselves as so ordered.

Such a conception of phenomenology seems far removed from the thought of Husserl himself, even in the *Crisis of European Sciences* volume, although it might be said that the very title of that volume, as well as its contents, indicates a new concern on Husserl's part to reflect on actual historical events rather than simply to withdraw to the plane of "pure science". Even in the earlier chapters of Merleau-Ponty's own *Phenomenology of Perception*, there is not much evidence of this kind of "historicist" or "hermeneutic" phenomenology. So has Merleau-Ponty simply allowed himself to be confused and carried away by his interest in Hegel, together with his political and social concerns, to seek to turn Husserlian phenomenology into something that it is not and cannot be? I want to suggest that the answer to that question is "No"; there is no confusion here, but a perfectly natural development.

Once one rejects, as Merleau-Ponty did, the Cartesian notion of the human subject as isolated and detached from the world that he or she (and gender differences hardly make sense in this context) can do no more than contemplate, then one is necessarily committed to a much richer view of human experience as actively involved with the world. The "phenomena" with which human beings are presented in their experience are then no longer the contents of the "inner self", but are the things themselves, as they appear, not simply to me, but to any human perceiver who occupies the same position. And I, as perceiver, am a concrete human being, whose ways of experiencing these phenomena are at least in part those of my own historical epoch and social setting. In these circumstances, phenomenological description cannot be of some sort of "human experience in general", but must be of a particular historical human being's or human group's way of being in the world. This does not preclude the possibility that there are general features of perceptual experience as such, of the kind described by Merleau-Ponty in the early chapters of *Phenomenology of Perception*, but it does imply that that general description must be no more than a basis for, and must eventually give way to, a phenomenology of particular ways of being in the world that in turn must lead to a philosophy of history and society.

Human experience is, as we have seen, on Merleau-Ponty's view essentially meaningful. Our involvement with our natural and human milieu implies that we cannot regard that milieu as a purely "objective", value- and meaning-free, set of states of affairs, but must see the things and people with whom we deal as having a "meaning" for us related to our dealings with them. If so, then human history must have a "meaning" too, for it is the succession of such meaningful experiences, and the meaning that we find in our contemporary experience must have a place in the unfolding of history itself. As Merleau-Ponty puts it, we are "condemned to meaning", and everything we say and do is part of history. The claim that we are "condemned to meaning" sounds very much like a riposte to Sartre's well-known slogan that we are "condemned to be free", and is a neat encapsulation of the difference between the two men's philosophies, which will be explored in more detail later in the book.

The notion of phenomenological understanding is inseparable from the clarification of what is involved in human rationality. Husserl's earlier phenomenology sought to elucidate rationality in a more or less Kantian fashion by uncovering the a priori rational structures of human experience as such. But a historicist or hermeneutic phenomenology of the kind developed in the Preface to *Phenomenology of Perception* must approach this task differently, by working through human experience to a concept of rationality that emerges from the dealings of human beings with each other in society and history. What is rational, on this view, does not consist of the eternal truths about "true and immutable natures" that might be evident to the "clear and distinct perception" of a transcendental ego; it cannot, since there is no such thing as a "transcendental ego" in that sense. Our subjectivity is irredeemably located "in the world", in time, space and history. Rationality must therefore be something that emerges from the human processes of reasoning to a conclusion that all those involved in the argument are able to share.

The rational structure of the world that we inhabit, or the rational meaning of the history of which our lives form part, is thus not located in some other realm of Platonic Forms or Hegelian Absolute Spirit, but is discovered in the "intersection" of my views and those of other people, or of my past views with those of my present. In this sense, it is something created rather than discovered. "Philosophy is not the reflection of a pre-existing truth, but, like art, the act of bringing truth into being";[20] the comparison between philosophy and art is a recurrent theme in Merleau-Ponty's writings, and will be discussed further in Chapter 7. As such, we should not expect philosophy, the establishment of rationality, ever to achieve completion, or to be immune to the influences and problems of its own time. But rationality, Merleau-Ponty insists, is not problematic: we find what is rational every time we engage in debate with others and manage to arrive at conclusions that are agreed on the basis of argument. Philosophy, as he conceives it (following Husserl, as he himself would claim), is not a discovery of transcendent or eternal truths, but the adoption of an attitude of wonder, of being a "perpetual beginner": "True philosophy consists", he says, "in relearning to look at the world."[21]

VI

So what has emerged from this discussion about Merleau-Ponty's view of phenomenology? In what sense was he, as he claimed to be, a follower of Husserl? It seems clear that his visit to Louvain in the late 1930s and his work in the Husserl Archive there had an influence on his own thinking, but what he meant by "phenomenology" was very definitely his own *interpretation* of what Husserl said even in his later works. As he himself says (and emphasizes by putting in italics), *"phenomenology can be practised and identified as a manner and style of thinking, . . . it existed as a movement before arriving at complete awareness of itself as a philosophy"*.[22] It is this "manner and style of thinking" that Merleau-Ponty seeks to identify in the writings of Husserl and then to make his own and adopt for his own purposes. He was not, and never set out to be, a "disciple" of Husserl in the sense of one who merely did further work along the lines and using the methods of the master. Husserl for him was rather a source of certain lines of thought that he could then develop in his own way; what he wanted, as he himself says, was a *"phenomenology for ourselves"* (the italics are again his own).

So what did he see as the main features of the phenomenological style of thinking? The discussion in this chapter should have made that clear. At its heart was a preference for the concrete and experiential over the abstract and theoretical. To think of the general explanatory theories of the sciences and of traditional metaphysics as expressing the only or the ultimate truth about the world and ourselves must be a mistake, he thought, if only because these theories get whatever meaning they have only by being related to our pre-reflective experience of the world. In this respect, Merleau-Ponty was part of a general modern mood of suspicion for grand theory, represented by Kierkegaard, Nietzsche, Heidegger, Sartre and Marcel (and in a different way by the later Wittgenstein). An important part of what a "phenomenological" style of thinking meant for Merleau-Ponty, therefore, was an attempt to get behind scientific and other theoretical accounts of ourselves and the world to their roots in experience. The purpose of doing so was not to attack science, but to understand better the significance of its findings for our general view of human beings and their place in the scheme of things; the enemy is not science itself, but misguided *philosophical* conclusions from it.

From the other side, the phenomenological manner of thinking, as practised by Merleau-Ponty, implies that the subjects of experience are not "transcendental egos", but ordinary human beings, located in time and space and at a particular point in history. Their accounts of the world and themselves are therefore their attempts to make sense of their own experience from that point of view, and give rise to no timeless a priori truths of the kind claimed by traditional metaphysics. The results of philosophical reflection must be provisional. Human beings are faced with a reality that is, in Merleau-Ponty's word, "inexhaustible", never to be fully comprehended by them, and yet they inevitably live in a world that is meaningful for them in its relation to their projects and activities in it. Our being in the world humanizes the world, makes it always *our* world, but, paradoxically, an essential part of its being a human world is that it stretches indefinitely beyond any human attempt to encompass it. There is a necessary gap between ourselves as subjects and the objective world of our experience, but it is never a gap that amounts to total detachment. This is the source of the "ambiguity" in Merleau-Ponty's picture of the relation between our experience and the world, which Alphonse de Waelhens, in the Foreword that he wrote for the second French edition of *The Structure of Behaviour*,[23] took to embody the core of what was distinctive about his philosophy.

Is phenomenology, conceived in Merleau-Ponty's fashion, a good, that is, an illuminating, way of doing philosophy? That can be judged only by seeing it in use, as we shall in the remaining chapters.

CHAPTER THREE

Being-in-the-world

I

Phenomenological philosophy, as Merleau-Ponty conceives it, "consists in re-learning to look at the world".[1] We need to re-learn to look at the world because we are "held captive" (to use Wittgenstein's phrase) by a picture of the world derived from the impulses that give rise to science – an *objectivist* picture of the world (including even our own bodies) as existing entirely independent of ourselves and interacting with our experience in a merely causal fashion. There is nothing wrong with this picture in its own context; if we are to study the world scientifically, then we need to set aside our own place in the world, to view the world not from where we happen to be, but as if we were completely outside it. Recent Anglo-American philosophers have referred to this purely detached scientific viewpoint by talking of "the view from nowhere" (Thomas Nagel[2]) or "the absolute conception" (Bernard Williams[3]); others have spoken of adopting the "God's-eye view". Merleau-Ponty is not in any sense opposed to science, as we have seen. What he is opposed to is the idea that this scientific picture represents a complete and self-sufficient view of reality. It cannot be self-sufficient, he argues, because it depends for its own significance on a prior view of reality; its concepts derive their meaning from our ordinary pre-reflective experience of the world as participants in it. The "view from nowhere" is an abstraction based on our many different "views from somewhere".

The very notion of "experience" implies that the experiencing subject is not contemplating the world from some position outside it, but is itself *part* of that world, and conversely that what we mean by a "world" is not something we merely contemplate but something we *inhabit*. This is, in the vaguest and most general terms, what Merleau-Ponty means when he asserts, as a central theme of his philosophy, that as experiencing subjects,

45

our being is necessarily "being-in-the-world". In this chapter, I shall be exploring what he means by that phrase (and by related terms like "body-subject" and "perception"), and why he insists on this account of our being. These notions are complex, so the manner of the exploration will not be a linear exposition, but more of a circling around about them, approaching them from different directions, continually coming back to a point near to (but not identical with) the one from which the movement started. In this way, I hope, we shall gradually build up to a fuller understanding of these terms and the role they play in Merleau-Ponty's thought.

We may start with our experience of being-in-the-world. Merleau-Ponty's term for our pre-reflective experience of being-in-the-world is "perception"; and if phenomenology, as he conceives it, is the description of pre-reflective experience, it follows that the heart of any phenomenological philosophy must be the description of "perception", or of the world as perceived. This is why Merleau-Ponty's major work is called *Phenomenology of Perception*, and why he speaks in the title of one of his essays of "The Primacy of Perception".[4] Perception is "primary" for Merleau-Ponty in that its description is the basis of a phenomenological account of all the other main concerns of his philosophy, many of which are indeed discussed in the later chapters of *Phenomenology of Perception* itself: in "The Primacy of Perception" he says "The perceived world is the always presupposed foundation of all rationality, all value and all existence."[5]

But this emphasis on perception may be misleading for English-speaking philosophers reared in the empiricist tradition, since what he means by the term is significantly different from what empiricists mean by it. Indeed, "empiricism" is one of his two main targets of attack (along with "intellectualism", of which more later) in the first part of *Phenomenology of Perception*, and the nature of his criticism of it there must be understood if we are to grasp the full significance of the claim that human being is being-in-the-world. What he is opposing is a whole tradition of philosophical thinking about the relation of the human subject to its world. This tradition does not consist in Descartes alone, and Merleau-Ponty's critique is therefore not simply a standard piece of anti-Cartesianism: it is directed rather at the whole tendency of Western culture to give an exaggerated significance to "scientific" or "objective" views of reality. Most philosophers, at least from the time of Descartes until the twentieth century, tended to make epistemology, the analysis of the conditions under which knowledge is possible, central to their thinking, and thus to treat theoretical or propositional knowledge as our primary relation to the world. But it is part of the very concept of knowledge (as Williams points out in his discussion of the "absolute conception") that knowledge is of "what is there anyway": that is, that knowledge presupposes a world that already exists to be known about, so that the "knowing subject", purely as such, is related to the known world more or less in the way a window is related to the scene on which it opens.

The empiricist strand in this tradition took sense-perception to be the basis of all genuine knowledge: that is, empiricists considered perception purely as part of this knowledge-relation to an independently existing world. But this is contrary to the whole aim of phenomenology, as Merleau-Ponty understands it, since it makes it appear that philosophy, like science, is interested only in (causally) *explaining* perception – as if perception were one kind of object in the world, to be explained, like other objective phenomena, "from the outside", rather than a human experience that we are all, including philosophers and scientists, necessarily familiar with "from the inside". Thus both empiricism and intellectualism, according to Merleau-Ponty, approach perception from the objectifying viewpoint of science. From this point of view, perception must be seen as the effect of the causal activity of external, independently existing objects, or rather their determinate qualities, on our sense-organs, nervous systems and brain or mind. For science is essentially concerned with *explaining* in terms of causal generalizations how perception can take place for any subject whatsoever, and that seems to require some such general analysis, however it may be filled in in detail in particular theories. A phenomenology of perception, by contrast, would set aside all questions about how we causally explain perception as an objective physiological phenomenon, and start from our own subjective experience of being perceivers; it would *describe* that experience, although in a way that increased our understanding of what it *means* to us to "perceive a world".

Empiricists might ask what is wrong with the objectifying approach of science, and what is the value of phenomenological reflection in this sense. We are back at the questions about phenomenology raised earlier. In our culture we generally assume that an objectivist or scientific account of reality must be primary, since we surely want to comprehend the reality of things, and the way things really are is typically contrasted with the way they may appear to particular subjects. Why should not this apply equally to ourselves and our experience? We are also parts of reality, so why should not the primary account of what we and our experiences are like be the objective view, the view from outside ourselves? It may be that we have to *start*, in giving any account of reality, from how things appear to us subjectively (and in that sense from "phenomenology"), but what is more important is where we finish. On this conception, it is only an account of *reality* when we have succeeded in getting above subjective appearances to a view, even of our own perceptions, from the outside, a view that can be shared by other rational beings apart from ourselves. If we think in these terms, as we commonly do, a philosophical analysis, if it is to be genuinely realist, must be as objectivist in this sense as a scientific account.[6]

The response of the phenomenologist to this argument is that the very notion of an objectivist account of reality as a whole *presupposes* a non-objectivist account of our own experience. For the objective account is not really a "view from nowhere", which would be a contradiction in terms, a view that was yet not a view; an objective view is one that can be shared with others because it expresses what is common to the views of everyone. It is, as it has been put, a "view from everywhere"; "everywhere" is certainly nowhere *in particular*, but it presupposes an indefinite number of "some-wheres", and the view from everywhere can therefore be arrived at only by starting from somewhere. If so, it would be impossible to formulate an objective view of other things unless we could each start from our subjective view, which by definition does not include our own subjectivity as one of its objects. Thus it would be impossible to experience objects unless, for each of us, our own experience were not itself one of those objects.

It follows from this that, in order for us to "have a world", we need to regard our relationship to objects in "perception" or "experience" as different from the relationship of one object to another. It is true that we can for certain (e.g. scientific) purposes treat perceptions as if they were objects like any others; but we could not even have the notion of a perception in the first place unless we had the first-person experience of perceiving, unless perceiving were not an object we contemplated, but our own *involvement* with the world. Without that first-person experience we could not distinguish as we do between perception-*like* phenomena, such as the responses of light-sensitive robots, and genuine perception, in human beings or in other animals; the purely objective features of the phenomenon in both sorts of case might well be virtually the same, but the difference would lie in the first-person experience of perceiving that is present in one case but assumed to be absent in the other.

How does this help our understanding of what Merleau-Ponty means by "being-in-the-world"? Above all, this argument implies that our primary relation to the world as experiencing subjects is not a *cognitive* relationship to a purely objective reality: that our relation to the world is neither a detached "view from nowhere" nor like that between objects in the world. Objects are "in the world" in a perfectly straightforward sense, the same sense in which biscuits are "in the tin": that is, they are spatially contained in it. But the sense in which experiencing subjects such as ourselves are "in the world" is different. We could not be in the world at all unless we had a position in space, and to that extent we are ourselves objects like any others. But "the world", for us, is more than simply the spatial container of our existence. It is the sphere of our lives as active, purposive beings: beings who have thoughts about it, who respond to it emotionally and imaginatively, who act on it (sometimes deliberately, sometimes unthinkingly), who are acted on by it and capable of being conscious of its actions on us, and so on. In all these ways, the world is, as was said earlier, the place that we "inhabit", rather than simply a set of objects that we represent to ourselves in a purely detached way.

What it is to "experience" the world, therefore, can be explained only in terms of such "inhabiting", rather than simply in terms of representation: indeed, we can "represent" the world only because we are already present in it and involved with it. We can formulate the idea of an "objective world" only as an abstraction, necessary for certain purposes, from our primary idea of the world as the scene of our own activities; we can understand the concept of a "view from everywhere" only because we already know what it means to have a view from where we are. If so, then we must "be in the world" before we can have a science of the world, so that the science of the world cannot replace that primary being-in-the-world. Nor can the scientific account of the world take the place of a philosophical understanding of that underlying contact that gives the scientific account its meaning.

This may sound like a variety of philosophical idealism, as if what we call the "objective world" were merely a human construct out of our inner experiences, but Merleau-Ponty denies this. If our being is "being-in-the-world", then that implies rejection of any dualist distinction between purely interior experiences and purely external objects. Perception is not an inner representation of an objective world, but a relation of inhabiting a world; and we can only inhabit a world that we find already there when we begin to experience it. If perception were some interior process, then it would be impossible to describe our perceptual experience, since "inner impressions" are by their very nature inexpressible.[7] No such problem faces a conception of perception understood as part of our being-in-the-world. The immediate objects of perception are then no longer "visual data", the internal end-products of a causal process which started with the object seen, but "the meaning, the structure, the spontaneous arrangement of parts".[8] The rejection of "objectivism" by Merleau-Ponty thus does not imply subjective idealism, in the sense of a denial of the independent reality of the objects that we experience. As he says in "The Primacy of Perception", "our relation to the world is not that of a thinker to an object of thought, and ... the unity of the perceived thing, as perceived by several consciousnesses, is not comparable to the unity of a proposition [*théorème*], as understood by several thinkers".[9]

II

The ultimate justification of Merleau-Ponty's account of perception, however, depends on the validity of his criticism of the alternative accounts given by empiricists and intellectualists. So let us return to that critique. A philosophical view based on the objectified picture required by science must take our perceptual experience to consist of "sensations" (Merleau-Ponty's preferred term – other common terms are "sense-data", "ideas", "impressions"); each sensation is to be thought of as a mental representation of a particular determinate quality in external objects, the ultimate result of a causal connection between that quality and ourselves as experiencing subjects. In the empiricist version, any connection between one sensation and another is purely contingent: for instance, we come to see various qualities as all being connected in being qualities of the *same thing* or "substance" simply because they are regularly associated with each other in our experience.[10]

This notion of a "sensation", and the whole account of our perceptual experience of which it forms part, sounds, Merleau-Ponty admits, perfectly obvious and commonsensical. Surely, perception *must* be something like this if we are to make any rational sense of how it is possible: doesn't science in addition confirm that this is roughly how it does take place? But if we set science aside for the moment and learn to look at perception, not as it must be thought of for purposes of scientific explanation, but as we actually experience it, then we shall see, he thinks, that the whole notion of "sensation" is thoroughly confused, and corresponds to nothing in our experience. "Sensations" are supposed to be parts of an objective account of the world, and as such ought to be one of the objects we can identify in the world. But at the same time, sensations can fulfil their function as units of experience of the world only if they are states of the self; I am, as Merleau-Ponty puts it, supposed to "coincide with" my sensations, and that is surely inconsistent with treating them as items I can identify in the objective world. Indeed, one might say that the source of the whole confusion is that the notion of "sensations" is an attempt to combine the *subjectivity* of perceptual experience with the scientific view of it as one kind of item in an *objective* world.

Items in an objective world are by definition precisely demarcated from each other; they have boundaries between themselves and other items. Hence, "sensations", considered as such items, would be equally determinate; each would represent a distinct quality. But, says Merleau-Ponty, nothing in our actual perceptual experience corresponds to this. Such a "pure impression" would necessarily be imperceptible, because of the very definition of "perception". What we perceive "always forms part of a 'field'".[11] Merleau-Ponty refers to the "Gestalt psychologists", who mistakenly treat this as a contingent, empirical fact about perception, when it is rather a necessary condition for calling anything a "perception". We could not properly use the term "perception", he would argue, unless the *objects* of perception formed a structured and unified whole; that is how we learn to understand what it is to "perceive" something. It is thus, he argues, a logically necessary truth that, even in the simplest perception, such as that of a white patch on a homogeneous background, "Each part arouses the expectation of more than it contains, and this elementary perception is therefore already charged with a *meaning.*"[12]

The principal criticism of empiricism is therefore that, if we set aside the prejudices of objectivism and re-learn to look at what we mean by a "perceptual experience", prior to all scientific and similar theorizing about the causes of such experience, then we see that the world as we perceive it does not consist in an atomistic collection of "sensations", but is a unified *whole* in which elements have no more separate an existence from each other than do the various parts of a painting. What each element is can be understood only in the light of its relations to other elements and to the whole, and it is this that Merleau-Ponty refers to when he says that even the most elementary perception is "charged with meaning". In this context, then, "meaning" means simply "contribution to a whole" or "place in a structure".

Empiricists do show some recognition of this: we have already seen (see note 10) how Locke, for instance, despite his rejection of the scholastic notion of "substance", does feel the need to account in his own terms for the fact that we perceive "qualities" as belonging to "things", so that our ideas of the various qualities of a single thing do seem to have a closer relationship than mere juxtaposition. But we have also seen how Locke contends that we have to recognize, if we are not to be misled into scholastic metaphysics, that this is a mere matter of convenience and reflects no underlying real connection between the ideas in question. Locke's account of the idea of substance is thus an example of what is called the "association of ideas", the forming of ideas of relations between ideas on the basis of an essentially contingent conjunction between them. Merleau-Ponty's fundamental criticism of the doctrine of association of ideas is that "the significance of the percept, far from resulting from an association, is in fact presupposed in all association".[13] That is, in order, for example, to recognize the particular kind of "association" between qualities that we call a "thing" (to distinguish it from other, purely chance, associations), we *already* have to have the concept of a "thing" or "substance". In short, empiricism can seem to work only by taking certain things for granted that ought not, simply in terms of its own theory, to be so taken.

"Empiricism" is a familiar term to anyone with even a nodding acquaintance with the history of philosophy, and it is easy to think of examples of philosophers who have held views similar to those described above. Merleau-Ponty's other main opponent is what he calls "intellectualism". "Intellectualism" in the sense in which he uses the term is not such a common label, but the way in which he describes this position makes it clear that what he has in mind are views like those of Kant and his many followers, including Merleau-Ponty's own teacher Léon Brunschvicg; he also refers to some aspects of Descartes's thought. "Intellectualists" recognize, as clearly as Merleau-Ponty, the defect in empiricism just mentioned: that its atomism fails to account for the necessary unity of anything that is to be called an experience, even when it brings in the "association of ideas". But they attempt to remedy that defect while retaining the very feature of empiricism that gives rise to it: the doctrine that our experience consists in discrete "sensations". If our experience is nevertheless structured in an intelligible way, if, for instance, we can distinguish things or substances and their qualities, then this, according to the intellectualists, is because *we* give it such structure. Intellectualism thus goes along with idealism, in that it implies that the world of our experience is a construction by our consciousness out of the sensations which are the immediate data of that experience.

Merleau-Ponty's objection to intellectualism is precisely that it has too much in common with empiricism, that it fails to address the fundamental problem in empiricism. Both traditional philosophical doctrines, he claims, share an acceptance of the "objectivist" world-picture of science, according to which the world consists of fully determinate and independent objects, with purely external relations between them. Such a world cannot have "meaning" in the sense that Merleau-Ponty is talking about here, since that would require a kind of unity that can come only because objects are not fully determinate or distinct, but are what they are only in virtue of their relations to other objects. The kind of relations between things that help to constitute those things as what they are have traditionally been called "internal" relations, as opposed to purely "external" relations like causality, the existence of which does not affect the character of the things related.

Merleau-Ponty's point could therefore be made by saying that we could not even speak of a "world" unless the objects making up that world formed a unified whole, and so were internally related to each other, but that, on the other hand, it could not be called a "world" at all unless the existence of the objects in it were prior to and independent of our experience of them. If the latter condition holds, then we cannot simply *impose* unity on the world, in the way that an artist, say, might impose unity on a painting by choosing to create a certain composition. From this perspective, empiricism and intellectualism are alike in failing to account for the existence of a "world", and so to give meaning to "perception" of such a world. Empiricists make the relations between objects purely external (and assimilate our relationship to the world to that between objects in the world), so denying the necessary unity of anything that is to be called a "world". Intellectualists substitute internal relations between our concepts of objects for internal relations between objects themselves, that is, reduce the world to our concept of it (and so reduce perception to *thought about* perception), so denying the independent reality that is equally necessary for anything which is to be called a "world".

If so, then an adequate account of perception, as well as a genuine realism that escapes the pitfalls both of intellectualist idealism and empiricist objectivism, will have to start from an entirely different point. Instead of taking for granted the scientific picture of the world and of our place in it based on the "view from nowhere", it will have to start from the position that we could not even speak of "perception" unless there were perceivers such as ourselves who "viewed" the world from *somewhere*. If we, as perceiving subjects, are necessarily somewhere, then it seems to follow that we as perceiving subjects are *within* the world that we perceive: that is, the world is not something distinct from ourselves who perceive it, and neither are we who perceive the world distinct from what we perceive. The relation between perceiving "subject" and perceived "object", in short, is an internal rather than a purely external one; the world is a "world" only if it can be perceived as such, and "perception" is possible only as a relationship to a world.

III

So we return to the notion of "being-in-the-world". For to say what has just been said is to say that our being as human subjects is "being-in-the-world", in a sense that goes beyond that in which the biscuits "are in" the biscuit tin. Despite any superficial appearances to the contrary, this is not, as was said earlier, a form of idealism: Merleau-Ponty is not saying either (in the manner of Berkeley) that the *existence* of the objects of perception depends on their being perceived or even (in the manner of the "intellectualists") that we *impose* their meaningfulness, their character as forming a "world", on objects. He could not be saying the former, since his view is that we can be perceivers only in relation to a world that is already there; the world is something that we find, not something we create. And he could not be saying the latter, since again the "meaning" that we can give to any object depends on its pre-existing properties: we could not (rationally) choose to regard a pool of (liquid) water as a writing desk or a fox as a sheepdog. Describing something as a "writing desk" is *finding* a meaning in it, even if that meaning is necessarily related to a human purpose.

The sense in which our being is "being-in-the-world", then, is, first, that we do not simply "represent" the world as a pure object of knowledge from a point outside the world, but actively participate in it; secondly, and consequently, that even our cognitive or representational relation to the world can exist and get its sense for us only as part of our "inhabiting" the world with the whole of ourselves; and, thirdly, that "inhabiting" a world in this sense implies that the world exists independently of our participation in it, sets its own limits to the ways in which we can participate in it, and extends far beyond any "meanings" that may emerge from the ways in which we currently inhabit it. To have "being-in-the-world" in this sense is neither to be a mere object, passively suffering the influence of other objects, nor to be in the God-like situation of creating the world from a position that transcends it; it is to be part of a two-way interaction between ourselves and the rest of the world out of which a meaningful structure to the world emerges. "Meanings" are thus both "found in" the world and "created" by our active dealings with objects. This may sound paradoxical, but the paradox disappears when we think about what is being said here. It is no more paradoxical than saying that my computer's being what it is depends both on my (and other human beings') seeing it *as* a computer and on certain features that it has independently of my awareness.

In this context, "perception" refers not simply to the consequences of the impact of "external objects" on our sense organs, but to our whole involvement with the world, emotional and practical as well as purely intellectual. That affects our understanding of the nature of the perceiving subject also. For a subject who is "in-the-world" in this sense – not simply located at a point in space, but actively involved with his or her world – cannot be the disembodied subject of the Cartesian tradition, since a Cartesian subject would be incapable of *acting* on objects. The Cartesian subject, being conscious, could attribute "meaning" to objects, but those meanings would be simply *ideas in the mind*, not real features of the "external" world, since the Cartesian subject is *detached* from that world. But neither, and for similar reasons, could it be the "brain", conceived, as in certain forms of materialism, as a purely material system, functioning according to the laws of physics alone, and capable of existing on its own. The brain can and does interact causally with other objects, but conceived in this fashion it lacks consciousness, and so cannot interact *meaningfully* with the rest of the world. The subject of experience must be an *embodied person*, a human being rather than a mere "mind": what Merleau-Ponty refers to as a "body-subject". There will be more to be said about the concept of the body-subject in the final section of this chapter and in later chapters, but for the moment it is sufficient to say that only a subject who was fully "embodied" could have "being-in-the-world" in the sense that Merleau-Ponty intends. Only a subject could have *experience* of the world, and only an embodied subject could have the kind of experience that consists in active involvement with objects, in which "representation" is only an element.

It has already been said several times that the whole concept of the subject's being as "being-in-the-world" entered twentieth-century philosophy through Heidegger, and that therefore Merleau-Ponty's use of the term is a borrowing from Heidegger. But it often happens in philosophy that such borrowings take on a different character in their new home, and I hope to show that there are sufficient differences in Merleau-Ponty's use of this concept to justify us in saying that he was not a mere unoriginal follower of Heidegger. Indeed, no one who read *Being and Time* and *Phenomenology of Perception* with any care could possibly come to the conclusion that the latter work was merely derivative from the former: the whole atmosphere of the two men's thought is worlds apart, and in this different atmosphere the notion of "being-in-the-world", while not changing in its essential definition, functions in a very different way. It is this difference in the mode of functioning that we need to understand if we are to see what is distinctive and original in Merleau-Ponty's philosophy.

For both philosophers, talk of "being-in-the-world" is intended to emphasize *activity* and *engagement* rather than pure *contemplation*, and consequently the "world" is not a mere collection of externally related objects, but is a realm of *meaning*, in some sense of that word. But the philosophical context for the discussion of that engagement is completely different. As the very title of his major work implies, Heidegger's primary philosophical concern was with Being. He was, as was said earlier, a phenomenologist, or at least claimed to be, but phenomenology for him was subordinated to ontology, the study of Being as such. Phenomenology was simply the best method for studying Being, the method of allowing Being to "show itself"; the focus was not on the human consciousness or subjectivity, to which "phenomena" appeared, but on what was revealed in this way. The essence of humanity, according to Heidegger's later work, "Letter on Humanism", is "its relation to Being":[14] not, notice, to "beings", i.e. to individual objects in the world. Heidegger's philosophical concern is not with the experience that individual human subjects have of the world in which they exist. As we saw in Chapter 2, he does not even speak of the "subject", but of Dasein, which is an ordinary German word for "existence", but whose literal meaning, which Heidegger exploits, is "being there". It is the general relation between Dasein and Being as such that Heidegger wants to describe in his "analytic of Dasein" and that seems to be the context in which we have to understand his talk of "being-in-the-world". The aim of his philosophy is not to reveal the roots of objectified thought in ordinary subjective human experience, but, as he would express it, to get away from such "humanism" to enable man to find "a home for dwelling in the truth of Being".[15]

One might well be unclear about what exactly Heidegger means by this, but whatever it means, it is certainly very different from Merleau-Ponty's concern with "being-in-the-world". Merleau-Ponty is precisely (or at least was at the time of writing *Phenomenology of Perception*) one of the "existential" phenomenologists, like Sartre, whom Heidegger attacks in "Letter on Humanism". His concern is to describe concrete human experience, the experience of individual human subjects who contingently exist in particular places and times, which gives meaning to the objectified structures of science and metaphysics that are erected on that foundation. His talk of "being-in-the-world" is thus not intended to get away from human subjectivity but to clarify the nature of that subjectivity, as existing only in an interactive relationship with its world. His phenomenology is not, like Heidegger's, aimed at letting Being reveal itself, but at describing the way in which meaning emerges in the world from the interaction between human subjects and the objects of their experience. Because of that, it is not a description of an "inner" world of pure consciousness, but of human modes of being-in-the-world; nevertheless, it is focused on the analysis of pre-theoretical human experience rather than on an analysis of Dasein. That is the sense in which it is a phenomenology of *perception*.

IV

We can still talk of "subjects" and "objects" in the traditional way, but the relation between "subject" and "object" is to be conceived in a very nontraditional way. It follows from the very concept of "experience" that a "subject" of experience cannot exist without "objects" to experience. Putting it another way, a subject can have being only *in* a world, as part of the same world as the objects which that subject experiences. But at the same time a subject, as such, must be in that world in an importantly different way from objects, for a subject, by definition, *experiences* the world. The world as experienced by a particular subject cannot be a mere collection of independent and merely externally related objects, but must be conceived of as unified by its relations to that subject and his or her projects in it: as a system of meanings. That is the sense in which, for each of us, the world is "my world". Thus, the subject can be conceived of only in relation to a world, and the world can be conceived of only in relation to a subject. The subject must be "in the world" both in the way that objects are and in a way that transcends the mode of being of objects.

At this point we can return to something that was said briefly earlier, since we can see more clearly now why the subject of experience, for Merleau-Ponty, cannot be either a disembodied Cartesian mind or a brain, seen simply as a material, mechanistic system capable of existing and functioning on its own. We can also see why the only kind of subject that could be "in-the-world" in Merleau-Ponty's sense is a *living human being*, since only that could be both one of the objects in the world (as a certain kind of living organism) and also (because human beings are conscious of their environment) interact with objects in a *meaningful* way so that those objects become the kind of meaningful unity that we call a "world". The human being is not a pure consciousness, but a living organism, a body. Unless human beings were embodied, they could not have conscious experiences of the world: without eyes, we could not see; without ears, we could not hear; without limbs, we could not act, and so could not in a sense have real intentions; and so on. A particularly important condition of our being able to interact consciously with objects is our possession of a functioning brain and nervous system, which integrates the activities of our sense organs and the movements of our limbs, and so makes possible the particular kinds of interaction with our world that are characteristic of human beings. In this sense, having the kind of brain that we have is crucial to being a conscious human being, a "person" in the way that human beings are.

It does not follow, however, as some philosophers would claim, that "consciousness" or "personhood" is *identical* with the brain, that my brain *is* me.[16] Being a conscious subject is engaging in complex relations with objects, and these relations depend on the whole human being, not simply on the brain; a disembodied brain could not be said to have conscious experiences of objects, but only to provide some of the necessary, but not sufficient, conditions for such conscious experiences. The subject of experience is, to repeat, the whole human being; *I* experience the world, not my brain, even though I need a brain in order to have any experience at all. There is a sense in which Merleau-Ponty is a "materialist", namely, that he makes no appeal to any non-material substance in order to explain human experience: but he is not a "materialist" if that means that he thinks of human beings as nothing more than lumps of matter whose behaviour can be explained entirely in terms of the laws of physics and chemistry. The unit of study for a phenomenologist of Merleau-Ponty's kind is not "consciousness" as such, but the particular human being's experience of the world, through action and emotion as much as through representational thought. All this is contained in Merleau-Ponty's key concept of the "body-subject", which is key in the sense that an understanding of it is central to grasping what Merleau-Ponty is about in his philosophy as a whole. In this final section of the chapter, I want to concentrate in particular on this concept.

If the subject of experience is not a disembodied Cartesian ego but a conscious but embodied human being, then that implies, first, that subjectivity is not co-extensive with consciousness. In Descartes's conception of the self, the "I" is a "mental substance", whose "essence consists solely in the fact that I am a thinking thing":[17] I am my mind, and the sole essential property of mind is "consciousness". I thus have a "much truer and more certain" awareness of myself as a thinking or conscious being, so that "I can achieve an easier and more evident perception of my own mind than of anything else".[18] A Cartesian subject is thus fully in possession of itself; it is wholly transparent to itself and the boundaries between itself and the world of material objects (including the body to which it happens to be attached) are clearly drawn. Merleau-Ponty, by contrast, believes it is necessary to show that consciousness "cannot take full possession of its operations".[19] But this would imply a wholly different conception of consciousness, such that our experience, our subjectivity, is not fully conscious in the Cartesian sense – as Merleau-Ponty says (same page) it implies "a new *cogito*". A new *cogito* in turn implies a new conception of the relation between the thinking self and matter; my own body ceases to be another object in the world and becomes instead "the visible expression of a concrete Ego". (This new conception of mind–body relations will be explored in more detail in Chapter 4.)

For the moment, let us concentrate on our relation to our world as "body-subjects". If we, as body-subjects, necessarily inhere in the world that we experience, that is, if our relation to objects is internal in the sense explained earlier, then it follows that it cannot be simply explained as a matter of "psycho-physiological mechanism". That would effectively reduce experience to something that was not really "experience" at all, but just a set of objective processes impinging on an equally objective "interiorless thing".[20] Whereas the notion of experience implies a *first-person* perspective, an "I" who has the experience, this scientistic picture attempts to deal with the phenomena of experience entirely in "third-person" terms. Perception becomes "a window on to things", as if we were permanently locked in a room in a house from which we were gazing on to the world outside, a place in which we ourselves played no part at all. But as soon as we recognize that the subject of experience is a "body-subject", whose being is essentially *in* the world experienced, then the objects of our perception cease to be simply objects that causally affect our sense organs and constitute instead the "field" in which we move about and act and to which we respond. The "meanings" that we find in the world are no longer, as they were for Descartes and his empiricist and intellectualist heirs, the simple result of causal processes whereby situations in the world give rise to processes in the central nervous system that we experience as sensations of pleasure and pain. Instead, they become part of a reciprocal relationship in which the human body becomes the expression of a certain way of being-in-the-world.

The world that we perceive, on Merleau-Ponty's view, is not the world of "truth in itself", which it is the ultimate goal of science to reveal to us: a world entirely independent of our wishes, values and plans; a world of determinate, sharply outlined objects and relations in an impersonal geo-metrical space, which can be precisely delineated in equally determinate judgements. It is important that we should aspire to such a conception, but it is also important to recognize, Merleau-Ponty argues, that we do not and cannot *start* from it. "We shall no longer hold", he says, "that perception is incipient science, but conversely that classical science is a form of perception that loses sight of its origins and believes itself complete."[21] The world with which we make contact in ordinary pre-scientific experience is not clearly defined and complete, but at the same time it is boundless, extending way beyond our awareness of it, and charged with meaning in virtue of the fact that it is *our* world, the world with which we engage. A sensation is not, as empiricists and intellectualists would hold, a confused version of an intellectual idea or judgement. Rather, Merleau-Ponty sides with "ordinary experience", in distinguishing sharply between "sensation" and "judgement": judgement involves "taking a stand", making an assertion about what are alleged to be the real properties of things, whereas sensation involves "taking things at face value".[22]

Our own bodies *can* be viewed scientifically, as one kind of object in the world, whose causal relations to other objects can be studied in exactly the same way as any others; but more normally they are not so much perceived as experienced as expressing our way of being-in-the-world. Similarly, the bodies of other human beings can be studied scientifically (e.g. in physiology or anatomy) as one kind of object in the world, but more normally we experience them as expressions of a person's manner of being-in-the-world; we can no more separate other human subjects from their embodiment than we can separate ourselves from our own bodies. In this way, the world as we perceive it is again a world of *meanings*, which include our own bodies and other embodied persons as having particular sorts of meaning for us.

Perception, as the pre-reflective contact of an embodied subject with its world, is necessarily perspectival. I see the world from where I am, both literally (from the point in space and time in which I happen to find myself) and in a more metaphorical sense (as being a person with a certain sort of body, a certain life history, and so on). An empiricist or scientifically minded philosopher might be prepared to agree with that; many such philosophers have spoken, for instance, of the way in which memory of past experience helps to shape present experience. But because of their preconceptions, they would mean by that that there is a causal relationship between my past memories and my current perceptions. That is not what Merleau-Ponty means. The connection of my present perception with my past experiences is not causal, but "existential". Empiricism "mutilates perception from below", by "treating it immediately as knowledge and forgetting its existential content".[23] That is, perception can only be properly understood if it is seen as referring to the way in which persons as a whole make contact with the world; persons as a whole are beings with emotions, values and purposes, and (importantly) they are *temporal* beings, beings who interact with their worlds in these ways *over time*. Thus, my present perception is not something separate from past perceptions, to be causally affected by them, but part along with them of a continuing life history and to be understood as such. It is only in the context of that existential contact that the purely *cognitive* relations with objects, which are isolated and made central by empiricism, can have any significance.

Just because of this, the world that is presented to us in sense experience is necessarily both charged with meaning and "ambiguous". Merleau-Ponty gives some examples of the "rich" (meaningful) notion of sense experience at the beginning of Chapter 4 of the Introduction to *Phenomenology of Perception*:

> A wooden wheel placed on the ground is not, *for sight*, the same thing as a wheel bearing a load. A body at rest because no force is being exerted upon it is again for sight not the same thing as a body in which opposing forces are in equilibrium. The light of a candle changes its appearance for a child when, after a burn, it stops attracting the child's hand and becomes literally repulsive . . .[24]

As these examples show, Merleau-Ponty's claim is that if we understand perception properly as the experience of an embodied subject, then we shall treat the values and meanings that we find in objects as a result of our practical and emotional dealings with them as just as much *real properties of the objects* as the "sensible qualities" to which empiricist and intellectualist philosophers devote all their attention. It is just as true to say, from the point of view of a phenomenological description of pre-reflective sense experience, that the light of the candle, as seen by the frightened child, is "repulsive" as that it is "bright".

We shall return to this point a little later on; but in the meantime it is worth pointing out that Merleau-Ponty's use of the notion of "meaning" has taken a new turn here. As we saw earlier in this chapter, he first introduces the idea of meaning into his account of perception by arguing that nothing could count as a "perceptual experience" unless its objects formed a structured whole. In this context, then, to say that the perceptual world is "meaningful" is simply to say that it is such a structured whole, and to talk of the "meaning" of an object is to talk of its contribution to such a structured whole. But in the passage we are considering now, "meaning" seems to be equated with "value", in a broad sense of that word which includes not only moral and aesthetic, but also instrumental, values (like a body's quality of being one in which opposing forces are in equilibrium) and emotional values (like the repulsiveness of the candle flame for the frightened child). These two senses of "meaning" are not, of course, incompatible, but they are certainly different from each other, and the argument for saying that the perceptual world is meaningful in the first sense could not establish that it was in the second. The argument for the meaningfulness of perception in the second sense depends essentially on the further claim that the subject of perception is a *body*-subject, one who actively "inhabits" the world that she perceives, and in so doing necessarily finds that the objects perceived have a significance for her related to her practical and emotional dealings with them.

The world of perception is not only meaningful; it is also "ambiguous". That is, we are confronted, in perception, not with a fully determinate world in which clearly defined objects stand in definite relations to each other, but with a world that is "inexhaustible". The world, as Merleau-Ponty says in a passage already referred to from the Preface to *Phenomenology of Perception*, "is not what I think, but what I live through. I am open to the world, I have no doubt that I am in communication with it, but I do not possess it."[25] It must be so, if we have our being *in* the world, since that implies that we perceive the world, not from a God's-eye view located somehow outside it, but from somewhere within it. As was said earlier, one of Merleau-Ponty's central criticisms of both empiricism and intellectualism is that neither "can grasp consciousness *in the act of learning*": the truth about the world, for them, is supposed to be (in principle at least) fully graspable in a single act of apprehension. But real human experience of the world necessarily involves learning, exploring the world from where one is and only gradually (if successful) coming to some kind of clearer understanding of things and how they are related to each other and to ourselves – an understanding that, since we can never see the world as a whole, will never, even in principle, be complete. The metaphor of "communication", which Merleau-Ponty employs in the passage cited above, is apt. When we are conversing with someone else, especially about some difficult personal issue, we can, if we are lucky, come to some kind of an understanding of what each other is saying. But since we are each speaking from our own point of view, understanding is something that has to be *come to*; it is not possible for it to be present from the beginning. Nor, since each increase in our understanding is a change in ourselves and in our interlocutor, can we ever come to anything that might count as a "complete" understanding of what the other is saying.

In this way, human experience is a kind of never-ending dialogue with the world that we inhabit, including, of course, our fellow human beings, both as individuals and as fellow members of society, for our own dialogue with the world is necessarily also a dialogue with other subjects about the world that we share with them. If the world, as the intentionality of consciousness entails, is distinct from anyone's consciousness of it, then my perspective on it also implies the existence of other perspectives, and my own attempt to understand it better must involve comparisons with other perspectives. "The phenomenological world is not pure being, but the sense which is revealed where the paths of my various perspectives intersect, and also where my own and other people's intersect and engage each other like gears."[26] Dialogue with other perspectives necessarily involves understanding the perspectives themselves better, since it involves grasping the meaning that other people's "worlds" have for them in relation to their own situation (e.g. understanding the repulsiveness of the candle for the child in the light of her past frightening experience of being burned). And it also involves coming to an agreement on certain principles of rationality – not in the sense of formal logical principles, which may be regarded as implicit in the very possibility of any dialogue at all, but in the sense of principles of what "makes sense", what counts as "evidence" for and against particular sorts of claims, where we distinguish between fantasy and reality, metaphor and literal truth, and so on.

We come back to the contrast between the world of pre-reflective perceptual experience, which the phenomenologist tries to describe without presuppositions, and the world of science. Science presents us with a world that is fully objective, totally detached from ourselves as perceivers, and so as having no properties that depend for their sense on a relation to a perceiver. In the world of science, no candle flame is "repulsive", only "bright" or "dim" or "capable of burning flesh or melting wax". And in the world of science every object is fully determinate, in its properties, boundaries and relations to other objects, with no element of ambiguity in any of these respects. Furthermore, the principles of rationality are taken as equally clear and self-evident. As scientists, what we have to do is to use these principles of rationality in order to produce judgements that "mirror" pre-existing truth about the objective world, to transcend our own subjective perspectives in order to arrive at an equally detached and unambiguous account of how the world, including ourselves and other people, actually is.

Empiricist and intellectualist philosophers, as we have seen, together with perhaps most of us living in modern Western culture, take it for granted that that scientific picture is the most fundamental account of how things are, and that the subjectivity of ordinary perception must somehow be subsumed and explained within that objective picture. It is part of phenomenology as Merleau-Ponty understands it, however, to claim that that assumption gets things entirely the wrong way round. It is only because we already exist as embodied beings in the world and so interact with it at a pre-reflective level that we are subsequently able by reflection to conceive of it as independent of our perceptions, as a fully determinate "objective world" in the sense required by science. To use Merleau-Ponty's own analogy, it is only because we have already experienced the countryside as a place in which we have explored forests, prairies and rivers that we can even make sense of the geographer's map, in which all these features are reduced to abstract symbols.[27]

Of course, there is a sense in which this scientific objectification is already implicit in the very nature of perceptual experience: perception is, after all, a communication with *the world*, with things that exist independently of ourselves. But a *communication with* the world is not in itself a *hypothesis about* the world. The world of perception is "already inhabited by a significance",[28] related to our existence in it, and it is this significance that ultimately gives meaning to the scientific hypotheses that we may formulate about it, and in which we treat as fully determinate what is indeterminate for perception. The role of the phenomenological reduction, in Merleau-Ponty's conception, is not and cannot be to set the world of "phenomena" at a distance from "consciousness" – cannot be, because phenomena and our consciousness of them are not ultimately separable. Rather, it is to slacken as far as possible those ties in order that we can understand in a more detached way their nature, and so correct misunderstandings of the implications of the concepts of science and other more abstract ways of thinking of the world by finding their origins in direct, pre-reflective experience of the world.

There might seem to be two closely connected problems for Merleau-Ponty here. First, given that our experience is "in-the-world" in his sense, how is it possible to detach ourselves even to a limited extent from our involvement with things? And, secondly, even if we could, how could we have a language to describe that pre-reflective experience to others, when the possibility of such a language seems to presuppose a world that is "objective" in the sense at least that it is accessible to more than one subject, so that expressions can have a shared public reference? Merleau-Ponty's response to both is to say that they arise only if we think of the "immediate data of consciousness" as internal, purely private, states. The world of perception may not be a fully determinate and impersonally objective world like that of science, but it is already an *intersubjective* or public world. This follows from the idea of "being-in-the-world", in which my consciousness is necessarily involved with a world that is shared, or at least shareable, with other conscious beings. We can thus detach ourselves to some extent from our ordinary involvement with the world by describing our purely individual perspective on the world; in that description we can use a language that is derived, by contrast, from that used to describe the more "intersubjective" aspects of our experience, and that is therefore intelligible to others. But in order fully to understand, and to judge the validity of, Merleau-Ponty's response to such problems, we shall need to wait until a later chapter, in which his view of the relations between subjectivity and intersubjectivity will be discussed at greater length.

The clear implication of the claim that our being is "in-the-world" is thus that we can think and reflect only *within* a situation; any analytic thought must start from where we happen to be. Human existence and human thought are inescapably *historical*, in the sense that no one can survey reality from a point outside time, *sub specie aeternitatis*. If so, then that particular sort of human thought called "philosophy" must equally be historically limited. The philosopher is not and cannot be a "transcendental ego", reflecting on the world from an absolute position and ordering it in accordance with eternal principles of reason derived from that transcendental subjectivity. Unlike Descartes's *cogito*, which is supposed to represent the position reached after stripping away by methodological doubt all those excrescences of personal, local and temporal existence to arrive at pure "mind", Merleau-Ponty's version will be genuinely personal, genuinely entitled to use the first-person pronoun "I", because the power of thinking will be seen as inseparable from the particularities of human existence. "The core of philosophy", he says, "is no longer an autonomous transcendental subjectivity, to be found everywhere and nowhere: it lies in the perpetual beginning of reflection, at the point where an individual life begins to reflect on itself."[29] It is in the nature of reflection that, in attempting to make explicit what is implicit in our existence, it will transcend, that is, "go beyond" such unreflective involvement and so will "change our existence": but "transcendence" in that sense does not involve stepping outside time and history.

The principles of rationality will then be seen as emerging from our reflections on our dealings with the world and each other in the course of our historical experience. This has implications also for thinking about, and changing the conditions of, our social and political experience. For we cannot, if we accept this emergent view of rationality, see any existing society as based on permanent and absolute principles of reason: only, Merleau-Ponty argues, in certain very favourable historical conditions are we even tempted to do so. "The experience of chaos", he goes on,

> both on the speculative and the other level, prompts us to see rationalism in a historical perspective which it set itself on principle to avoid, to seek a philosophy which explains the upsurge of reason in a world not of its making . . .[30]

This quotation encapsulates the link between Merleau-Ponty's phenomenology of perception and his social and political philosophy, which will be further explored in Chapter 6.

CHAPTER FOUR

Embodiment and Human Action

I

For the Cartesian dualist, our being is not strictly *in* the world at all; the subject of experience, "the mind by which I am what I am", as Descartes puts it, is a conscious mind, which is independent of the world of matter, even of the body to which it is for the time being attached. The subject, being unextended, is not even in space; the world is a spatial system of objects that the subject contemplates from a "position" that is not part of that system. The main traditional alternative to Cartesianism has been a materialistic monism, which rejects one of Descartes's two substances, mind, and retains only matter. For this kind of materialism, human being is certainly in the world, but in the sense that human beings are simply one kind of material object and, as such, are spatially located in the world of matter like every other kind of object. But this sort of "being in the world" rules out any ultimate distinction between subjects and objects; what we call "subjective experience" is, on this view, merely a way of referring to the causal impact of other objects on the sense organs and brains of certain kinds of living organisms.

As these illustrations show, it is impossible ultimately to separate the question of the nature of our minds and their relation to our bodies from that of the relation between our experience and its objects. Merleau-Ponty rightly says, "The theory of the body is already a theory of perception"[1] (and the converse is, of course, equally true). But the dualist and classical materialist theories of the body entail equally unsatisfactory theories of perception from a phenomenological point of view. The dualist theory reduces perception to its purely *cognitive* aspects: in effect, it equates perceiving or experiencing with perceiving *that* some proposition or other is true. It must do so, because the subject of perception is essentially distinct from its objects, and can have no relation with them except a detached cognitive one. But this, the phenomenologist would say, is to ignore something that is clear about the nature of our experience when we consider it without theoretical presuppositions, namely, that we perceive the world always from a certain individual point of view that embodies not only our literal spatial position but our active purposes and emotions; the objects of our awareness are thus experienced by us in their relation to those goals and feelings, and in that sense as having a *meaning* for us. Because of this, even the cognitive aspects of our perceptual experience cannot be considered in isolation from the personal meaning that what we perceive has for us in virtue of our individual perspective. Our relationship to the world of experience is not an external one; the world that I experience is, in an important sense, *my* world, a world that I "inhabit" rather than simply contemplate.

The classical materialist theory of the body is, if anything, even more unsatisfactory. For the materialist, as was said earlier, the perceiver is simply one kind of object in the world, whose interactions with other objects are straightforwardly causal. To experience the world is on this view not actively to inhabit it but passively to respond to external stimuli. There is no sense in which I can perceive my world as meaningful in relation to my individual projects in it, since there is nothing specifically *mine* or *individual* about these projects: they too are simply complex reactions to external stimuli, explicable in terms of general causal laws. But this, even more than the dualist theory, flies in the face of a presuppositionless account of what experience is actually like. We *do* experience our world as meaningful in relation to our individual projects, and this meaning is not merely something that we *impose* on a basically meaningless set of data, but an essential part of a description of what we actually perceive. The computer at which I am working now, to take a simple example, is perceived by me as just that, a computer and word-processor on which I can pursue my project of writing this book. In this sense, what I see may well be different from what others see, even when those others are looking from the same spatial position as me. The classical materialist account cannot allow for subjectivity in this sense, the sense in which different subjects have a perspective in other than the literal spatial sense.

If, then, we are to have a theory of the body that is also an adequate theory of perception, it must clearly be different from both Cartesian dualism and classical materialism. Or perhaps it would be better to say that if we are to do justice to the *phenomenology* of perception, we need to pay attention to the *phenomenology* of our relation to our own bodies: not to construct a "theory of the body" at all, but to describe without theoretical presuppositions what it is like to be embodied. If we do that, Merleau-

Ponty would say, we shall see that we do not, except in very special circumstances, experience our own bodies (or those of other human beings) as *objects* at all. Rather, our own bodies are for us the means by which we are in the world, engaged in a particular set of circumstances in which we have particular "projects" of our own to which we are committed. By the same token, to be a "self" is to be a living creature that is "in the world" through the vehicle of one's body. There is no suggestion in this account that "self" and "body" are the names of distinct "substances", as in the Cartesian theory; they are elements in a single human being's involvement with his or her world. To put it differently, there are not "minds" and "bodies"; there are only *human beings* who form various projects in relation to the environment in which they find themselves and who realize those projects by making appropriate bodily movements (including the processes in their brains and nervous systems that precede and causally determine the external bodily movements).

Is this not a form of materialism? In a sense it is, the sense being that it does not postulate any separate non-material substance in order to explain the possibility of human beings' forming projects. But that is because it is not concerned with the ontological issue of how many substances we need to postulate in order to *explain* the phenomena of human experience; it is a phenomenological account that aims simply to *describe* those phenomena themselves. (Phenomenological description in this sense, although not itself explanation, gets its point in part because an adequate description of what we are to explain seems a necessary preliminary for a satisfactory explanation even in science.) The phenomenological account that Merleau-Ponty offers is that we experience ourselves, not as distinct "minds" and "bodies", but as unified persons who form intentions and act in the world, but can do so only because our bodies function mechanically in certain ways. Because it is not concerned with matters of ontology and metaphysical explanation, it is not a version of the classical materialism described above, which, in denying the existence of the dualists' "mental substance", thought that human beings were "material substances", a kind of physical object, and "in the world" only in the sense in which physical objects are.

The use of notions like "purpose", "intention'", "meaning", "project" and so on in itself implies a "subjective" dimension to human being-in-the-world, which must be taken into account in any adequate description of human perceptual experience, even for the purposes of science. To have the intention of eating that juicy apple on the tree in the garden involves conceiving of it as an apple and of an apple as something for me to eat, either in order to satisfy my felt hunger or in order to give me sensual pleasure (or both, of course). It also involves the notion of it as a *physical object*, existing independently of me and my wishes, so that, for instance, I can eat it only if I take steps to appropriate it and put it into my mouth. To see the apple in these ways (even to see it as an independently existing physical object) is to see it as "meaningful" in relation to me as a subject, a being with feelings, desires and so on of my own: indeed as a being capable of *seeing things as* related to me in such meaningful ways, rather than simply responding mechanistically to their impact on my nerve-endings. And to act to realize this purpose – for example, to reach out, pluck and eat the apple – has to be explained differently from such a merely mechanistic response (an example might be blinking because of the intensity of the light reflected from the apple). The explanation, because of what it is we are seeking to explain (an *action* rather than a passive *response*), must be in terms of reasons: purposes, goals, intentions, etc.

Because classical materialism is an *ontological* theory, concerned to reject one of Descartes's two substances, and because the separate existence of the "mental" substance they rejected was supposed by Descartes to be the only way in which the possibility of using such concepts as "purpose" could be explained, classical materialists felt obliged to deny the validity of such concepts or their usefulness in a scientific account of human behaviour. They concluded that human actions, like the movements of other objects, must be treated as nothing more than changes of spatial position, fully explicable in terms of the mechanistic laws of natural sciences. In the case of human beings, as of other living organisms, that meant that they must be explicable in terms either of neurological mechanisms or of dispositions to external bodily movements.[2] But if we leave aside questions of the ontological conditions of the possibility of forming purposes and intentions and simply examine our experience without philosophical or scientific preconceptions, it is clear that we *do* form them, and that in that sense we are subjects who are "in the world" in a way that is significantly different from that in which objects are. Indeed, even to say that we "experience" or "respond to" the world, as opposed to merely "being affected by it" is to say that we are in the world as subjects rather than simply as objects.

If so, then any account of human beings and their behaviour, including the account given in scientific psychology and physiology, must, if it is to be adequate to the facts of experience, make use of the concepts that materialists rejected: "purpose", "intention", "goal", "meaning" and the like. This is the central argument of Merleau-Ponty's first major work, *The Structure of Behaviour*,[3] and is a major theme of *Phenomenology of Perception* itself. If Merleau-Ponty can show that it is impossible to construct even an adequate scientific theory of human behaviour except by treating human beings as both *subjects* and *embodied*, then that will provide powerful further support for the correctness of the account of human being-in-the-world derived from phenomenology. In the next section, therefore, I shall examine some of the main elements in his argument in *The Structure of Behaviour*.

II

The goal of *The Structure of Behaviour* is announced in the Introduction as being "to understand the relations of consciousness and nature: organic, psychological or even social".[4] "Nature" is defined in the next sentence as "a multiplicity of events external to each other and bound together by relations of causality". This is nature as conceived in natural science, which studies the world as a system of objects distinct from our consciousness of them and with only external, causal, relations to our consciousness and to each other. Merleau-Ponty's aim might in fact be described as that of showing that we cannot "understand the relations of consciousness and nature" without *abandoning* this concept of nature in favour of a different one. As he says further down the same page, psychology, in so far as it has sought the status of a natural science, has accepted this picture of the relations between consciousness and nature; it "has remained faithful to realism and to causal thinking". This attempt had led the French psychologists who are Merleau-Ponty's main concern in one of two directions. Some adopted a version of materialism in which consciousness was identified with certain events in the brain. These events had the peculiar feature of existing both "in themselves", like other material objects, and "for themselves", that is, with a private subjective dimension; they were thought of as causally related to other events. Others adopted what Merleau-Ponty calls "mentalism", in which consciousness is treated as "the analogue of a force",[5] although of a non-physical nature; then the impact of consciousness on the body had to be reduced to a minimum, in order not to disturb too much the idea of a closed physical universe in which energy was conserved. In either case, contemporary science, at least in France, saw "the organism and consciousness as two orders of reality and, in their reciprocal relation, as 'effects' and 'causes'".[6] The terms in which this discussion was conducted may sound rather outmoded now, but if we can look below the surface of language, we can recognize here essentially the same problems about the way in which consciousness can be fitted into the facts of neuroscience that now engage so many philosophers and scientists.

Materialism and monism are plainly not themselves parts of empirical science, but philosophical assumptions made by scientists about their work. Because they are simply assumptions, they are not clearly thought out and argued for as they might be by philosophers. In French philosophy proper in his time, the dominant view according to Merleau-Ponty was what he here calls "critical thought" (what he calls in *Phenomenology of Perception* "intellectualism"), which rejected the scientific "realism and causal thinking" on which both materialism and mentalism were based. "Critical thought" was a form of idealism in the Kantian sense according to which "there is nothing in the world which is foreign to the mind".[7] On this view, nature, the objects in it, the distinctions between kinds of objects, and the causal relations between objects, were all constituted by consciousness, and this was seen as the only way of avoiding the intellectual problems in a realistic and causal analysis of the relations between consciousness and its objects. But Merleau-Ponty was dissatisfied with this proposed resolution (or perhaps better, dissolution) of the problems, which seemed to him to allow only an impoverished sort of psychology in which the study of the phenomena of consciousness was separated from that of the mechanics of the brain and central nervous system and in which the phenomena of consciousness were seen as consisting only in the "judgements" by which consciousness constituted nature.

Surely it must be possible, he argued, to accept the criticism that these philosophers made of realism and causal thinking, but yet to pose the question, "is there nothing justified in the naturalism of science – nothing which, 'understood' and transposed, ought to find a place in a transcendental philosophy?"[8] This well describes his own aims in *The Structure of Behaviour*. What he seeks to show is that there can be a science of psychology that is capable of doing greater justice to the complexities of human behaviour and what it might be like, while yet not abandoning the original insights of naturalism. The superiority of this different sort of psychology would rest on a view of human beings and their place in nature distinct from those both of "realism and causal thinking" and of "critical thought", while taking over from the former a (suitably transformed) naturalism and from the latter elements in its critique of scientific objectivism.

The approach, as the title of the book suggests, is to consider the notion of "behaviour", which is in itself *neutral* in regard to the mental/physical distinction, but which Watsonian behaviourists in psychology have identified with certain observable physiological movements, at the most basic level natural and "conditioned" reflexes. This is in line with the objectivist realism that treats as "real" only those things that are observable by more than one person and thus admit of scientific verification, and consequently denies any notion of consciousness as an "internal reality".[9] The result is that our ordinary inner experience of our own behaviour as directed, intentional and meaningful, is rejected as mere "appearance", of which science reveals the deeper reality. Behaviour is really nothing but a physiological response to the action of a stimulus on a given receptor, explicable solely by the laws of physics and chemistry. For example, in classical reflex theory, the apparently intentional character of behaviour is explained by saying that "it is regulated by certain pre-established nerve pathways in such a way that in fact I obtain satisfaction".[10]

One obvious problem with this, even from a strictly scientific point of view, is that we rarely find, even in non-human animals, simple classical examples of reflexes in which a single defined stimulus produces a single defined response; and complex responses do not seem to be analysable as a summation of independent responses to distinct elements in the stimulus. The only cases in which we find reflexes as defined in the theory are the product of highly artificial laboratory conditions, where the very stimuli to which the animal has to respond are determined, not by nature, but by the decisions of human scientists. In less artificial situations, what the facts suggest is a picture of even the simplest animals (even dung beetles, to use Merleau-Ponty's own example) as *active problem-solvers* rather than as mechanistic systems in which isolated "receptors" are passively affected by equally isolated "stimuli". The animal's response varies according to the nature of the external situation and its relation to the animal's own internal needs. In this sense, the organism itself "chooses the stimuli in the physical world to which it will be sensitive".[11] The use of the word "choose" here is not, of course, meant to imply some kind of conscious decision on the part of the organism; it is a way of saying that we cannot fully understand the behaviour except by using concepts such as "adaptation", "the good of the animal" and the like.

It is important to understand the nature of Merleau-Ponty's argument here, and especially to be clear what he is *not* saying. He is not advocating a "vitalist" metaphysics in the style of Bergson (what Merleau-Ponty calls "finalism"), according to which there are inner purposes in living organisms, an *élan vital* or "life-force", to use Bergson's term, which constitute "life" as a separate ontological domain from mechanistic matter. Nor, certainly, is he suggesting, in the style of the intellectualists whom he criticizes, that the categories of purposive explanation are imposed by our own transcendental subjectivity on the phenomena. He is not making any metaphysical proposals of any kind, but on the contrary is arguing that we should set aside metaphysics and let the phenomena speak for themselves (fully in accordance with his conception of phenomenological method). Physics, the very paradigm of a natural science, has, he says, made progress precisely because physicists do not regard themselves, in their scientific work, as having to choose between different *ontological* claims, and physiology should follow suit.

Once we set aside the a priori metaphysical assumption that explanations in a natural science must be mechanistic in form, we can allow ourselves to accept the natural reading of the phenomena. The answer to "finalism" or "vitalism" is not to deny the facts to which the finalist draws attention, but to find a better way of accounting for them. The need to understand animal behaviour in purposive terms, even at the simplest and least conscious level, does not require the adoption of a "finalist" metaphysics, but an expansion of our conception of the possibilities of scientific explanation, a need to recognize "a directed activity between blind mechanism and intelligent behaviour which is not accounted for by classical mechanism and intellectualism".[12]

Because this recognition does not rest on any ontological distinction between "mind" and "matter", or between "life" and "dead matter", it does not imply any denial of the role of mechanism in animal or human behaviour, or any claim that behaviour does not also have an essential anatomical, physiological or chemical dimension. The claim is rather that the organism's behaviour can only be understood by using "finalistic" concepts, but that these concepts themselves get their meaning from the way in which neurological processes naturally operate as unified wholes. To achieve an adequate scientific understanding of the organism's behaviour, we have to see it as a response of the organism *as a whole*, and so to understand the nervous processes involved as working together to achieve the goals of the organism. But they can do that only because each process involved works in its own way, which can be understood in terms of ordinary laws of physiology. We must remember also that, at the level we are concerned with, this "directed activity" is something *between* "blind mechanism and intelligent behaviour". There is no suggestion on Merleau-Ponty's part that the organism *consciously directs* its responses, or that it has a concept of its own goals in mind; indeed, Merleau-Ponty explicitly rejects "finalistic realism" as well as "mechanistic realism"[13] – that is, the belief in either mental or material causes of the organism's behaviour. Intentionalistic explanation – explanation in terms of goals or purposes – is primary because we have to experience organisms as wholes actively engaged with their environment before we can, as a further step, analyse those total reactions into the mechanisms by which they are achieved.

If this is true of simple reflexes in organisms as primitive as the dung beetle, it must clearly be even more so when we move to the more complex reactions that are found only in more sophisticated animals such as ourselves. Pavlov notably attempted, as Merleau-Ponty says, to extend reflex theory to cover these more complex reactions, by introducing the notion of the "conditioned" reflex in an effort to account for the element of learning in responses to a more varied surrounding environment without departing from the underlying assumptions of the theory. But it is precisely this refusal to abandon the assumptions of reflex theory, in Merleau-Ponty's opinion, that is responsible for the inability of Pavlov's account to do justice to the actual phenomena of behaviour. The theory of the conditioned reflex, he argues, is not derived from empirical observation or the needs of science itself, but is a philosophical construction introduced in order to make organic phenomena fit into a mechanistic picture that may be appropriate to a science of inanimate objects but is inappropriate to the living world. Observation of the phenomena shows, Merleau-Ponty argues, that what animals learn is not to respond in a constant fashion to particular stimuli that could be independently defined, but to react variably to stimuli in accordance with the animal's own needs. Pavlovians can pretend otherwise, he says, only because they present as evidence for their interpretations allegedly directly observable "physiological facts" that can only be, at least in the present state of knowledge, the results of inference to what *ought* to be the case in terms of their own theory.

In this case, too, then (and even more obviously) paying attention to the phenomena themselves rather than attempting to fit them into a preconceived metaphysical framework requires us to see behaviour as a purposive engagement of the animal as a whole with a milieu that is meaningful to the animal in relation to its own purposes. A *learned* response is not simply a *conditioned* response, but one in which behaviour is varied to deal with situations that are different in content but the same in form. Mere "trial-and-error" processes, such as are postulated in Pavlovian theory, in which responses that *happen* to be successful are reinforced, do not constitute genuine *learning*; when an animal learns, it acquires a generally relevant principle that will *guarantee* success. Merleau-Ponty quotes from a psychologist called Guillaume who said "Everything happens as if the animal adopted a 'hypothesis' which 'is not explained by the success since it is manifested and persists before the success can confirm it'."[14] An example discussed by Merleau-Ponty is Wolfgang Koehler's famous studies of apes, in which the chimpanzees' use of tree branches as tools cannot be explained by the physical properties of the branches, since other sorts of objects are also used in the same way, but only by taking the chimps as seeing them as "meaningful" to themselves, as usable to achieve their own purposes.

This is not "anthropomorphism" in any undesirable sense; it does not require us to see the chimps as engaging in reflective thought in the way that adult human beings at least sometimes do. There are parallels to human behaviour, in that it seems we can understand what the chimps do only by analogy with our understanding of what we do when we use means to achieve an end. But the ends in the chimps' case are assigned by "the needs of the species, defined once for all". The difference in typical human cases is that our behaviour is *symbolic*: it involves the use of *signs*, which allow "a possibility of varied expressions of the same theme". Language-using animals such as ourselves can describe objects in different and individual ways, and these descriptions can have a truth-value; the conduct of such animals is therefore "open to truth and to the proper value of things".[15] When that stage is reached, behaviour has become fully meaningful, and intentional explanation is, even more clearly, the only satisfactory way of understanding it.

The attempt to arrive at an adequate conception of "behaviour" in this way illuminates the significance of Merleau-Ponty's notions of the subject as essentially embodied and of human being as being-in-the-world. The unsatisfactory character of reflex theory, of Pavlov's theory of "conditioned" reflexes and of Watsonian behaviourism, results, Merleau-Ponty argues, from the fact that the proponents of these theories did not pay attention to the phenomena themselves, but sought to fit them into a preconceived metaphysical framework. This framework presupposed a simple dichotomy between "mind" and "matter", "directedness" (intentionality) and "mechanism", with the implication that human behaviour either had to be "reduced" to the same level as the simpler mechanisms of more primitive organisms, or else had to be treated as radically different in kind from them. If we do attend to the phenomena, however, Merleau-Ponty suggests, we see no need for such dichotomous thinking. We need to think in *biological* terms, rather than in terms either of physics, or of the psychology of consciousness. Human behaviour *is* significantly different from that of dung beetles, and even of primates, but it also has important points of connection with these simpler forms. Neither they nor human behaviour can be understood as simple mechanistic responses to defined stimuli: the behaviour of organisms at any level is best understood as active problem-solving – attempts to resolve the problems that the organism's environment poses to it in its goal of satisfying its biological needs.

The difference in the case of human beings, as suggested above, is that their behaviour can be symbolic. The use of signs, as argued there, introduces a radically new element into both the behaviour and its understanding. As analytic philosophers have also recognized, human action is "under a description"; the same bodily movements can constitute different actions under different descriptions. To take a stock example, the same movements of my hand with a pen may constitute signing a cheque (and so buying something), signing a letter or simply doodling. To understand what I am doing and why requires more than observation of my bodily movements and their neurological or other causes; it is most important to know the description under which I am acting and the reasons for performing an action under that description. Human action is in this way significantly different from the behaviour of other animals. It is more *individual*; its meaning relates to individual conceptions of need rather than to the generalized needs of the species. The possibility that language allows of adopting different points of view on the "same" situation, Merleau-Ponty argues, frees the "stimuli" both from the particular context in which they present themselves to me in my current experience and from any generalized meaning that they may gain from a relation to the predetermined needs of the species as a whole.

Human behaviour that is fully self-conscious is thus both importantly different and at the same time fundamentally similar to the less conscious behaviour of human beings themselves and of other animals. It is similar in being "directed", in having a meaning related to the goals of the organism, but different in that its directedness is more individual; the goals of the organism are dictated not by the needs of the species but by the individual's own definition of his or her needs. This implies a certain continuity between pre-conscious and fully self-conscious behaviour; fully self-conscious behaviour, as it were, emerges from the pre-conscious background and cannot be understood except as a further development of what was already implicit in that background. This illustrates the point made earlier, that paying attention to the phenomena, which in this case means taking account of the specifically *biological* characteristics of human beings, liberates us from thinking in terms of a radical distinction between "consciousness" or "intentionality" and "matter" or "mechanism". Part of what is meant by saying that the subject is essentially "embodied" is that the "intentional" goes "all the way down", below the level of explicit self-consciousness; and that this is not incompatible with accepting that mechanism "goes all the way up", in the sense that the operations of intentionality presuppose neurophysiological processes, which can be causally explained in terms of the laws of physics and chemistry. Being-in-the-world, for embodied subjects such as ourselves, involves the interplay of both our "embodiment" and our "subjectivity", the expression of our way of seeing the world in our bodily movements.

III

The holistic conception of the organism developed in *The Structure of Behaviour*, according to which responses to the surrounding environment have to be understood in the context of an attempt by the organism as a whole to solve its problems, makes room for the use of a certain concept of *disorder* in application to behaviour, for if behaviour is seen as an attempt at problem-solving, then it can be evaluated as successful or unsuccessful; and an unsuccessful attempt can be regarded as "disordered". In the case of human behaviour, where the problems, as we have seen, are individual in character, then this suggests a way of giving sense to the difficult concept of "mental disorder" by seeing it as a particular way of being-in-the-world involving unsuccessful attempts to solve problems in the individual's existence. Conversely, thinking about mental disorder may offer further possibilities of clarifying the general notion of human being as being-in-the-world. There is a little discussion of mental disorder in *The Structure of Behaviour*, but much more in *Phenomenology of Perception*. In this section, I shall examine these discussions, both for the sake of their own intrinsic interest and for the light that they shed on Merleau-Ponty's conception of human embodied existence.

It is, says Merleau-Ponty, "perhaps the least contested idea of modern psychology" that the behaviour of a diseased subject cannot be understood by simple "disaggregation" of that of healthy subjects.[16] By this, I take him to mean that we cannot understand it simply as like healthy behaviour except in that it lacks some component that is present in the latter. Rather, as he goes on to say, we have to supplement physiological explanation with psychological description, to see a "qualitative transformation of nerve functioning" as the essential element in illness. Diseased behaviour, that is, cannot be adequately understood either by physiology or by psychology *on their own*; we need to understand both the disturbances to normal nervous activity (a task for physiological causal explanation) and the transformation in the goals that nervous activity serves (a task for psychological understanding in intentional terms).

To be clear what this means, we obviously need to consider how this analysis can be applied to actual examples, and the fullest discussion of such examples is to be found in *Phenomenology of Perception*. Some of these examples might not be considered cases of "mental disorder" on a narrow definition of that term, but they are disorders that clearly have a "mental" component, and so may help to shed light on the undisputed cases of mental disorder. Take, for instance, the phenomenon of the "phantom limb", which is discussed by Merleau-Ponty in several places. In such cases, a person who has lost an arm or a leg, either as a result of accident or of surgical amputation, continues to experience sensations that appear to be located where the missing limb used to be. Some of the facts about such phantom limbs appear to suggest a purely physiological explanation, in terms of the continuing functioning of the nerves that formerly conveyed "messages" from the limb in question. "For example",

Merleau-Ponty says, "if, in the case of a man who has lost a leg, a stimulus is applied, instead of to the leg, to the path from the stump to the brain, the subject will feel a phantom leg".[17] Other facts, however, suggest what Merleau-Ponty here calls "psychic" determinants, involving consciousness. Injured patients who had not previously had a phantom limb may develop one when they experience some situation that recalls the one in which they were injured. Or again, "It happens that the imaginary arm is enormous after the operation, but that it subsequently shrinks and is absorbed into the stump 'as the patient consents to accept his mutilation'."[18]

A purely physiological explanation could account only for the changes in nervous transmission from the periphery to the cerebral cortex produced by the injury, and this would not explain why the phenomenon depends also on how the patient *experiences* his injury. On the other hand, a purely psychological explanation could not account for the relation between these experiences and specific changes to the patient's nervous system. Can we overcome the problem by simply *combining* physiology and psychology? No, Merleau-Ponty argues, because that would require us to find some point of contact between physiological processes located in space and psychological phenomena like thoughts and emotions, which "are nowhere", and such a point of contact seems in principle impossible to find. The phantom limb seems to be a result neither of physiological causes alone nor of a conscious thought process. Understanding it requires us to get away from the dichotomy of "psychic" and physiological, intentionality and mechanism (a dichotomy that is still present even when we attempt to combine both sides of the divide). We need rather an "organic" mode of thought: essentially the "biological" way of thinking presented in *The Structure of Behaviour* and discussed above in the preceding section.

As we saw then, this requires us to conceive of the organism as a whole attempting to solve problems in its dealings with its environment. From this point of view, we can find parallels with the phantom limb phenomenon in the behaviour of non-human organisms, even much simpler creatures such as insects, when they lose a limb. An insect that has had one of its limbs cut off, for instance, may *substitute* a remaining sound limb if that is required in the performance of an instinctive act. This substitution is not the result of a standard nervous mechanism, Merleau-Ponty argues, since it does not occur in every case in which the insect is frustrated in making the relevant movement; it does not occur, for example, when the normal leg is merely tied, rather than cut off. Merleau-Ponty's explanation is that the insect continues to move about the world with no diminution of its capacities. It confronts its world as a whole organism, and the "current of activity . . . flows towards the world" through all its limbs.[19] What this seems to mean is that each of its limbs has, and is experienced by the insect as having, its own function as part of the insect's total response to its environment. Because the limb that is merely tied is still experienced by the insect as part of that total response, it does not feel the need to substitute another limb for it; but in the case of the amputated leg, which as such no longer "counts in the insect's scheme of things", the insect does try an alternative solution to its problem, by using another limb instead.

Does this view of the insect as a problem-solver involve an absurd picture of it as deliberating and making choices about which limb to use? No, Merleau-Ponty replies, any more than such an absurd picture is conjured up when we talk of a drop of oil as "solving a problem" about its flow. There is certainly a difference between the insect and the drop of oil. The oil does not have any inner needs to satisfy by its "solution" to its "problem", but simply flows in a way determined by external forces, whereas the insect, as a living creature, does have such inner needs, which determine both the nature of its problem and the sorts of solution that it can adopt. We can thus speak non-metaphorically of the insect as having a "scheme of things", in a way that is impossible in the case of the drop of oil; but having a scheme of things in this sense does not, in the case of any creature that lacks the capacity for symbolic thought, involve making a conscious choice.

Even in the case of creatures such as ourselves, who do have that capacity, not all our actions are the result of conscious choice. In virtue of our having that capacity, as was argued in the previous section, our way of being-in-the-world differs from that of the insect in being *individual*; the inner needs in terms of which we structure our world are not, like the insect's, an "*a priori* of the species", as Merleau-Ponty here expresses it, but are the outcome of fully individualized conceptions. But the raising of those individualized conceptions to full consciousness, their recognition as "my own", is a further stage resulting from reflection. If it is not so raised, our perception of the world remains "an intention of our whole being . . . [a modality] of a *pre-objective view* which is what we call being-in-the-world".[20] The experience of an amputated limb as still belonging to us is such an "intention of our whole being". We do not consciously choose to regard the limb as if it were still there: but we continue to "be-in-the-world" in the same way as we did previously when the limb was still attached and usable. In our "scheme of things", the limb is still experienced as a functioning part of our total response to our environment; this is a "disordered" way of being-in-the-world in that it involves a mistaken way of perceiving the terms of our problem and so an inadequate solution to the problem.

Such relatively simple disorders can be used as the basis for an approach to understanding much more subtle and complex conditions that can be clearly described as mental disorders, such as the case of Schneider, which Merleau-Ponty examines in great detail (making use of the extensive discussion in the psychological and neurophysiological literature). Schneider appears to have suffered an injury to the occipital region of the brain, the result of a wound from a shell splinter, which was certainly the beginning, and in some sense also the root, of his problems. These problems were partly motor, partly perceptual, and partly sexual; the common element was a kind of detachment from his own body. A normal person, according to Merleau-Ponty (and to the scientists from whom he quotes), "can immediately 'come to grips' with his body",[21] so that he doesn't experience it *intellectually* as an object; when he is touched, for example, he knows roughly where, without the need to work out the precise position on its "geometrical outline". Schneider, by contrast, had a "need, in order to find out where he is being touched, to convert the bodily area being touched into a shape".[22] Again, patients like Schneider find "abstract movements" difficult. If asked to close their eyes and then to move an arm, they become perplexed about how to do this, and have to work out intellectually a strategy for doing it; their body, in other words, is for them an instrument that they have to use, rather than "the potentiality of a certain world",[23] as it is for a normal person.

Closely connected with these motor problems in Schneider's case were certain disorders of sight, a kind of "psychological blindness". Merleau-Ponty quotes from Gelb and Goldstein's description of the case:

> The patient's visual data lack any specific and characteristic structure ... Before him he sees only patches in which his sight allows him to pick out only salient characteristics, such as height and breadth and their relation to each other.[24]

As this shows, Schneider's visual difficulties, like his motor problems, consisted in a detachment from the normal involvement with one's own body, and engagement, through one's body, with the world. The world as he perceived it had no structure or meaning, but consisted in meaningless patches, which it is an intellectual task to order into a workable picture of the surrounding environment.

Finally, Schneider also experienced sexual problems. He had no spontaneous sexual interest; he was not aroused by pornographic images, or by talk about sex or the sight of a human body. He still had sexual relations, but only in specific circumstances, and if his partner, for instance, experienced orgasm before him, then his own desire subsided. It was almost, as Merleau-Ponty says, as if he simply did not know what he had to do. In this case too, then, the heart of the problem is a detachment from his own body: here it is from the normal way in which we see the world as sexually charged, and the normal capacity to grasp without thinking the erotic character of a situation and to follow it through until we achieve satisfaction. Sexuality, for Schneider, had become, not a spontaneous reaction, but an intellectual problem which he had to work out how to solve.

How Schneider's condition should be explained depends on how we describe what is to be explained. If we try to fit it into the mechanistic framework usually thought to be the only one appropriate to a genuinely scientific approach, then we shall seek to exhibit it as an instance of general causal laws, based on inductive reasoning from observations of "constant conjunctions". The causes may be physiological: disturbances to the normal functioning of relevant nervous mechanisms, of which the effect is the observable symptoms. The fact that Schneider's problems began with a brain injury might appear to support that interpretation. Or we might try to formulate a causal explanation in terms of the relation between one "psychic fact" and another; our general laws might be *psychological* in character. What is wrong with this way of thinking about behaviour, according to Merleau-Ponty, is that the mere noting of correlations cannot in itself enable us to understand the behaviour better, since it does not in itself enable us to see *why* just this correlation has been selected out of the many we might observe. The different factors in any situation are intertwined with each other, and do not isolate themselves or identify themselves as "causes". We need to do this by finding a way of "correctly reading phenomena, . . . grasping their meaning, that is, . . . treating them as modalities of the subject's total being".[25] We have, as Merleau-Ponty also puts it, to abandon the "third-person", external, point of view implicit in causal thinking and to understand the behaviour "from the inside", as the subject himself or herself sees it, as an expression of his way of being-in-the-world. This is not a substitution of "understanding" for "explanation"; the point, Merleau-Ponty insists, is that genuine explanation of human behaviour is impossible *without* understanding it from a "first-person" point of view.

This implies a certain conception of what "illness" is (at least in cases of "mental" illness). It is not merely a breakdown in mechanical functioning, whether of the brain or of the "mind", but a disordered way of being-in-the-world, of relating to one's own body, or to other people, or to the world in general. In the case of the person with the phantom limb, emotion, memory and the limb itself are all part of the person's changed way of being-in-the-world. In Schneider's case, what had changed was "the very structure of perception or erotic experience".[26] None of this is incompatible with a recognition of the essential role played by physical disease or injury in mental illness; because we are embodied consciousnesses, we can have a world only through our bodies, so that a disturbance to our bodily functioning is necessarily involved in any disturbance of our way of being-in-the-world. "Consciousness", Merleau-Ponty declares (claiming to follow Husserl's unpublished writings), "is in the first place not a matter of 'I think that' but of 'I can'."[27]

IV

Merleau-Ponty is led by his discussion of Schneider's case to reflections on sexuality in general, which he says is always present in human life "like an atmosphere".[28] In this, he acknowledges, he is in agreement with Freudian psychoanalysis; and his discussion of the strengths and weaknesses of Freudianism adds further depth to his general account of human embodiment. Freud had seen knowledge of a person's sexual history as providing the key to understanding that person's life as a whole, but what, Merleau-Ponty asks, does this generalization of the notion of sexuality entail? Does it mean that everything about our existence has a sexual meaning or that everything about our sexuality has an existential meaning? The latter alternative seems, Merleau-Ponty argues, to deprive sexuality of any specific character of its own, distinct from other aspects of our existence. If the phrase "sexual phenomenon" is to have any real meaning, it must surely refer to *sexual* – that is, ultimately genital – activities. To see sexual history as the key to understanding the problems of neurotics, as Freud does, must mean something more than merely saying that our problems arise from our past lives; it must involve attaching special significance to the narrowly *sexual* aspects of those lives.

Merleau-Ponty believes we can do this if we think in terms of his own notion of subjectivity as essentially embodied, for then the personal dimension of our existence cannot be ultimately separated from its bodily dimension; being embodied means that our personal existence is necessarily rooted in an impersonal, physical world. We depend on that impersonal world both because it provides the necessary conditions for bodily survival, without which any kind of personal existence would be impossible, and because we must first belong to the world in general before we can "enclose" part of it as our own *human* and individual world. Personal existence, indeed, is only "intermittent", and much of our life is conducted on that relatively impersonal level; existence as a person is rooted in something "pre-personal".

As embodied subjects, in short, our subjective existence, our existence as persons, necessarily takes place in a certain "atmosphere", created by the character, structures and needs of our bodies. Our bodies "express" existence just in the same way that language expresses thought. Human existence, as "being-in-the-world", is essentially "ambiguous"; we cannot be defined either simply as bodies or as persons, but only as persons who "take up" our embodiment and as bodies in which our personal existence is "realized". Given the specific nature of our human bodies, that means that our "being-in-the-world" necessarily has a sexual dimension to it. The way in which we normally interact with the world, and especially with other persons, can be understood only if we take into account that sexual dimension. But at the same time, since sexuality, like other aspects of our embodiment, "expresses existence", our sexuality can be fully understood only in the light of its "existential significance".

Merleau-Ponty is at pains to point out that he is not any kind of "reductionist" in his view of sexuality; he is neither "reducing" existence to sexuality, nor "reducing" sexuality to a mere "symptom of an existential drama". That is, he is neither doing what Freud himself often seems to be doing (or at least what the latter's language often implies), namely, treating human beings simply as biological organisms, whose behaviour can be causally explained by "instincts" or "drives", mainly of a sexual nature; nor is he denying their biological nature and treating human sexuality simply as a manifestation of personal (non-biological) attitudes to the world and other people. He insists, as against the first kind of reductionism, that such phenomena as "modesty, desire and love" simply cannot be understood if we see human beings as nothing more than mechanistic systems or animals with instincts, but only if we recognize that they have consciousness and freedom. As against the latter kind of reductionism, he argues that our human existence necessarily realizes itself through our bodies and the form of our embodiment, so that the "existential drama" has its roots in our biological nature, including the bodily structures of our sexuality.

> The importance we attach to the body and the contradictions of love are, therefore, related to a more general drama which arises from the metaphysical structure of my body, which is both an object for others and a subject for myself.[29]

However initially plausible this view of human sexuality may be, if it is to be philosophically acceptable it needs some sort of supporting argument. One way of supporting it, found in Merleau-Ponty, is to seek to show that we can achieve a better understanding of some of the pathological phenomena with which Freud deals if we start from Merleau-Ponty's "existential ambiguity" than if we start from the biologistic or mechanistic assumptions of Freud himself (or of others). We can understand his point better if we start with a brief, and so somewhat simplified, account of Freud's approach. In the biologistic interpretation of Freudian theory, human beings have certain natural "instincts", notably an instinct of self-preservation and a sexual instinct, that are somehow "hard-wired" into the brain and nervous system and which we cannot help but seek to gratify. Human beings, however, are also social creatures, who therefore need to restrain their attempts to gratify their urges in the interests of orderly relations with other members of society. Because we start life as infants, the first and most crucial stages of this process of socialization take place at an unconscious level. Children, for example, pass through pre-genital stages in their sexual development, in which sexual interest focuses on the mouth and on the anus, which is socially disapproved of, rather than having its socially approved focus on the genitals. Again, male children are sexually attracted to their mothers and so feel hostile to their fathers, as sexual rivals: this is again socially disapproved of. In both cases, the disapproval of society as a whole is mediated through the disapproval of parents. Since the child is absolutely dependent, emotionally and physically, on parental approval, he or she "represses" the disapproved urge: that is, the urge is removed from conscious awareness and kept in the "unconscious mind". Adult pathologies of behaviour result, on this view, from the causal influence of these repressed urges on the adult's relations to other people and the world in general.

What is Merleau-Ponty's alternative story? Human beings, first of all, are for him not biological machines, collections of neurophysiological mechanisms operating in ways that can be explained by causal laws. Rather, they are embodied subjects, actively engaged with the environment in which they find themselves, trying to solve problems in their existence and adapting their behaviour in the light of the solutions they find to those problems. Because of the nature of human embodiment, many of those problems, perhaps all, will have an inescapable sexual dimension. On this view, the development of a human being has to be understood, not in causal terms, but as a "progressive and discontinuous structuration of behaviour".[30] Putting it more simply, we normally *learn* from our experience and so build a repertoire of ways of behaving, which are integrated with each other to enable us to live a coherent life in society. It follows that normal human development passes beyond infantile attitudes and the solutions to childhood problems that the infant adopts. Things go wrong when, for some reason, this does not happen. We may, for example, encounter an obstacle that we cannot overcome; because we equally cannot bring ourselves to abandon the course of action in question, we remain "imprisoned" in the attempt to overcome the obstacle. The rest of our lives goes on and develops. Parts of our existence, the parts of which we are explicitly aware, may operate in terms of adult conceptions, but these operations themselves are distorted by our continuing attempt to operate at an infantile level.

Because our personal existence arises out of our impersonal existence as bodies, our bodies represent the continuing influence of our past; our bodily habits of behaviour provide the material from which we create meaning and personal identity, but the body's impersonal character prevents us from being completely in control of our own identity. In this sense, our failed attempt to solve our problem continues to have an existence and influence on our lives outside the scope of our conscious choice of ourselves. That, in Merleau-Ponty's view, is the correct interpretation of what Freud had in mind in talking of "repression", freed from Freud's own misguided attempts to describe it in causal or mechanistic terms; the behaviour of the neurotic has to be *understood* in the light of his or her total way of being-in-the-world, rather than causally explained in terms of the actions of quasi-biological "forces".[31] Repression is an *intentional* act, something we *do* with our memories, but Freud is right to say that repression does not consist in a specific *rejection* of the memory (which would involve being conscious of it), but in distancing ourselves from a whole *type* or *class* of memories.

What is true in Freudian psychoanalysis, in Merleau-Ponty's view (and this will be explored at greater length in Chapter 5), is the picture of a human self as emerging from an impersonal bodily existence as the human being progressively integrates the actions and dispositions already inherent in that bodily existence to create a more unified structure. Pathology, the "complex", is then definable as a failure of integration, resulting from a return to a more primitive manner of organizing one's behaviour. What is false in Freudian psychoanalysis is that it fails to see that even the impersonal bodily existence of human beings is already "expressive" or "meaningful" – that our bodies are actively engaged with their world rather than merely passively or mechanically responding to it. Indeed, it is only because we are embodied, in Merleau-Ponty's view, that we have a "world" at all: that is, that we see objects and people around us as meaningful and related to each other, in virtue of a common relation to our projects. The inseparability of the impersonal, or bodily, and the personal or conscious in human existence is the basis of the essential ambiguity of that existence on which Merleau-Ponty lays so much stress. And, in the present context, it has implications for the appropriate mode of treatment of psychopathology. It means that it can never be enough to appeal to the patient on a purely conscious level, simply making him aware of what he has repressed. Such a purely cognitive awareness would change nothing: the patient needs to come to appreciate at an *existential* level the meaning of his disorder. For that to be possible, Merleau-Ponty goes on, a personal relationship with the doctor and the resulting change of existence are necessary.[32]

From this point of view, it is possible to see a way in which we can understand Schneider's sexual problems "existentially", while at the same time making full allowance for the role of his brain injuries in their origins. The problem that confronted Schneider *must* indeed be understood in the first instance as a problem in his existence, as an impoverishment of normal being-in-the-world, which for him has lost its erotic structure. For most human beings, the bodies of other human beings are not perceived merely as spatial objects, but also as potential objects of sexual desire, whose erogenous zones are emphasized. Perception, as part of our being-in-the-world, has an essential sexual structure. Schneider's problem was that his world was diminished through having lost this structure of perception, and that is an existential problem. But at the same time, it is no accident that this problem was precipitated by an injury to a certain area of the brain, for it is the way in which these areas function that makes it possible for us to experience the world as erotically structured. The existential problem cannot therefore be resolved merely by appeal to Schneider's powers of conscious recognition of its nature, since such recognition on its own could not restore the lost erotic structure of his world.

Another case discussed by Merleau-Ponty can further illustrate these points. This concerns a girl who has been forbidden by her mother to see the man she loves. The girl finds it impossible to sleep, becomes uninterested in eating and finally loses the use of speech. This was, however, not the first time in her life that she had lost the power of speech; she had had the same experience twice in her childhood after frightening events. An orthodox Freudian might therefore, as Merleau-Ponty says, relate this symptom to the "oral" phase of sexual development, in which sexual interest is focused on the mouth. But a more "existential" approach might recognize that the mouth has other than purely sexual meanings for us; above all, of course, it is the means by which we communicate with others. (Indeed, in so far as sexuality is not merely a matter of internal bodily sensations but also of relations with others, we might say that this connection with communication is part of the *sexual* significance of the mouth.) Loss of speech can thus be understood as a refusal to coexist with her family. In much the same way, the girl's inability to swallow food can be seen as a refusal to "swallow" her mother's prohibition. Her mother's refusal to allow her to see her lover has thrown her back into an earlier, childish phase of her development in which she had similarly broken with life as a way of avoiding the fearfulness of her situation.

The role played by her oral functions (speech, swallowing) in this refusal may well, as Freud suggested, have been due in those earlier cases to the sexual significance of the mouth at that stage of development. But the sexual significance of symptoms, Merleau-Ponty argues, is part of a more general meaning that they have which derives from very funda-mental structures of human existence, our relation to past and future, to ourselves and to others. Thus, in this case too, the problem is existential, but it does not follow that it is a problem only at the conscious level of existence, to be resolved by appeal to the girl's own cognitive resources. Like all existential problems, it arises from the ambiguous character of human beings as embodied subjects, in which the structures of our world cannot be understood apart from our character as biological organisms, but at the same time our character as biological organisms can be understood ultimately only in terms of the way our bodily characteristics are taken up into our personal lives. The discussion of these pathological cases thus leads naturally into a consideration of Merleau-Ponty's view of the self, its relation to other selves, and its capacity for free action, which will be the theme of Chapter 5.

CHAPTER FIVE

Self and Others

I

By means of his method of doubt, Descartes arrived at a basis for certainty of knowledge in the *cogito* ("I think, therefore I am"); the very possibility of achieving certain knowledge depended on starting from one's own conscious thoughts, which were both transparent (immediately self-revealing) and private (accessible only to the individual whose thoughts they were). There is an element of truth, Merleau-Ponty thinks, in this Cartesian return to the self. It is clearly true, for instance, that we can only have experience of objects if we are ourselves conscious subjects of experience, and if we distinguish between ourselves as subjects and an objective world that transcends our subjective experience of it. But consciousness is necessarily reflexive; to be conscious of anything else is also to be conscious of oneself as experiencing it. A love that was not conscious of itself, he says, would be a contradiction in terms, as would an unconscious thought or will.[1] So our experience of the world does, as Descartes implied, require as a starting-point our awareness of ourselves as subjects.

Nevertheless, there are serious problems in the Cartesian view. Above all, it is too one-sided; it is not just that I must first be aware of myself as a subject before I can be aware of other things as objects, but also that my awareness of myself as a subject necessarily presupposes awareness of other things as objects. Consciousness is by its very nature such that it actively *transcends* itself; it goes beyond itself, and has no inner content.[2] We are back with the doctrine that consciousness is essentially *intentional*, that to be conscious is always and necessarily to be directed outside oneself; we cannot therefore retreat into a self-enclosed subjectivity in which we doubt the existence of an "external world", since even our awareness of our own subjectivity is possible only if we are also aware of a world that transcends it. Subject and object of experience are inseparably bound up together; our being is "being-in-the-world". And we can no more doubt the existence of external objects than we can doubt the existence of ourselves and our thoughts. Radical doubt is impossible, since doubt itself is a form of commitment to the world. To doubt one thing presupposes that there are other things that one does not doubt: to doubt whether that is a real oasis or a mirage, a trick of the light, for instance, presupposes that one does not doubt that one is in a desert, that light and heat often play tricks with one's perception, and so forth. We have reasons for doubting things, which we share with and can expound to others, so that even the possibility of doubting some things implies the existence of a world which we share with others and about which we can converse with them. The real *cogito* is not the self-consciousness of some absolute mind which exists God-like and eternally distinct from the world it thinks about, but the self-consciousness of some particular individual, such as the reader of Descartes, who exists in a particular place at a particular time.

The Cartesian view of the subject as a special kind of inner object, distinguished from other objects by virtue of being fully transparent to itself, is incoherent also in another way, for to get to know an object, Merleau-Ponty argues, requires us to engage in a "synthesis", to experience first one aspect of the object, then another, and then another, gradually coming to know the nature of the object in question. This process must be endless in principle, since the nature of any object, by definition, is inexhaustible. So if the self were an object, even an inner object, the same would have to be true of it; if so, the self could not be fully transparent even to itself. But this seems to be a *reductio ad absurdum* of the notion of the self as an "inner object". If it is supposed to be *inner*, that can only mean that the self that knows and the self that is known are one and the same, so that the self must be fully transparent. But if it is supposed to be an *object*, that would entail, as we have just seen, that it is *not* fully transparent; in short, the concept of an inner object is self-contradictory, and we need a different conception both of the self and of self-knowledge.

If the self is not an inner object and self-knowledge is not a matter of perception of that inner object, what are they? "Self" or "subject", in Merleau-Ponty's view, are not names of any kind of object, but ways of referring to certain kinds of relations with objects (intentional relations); a self can exist only in its relations with a world that transcends it. If so, self-knowledge must be achieved in *action*, in our dealings with items (including other subjects) in the world. Since our dealings with the world are always ambiguous, our knowledge of ourselves can never have the kind of transparency that Descartes attributes to it. There is a certain *opacity* to the existence of a person; we can be ignorant of aspects of ourselves, and even suffer from illusions about ourselves just as we can about external objects.

Thus we are not, as Descartes implied, in full possession of ourselves. The self, to put it differently, cannot be identified with those aspects of itself that are explicitly conscious; they must exist as a pool of light in the midst of surrounding darkness, which is as much a part of the conscious self as the light is. My awareness of my own thoughts and feelings is not an immediate grasp of facts about an object. Very often, we have to *discover* what we feel; for example, I discover that I am in love by seeing certain facts about myself as a whole. The love that I thus discover is not some unconscious "thing" or an object of consciousness, but an impulse that carries me towards someone else, and a change in the way I think and behave.[3]

Similarly, when we speak of illusions about ourselves, or about "false" feelings, we are not talking of an intellectual mistake about a matter of fact. The falseness of our feelings is not that of a proposition, but rather an expression of a distortion in our way of being-in-the-world. For example, it may consist in the failure of the feeling to engage our whole being, to permeate all aspects of our relations with the relevant objects or people. The pain, sadness or rage of the hysterical subject, for instance, is not *feigned*: he is not a dissembler. They are distinguished from real pain, sadness or rage "because he is not wholly given over to them: at his core there is left a zone of tranquillity".[4] Similarly, whereas true love "summons all the subject's resources", mistaken love "touches only on one persona". In one sense, the feeling for the "beloved" is perfectly real – there is some kind of emotion there. What makes it false is that the emotion is not a total engagement with this individual *as this individual*, but a response to her in so far as she resembles someone else; or that it is not a response of my whole being, but a mainly intellectual recognition of a community of interests; or that in some other way what is felt falls short of what we mean by "love". All this fits with the view that feelings, thoughts, and so on are not objects of contemplation but experiences that we "live", and whose nature we therefore discover, not by inner (or outer) perception, but by reflection on the manner of our being-in-the-world. Freud's talk of the "unconscious" was essentially correct, even though he misdescribed it in typical objectivist fashion by conceiving of it as a region or part of a certain kind of object (the mind), rather than as referring to those aspects of ourselves on which we have not yet reflected, or perhaps find it difficult to reflect upon.

II

To conceive of the self, not as an object, but as a way of being-in-the-world, makes it possible to give non-Cartesian accounts of the relation of the self to its own body, of the development of the self over time, and of the relation between selves. Descartes himself saw that I cannot be located within my body like a pilot in his ship, but the Cartesian view of the self as a "mental substance" makes it hard to see what other account of the relation between self and body can be given. If what we are is a "project towards the world",[5] then the Cartesian *cogito* ("I think") becomes *I act*; my existence as a self is not that of a single continuing "consciousness", or a series of such consciousnesses, but a single "experience" in which I, as an embodied human being, engage with the world. My body is not, as objectivists might have it, an instrument loosely attached to me that I can use, but is me myself as involved with the world and as expressing myself in its movements. If I am an embodied subject, then the thoughts, feelings, intentions, wishes and so on that I have necessarily find expression in my body, not only in my actions and the objects I manipulate in them or the environment that I change by them, but even in the very characteristics of the body itself. Conversely, my body *for me*, or what Merleau-Ponty calls *le corps propre*, is not some kind of mechanistic system loosely attached to me, but is my mode of expression of my thoughts, feelings, intentions and so on. A person's body can become what Merleau-Ponty beautifully describes as "the eloquent relic of an existence".[6]

Descartes arrives at the *cogito* as his "Archimedean point", the one reliable foundation for knowledge that remains secure against radical doubt. But the very possibility of radical doubt, as we have seen, already takes for granted a fundamental distinction between a secure "inner world" of thought and an "external world" whose very existence it is possible to doubt. In conceiving of the self, not as an inner world to which we can retreat, but as embodied and so having its being *in-the-world*, Merleau-Ponty rejects this Cartesian assumption, and with it the notion of an absolute foundation for knowledge and of an ultimate distinction between "self" and "external world".

Moreover, if the self that we are is not a special kind of non-material substance located somehow within our body, but is what finds expression in the movements of that body, then it seems at the very least plausible to view it, not as an object with an "essence" that gives it identity and makes it the same object at different times, but as developing over time. That view is indeed, Merleau-Ponty argues, a necessary consequence of the conception of ourselves as embodied subjects. An embodied subject necessarily perceives the world from a certain perspective, not only, as is obvious, in space but also in time. The world that we perceive is not timeless, but *present*; our involvement with it is necessarily permeated with our habits of perception derived from our past experience and encoded in our bodies. Merleau-Ponty even identifies my body with my habitual familiarity with the world, the kind of knowledge that I have of the world which is implicit or "sedimentary" rather than the result of explicit reflection.[7]

This conception of the self as embodied and active, and so temporal, is distinguished not only from the Cartesian view of it as "eternal", a timeless contemplation of a world entirely distinct from itself, but also from empiricist views, like Hume's, in which the self is reduced to a sequence of externally related "impressions", or mental states. The Humean account is as dualistic as the Cartesian; a "bundle of perceptions" is as disengaged from the world as a Cartesian "mental substance". A self that is actively engaged in the world cannot be regarded as a mere series of externally related mental events; the self's present actions are the outcome of its past and create its future. The relations between past, present and future are internal, rather than external; none of these terms can be defined except in relation to the other two. Because of this, the human subject is temporal, not by accident but by a necessity of its nature.[8] If the human subject necessarily has its being "in-the-world", that is, if it is necessarily embodied and actively involved with the world, then it necessarily has a past, present and future; what someone has been in the past provides the reasons for her present actions, which are directed towards the future. Time, Merleau-Ponty says, "is not an object of our knowledge, but a dimension of our being";[9] in a sense, time "produces itself" in the process of our engagement with the world.

Merleau-Ponty quotes approvingly from Claudel, "Le temps est le *sens* de la vie" ("Time is the direction of life") and Heidegger, "Der Sinn des Daseins ist die Zeitlichkeit" ("The sense of human existence is temporality").[10] To see a human life as necessarily temporal in this way is to see it as having a direction, so that changes in a person are not merely in their superficial properties, leaving an unchanging essence, but genuine *developments*. A human self retains the past in the present, giving an inexhaustible depth and richness to that present. The "historicity" of human existence consists in the fact that it has a direction from the past into the present and so into an (at least possible) future, so that the present can be said both to "incorporate" the past and to "transcend" it, and, likewise, since the future, if it comes, will be the present, the future will incorporate the present and all its other pasts and transcend them. Or, to put it less abstractly, what I am now (and so what reasons for action have force for me now) depends on what I have been, while my present actions help to create the world in which I shall have to live in the future (if I survive). In writing the present sentence, for example, I am seeking to continue the argument of the previous sentences (an isolated sentence would make no kind of sense at all), and am also preparing the ground for the sentences that are to come.

In an individual's life, as in a passage of prose, the particular incidents get their meaning from their relation to what has gone before, so that the self that I am (whoever I may be) is not a mere "bundle of perceptions" bound together by timeless external relations, but something that develops over time, much in the way that a nation develops over its history, or (to vary the metaphor) in which the plot of a novel or a movie develops in its successive episodes. The comparison of personal identity with national identity may suggest to some the ideas of Derek Parfit,[11] who also compares persons to nations in this way. But the point of the comparison for Parfit is quite different: for him, it is a way of emphasizing his view that the question whether a person (or a nation) is or is not the same at different times is not one that admits of a simple "yes or no" answer, but one that requires a *decision*. The point of the comparison here, on the contrary, is to suggest that both nations and persons can have an identity that does not depend on the continuity of an eternal, unchanging essence. Their identity consists, paradoxically, in their becoming different, but in the successive differences being intelligibly related, in that each "develops out of" what came before; what we are is what we are in the process of becoming. Contrary to both Hume and Parfit, we do have an identity as persons, even if that identity has to be progressively constructed in the course of our existence. (And this applies, as we shall see shortly, not only to human individuals, but to human societies and indeed to humanity as a whole.)

A self that is "historical" in this sense cannot be identified with (although it includes) the self of which we are explicitly conscious. Merleau-Ponty says that the self who has a past, a present and a future is not the autonomous subject, but the embodied person who is able to explore the world with his senses. Embodiment and the temporality of our existence are thus, as has already been said, inextricably connected, and the fact that we have a history (or, as Merleau-Ponty prefers to say here, a "prehistory") gives an added dimension to the conception that most of the existence of an embodied self is *un*conscious, or at least *pre*-conscious. My existence as a *person* is something that develops out of a pre-personal existence as a part of nature, and my personal perceptions all presuppose therefore a natural background.

In order to understand who I am, therefore, I have to reflect on my past, and not only my conscious memories, but also those unconscious interactions with the world that constitute the major part of my existence. This brings us back to Merleau-Ponty's interpretation of Freudian psychoanalysis, already considered in Chapter 4, since it makes more explicit the temporal dimension to human existence that is implicit in Freud's very language (psychoanalysis is based on a view about the course of human development) and that Merleau-Ponty uses in his critique of Freud's biologistic or mechanistic distortion of his own insights. If human existence, individual or collective, is essentially historical, then there is a sense in which we construct ourselves as subjects by the solutions that we find to the problems posed to us by our own existence; but most of that problem-solving (especially in our earlier years, when the foundations of our self-construction are being laid) will not be a matter of *conscious* choice of solutions to explicitly conceived problems. The unsuccessful solutions to old problems will then linger on as habits, "sedimented" (as Merleau-Ponty sometimes expresses it) in our bodily habits of behaviour and presenting obstacles to a construction of an adult identity as an autonomous subject.

Interpreted in this way, Freudian psychoanalysis becomes, not a deterministic theory in which our present actions are the causal outcome of our "drives" or of biological forces repressed into the "unconscious", but on the contrary a way of making human freedom more concrete. Psychoanalysis is seen as a reading of someone's past, in which the meaning of their present behaviour is reinterpreted in the light of an uncovering of aspects of their past that have previously been hidden from view, "sedimented" in the habits of bodily response. Understanding ourselves better in this way makes our behaviour *more*, rather than less, free, since the recovered past has been reintegrated into ourselves, instead of acting like a semi-alien force from outside. As Merleau-Ponty expresses it in his essay "Cézanne's Doubt", which is included in his collection *Sense and Non-Sense*, "Psychoanalysis does not make freedom impossible; it teaches us to think of this freedom concretely, as a creative repetition of ourselves, always, in retrospect, faithful to ourselves."[12]

Part of what is wrong with Sartre's conception of the self and its freedom, in Merleau-Ponty's view, is that it makes it impossible to allow for this phenomenon of "sedimentation", which is so obvious when we reflect on human experience without theoretical preconceptions. Although Sartre sometimes insists that there can be freedom only "in a situation" – that is, that we can exercise genuine freedom of choice only if we have real alternatives between which to choose, which is possible only if the situation imposes constraints upon us – he immediately proceeds to undermine that requirement by saying that "there is a situation only through freedom".[13] This implies, as Merleau-Ponty sees (and as Sartre himself says), that even the alleged constraints on freedom are themselves the result of free choice and so not really *constraints* at all. But, Merleau-Ponty argues, an absolute freedom of this sort is not really freedom at all. If all our actions, and even our passive states, were indeed "free", then paradoxically *none* would be; there would be no such thing as free action, since that would have meaning only if we could distinguish free from unfree actions.[14] Sartre's doctrine of freedom reveals his underlying Cartesianism, which undercuts his own existentialist belief that "The concrete is man within the world in that specific union of man with the world which Heidegger, for example, calls 'being-in-the-world'."[15]

A self that is not constrained by its situation must be a Cartesian or disembodied self, and the experiences that it has, since they lack the sedimentation that comes from embodiment, must be, like Hume's "perceptions", a series of discrete, externally related, mental states. Significantly, Sartre speaks not of "transcending" our past, but of "negating" it, as if we could set at naught all our past experiences and start afresh at each moment. But this contradicts Sartre's own insistence on freedom in a situation. We can be free only in a situation because we can be free only if we have real choices, and we can have real choices only if constrained by a situation. But only a self that is embodied and that cannot simply disown its past existence is necessarily constrained in what it can choose by a situation that it did not choose. Merleau-Ponty considers Sartre's own example of the rocky outcrop that obstructs my onward movement, and which, Sartre says, acquires the meaning of "being unclimbable" only relative to my project of climbing it. This is certainly correct, as Merleau-Ponty admits, but what is not correct is Sartre's inference that I therefore *freely choose* to confer that meaning on the rock. Its unclimbability by me is a *fact* about that rock, given my physical powers; even given the same project, one rock can be unclimbable, and another climbable. Sartre's view that there is a situation only through freedom presupposes that our relation to the world in which we find ourselves is purely contemplative and external; but for embodied, active beings like ourselves things assume meanings that are not within our choice.

As with our physical environment, so it is with our own past, and for much the same reason. Our past is not something that we merely contemplate as a spectacle, but something that is "sedimented", through our bodies, in the background to the selves that we are now. The longer established a habit of behaviour or response is, the more it gains a kind of "favoured status" in our sense of ourselves, and the harder therefore it is to change. This does not imply that we are *determined* by our own pasts, any more than by our physical attributes; we remain free to reshape our lives, we may even in some cases be able to choose to discard our whole past or some aspect of it, but although change of this sort is possible, it is not probable.[16] Some habit of behaviour that has become so ingrained in us, in our very physiological patterns of response, as to become effectively part of what we are is not *likely* to be easily changeable, although, to repeat, nothing precludes the possibility of changing it, over time and with great effort. Despite this improbability of radical change, further-more, we retain a real freedom in relation to our past: our past presents us with the parameters of our choice, but does not destroy the power of choice itself.

III

Cartesianism has an inherent tendency towards solipsism, the view that I may be the only conscious subject in existence, or, more moderately, that I cannot *know* that I am not. If what I am is an inner object, transparent to myself but inaccessible to any other self, then it must follow that other selves, if there are any, are equally inaccessible to me. But if that is so, how can I know that there *are* other selves? From the point of view of "objective thought", of which Cartesian dualism is one manifestation, the whole idea of "other selves" seems self-contradictory, for it acknowledges only two kinds of existence: being-*for*-itself, the being of a self-conscious subject, who is necessarily aware of what goes on inside its own consciousness; and being-*in*-itself, the being of a mere thing, which has no consciousness at all. If this exhausts the possibilities, then other selves seem to be logically impossible, since they would have to be selves and yet at the same time mere objects of my experience.

If, however, we start, not from the preconceptions of objective thought, but from a presuppositionless phenomenological description of what we experience, then it is clear that there are other selves. If human being is "in-the-world", if human subjectivity is necessarily embodied, then my existence as a subject is not that of an "inner object", accessible only to myself, but that of an object in the world who manifests his consciousness in his observable actions. But then my existence as a self is on exactly the same footing as the existence of other selves. My experience of the world is an opening on to a *shared* world, a cultural world, in which objects have meanings that I share with other subjects. Merleau-Ponty gives as examples of such socially meaningful objects such things as roads, villages, churches, tools, pipes and so on. Other people themselves are experienced, not as mere physical objects, but as other embodied subjects. I *can*, of course, treat other people as mere objects, and for some purposes (e.g. some kinds of scientific work) that may even be appropriate, but outside those special contexts that objectifying attitude is essentially insincere, and as artificial as the conception of myself as a pure subject. Other human beings, like me, are both subjects and objects, and subjects who express their subjectivity in their dealings as objects with the world. Our selves (my self and other selves) exist, not "inside" us but in what Merleau-Ponty calls the "inter-world", the world of our dealings with each other.

This is so obvious that we can fail to recognize it only if we are obsessed by the objectivist prejudice that the scientific, physiological, concept of the body "from the outside" is primary, when in fact, Merleau-Ponty would argue, it must be derivative from our fundamental experience of the body as we "live" it, an abstraction for certain specialized purposes that is possible only because we create an interworld by giving expression to our lived experience. It is an "interworld" because it is a world that is *shared* with other subjects, who are also not mere physical objects, but lived bodies who give expression to their experience. This expression takes many forms – meaningful actions, bodily gestures, facial expressions, and so on – but its most obvious form is *language*. Our thoughts and feelings are expressed most explicitly in words, and it is in language that we formulate the concepts of which the objectivist view of the world itself consists: concepts such as "physical object", "causal relation", and so on. Even the terms in which we identify ourselves ("a bourgeois" or "a man", to use Merleau-Ponty's examples) are terms in the shared language: another indication of the way in which our lives as individuals are inseparable from our membership of a society. This is what gives our lives a meaning that we do not constitute: each of us is doubly "anonymous", both in the sense that each of is an absolutely individual subject and in the sense that each of us is just one among many subjects. The two kinds of anonymity are inseparable from each other: I am a subject only in so far as I am related to other subjects. This too is part of our being-in-the-world.

The phenomenon of communication in language illustrates both the element of truth in solipsism and its ultimate absurdity, for communication requires both the separateness of individual selves and the possibility of overcoming that separation. The very possibility of communication clearly implies a link between one self and another; it expresses a sense of connectedness with others that I have even before I begin to speak, and without which the whole project of communication or dialogue would be meaningless. But for that very reason the communication occurs in the space between us; communication implies the existence of two distinct selves between whom it takes place – I cannot "communicate with" myself. What is communicated is thus different from each person's experience of themselves: it is the purely outward, the "anonymous" expression of our thoughts and feelings, not the thoughts and feelings we each actually experience. Someone else's grief and anger have a different meaning for them from the meaning they have for me: to me, they are something that I observe; for them, something that they live through.[17]

The problem that the doctrine of solipsism brings to light is thus that each self is essentially individual and separate from every other self, which is what makes it difficult to understand how one self can know of others, and that is a genuine problem. But solipsism simply throws up its hands in the face of that problem, and ends up saying something absurd. It cannot be the case that there might be only one self in the world, for two reasons, both connected with language. First, I can identify myself only by using the first-person pronoun ("I"), and the first-person pronoun can have a use only if other personal pronouns ("you", "he", "she", etc.) also have a use, since its use is to distinguish me from other persons. In other words, the suggestion that I might be the only self in the universe is incoherent, since I can only give any meaning to "being a self" if it is not the case that I am the only self in existence. Putting it differently, I can regard other human beings as mere objects without consciousness only by regarding myself in the same way. But even in this case, this mutual "objectification" gets its emotional power for us only because we know that it would be *possible* for us to communicate, that is, to relate to each other as subjects. As Merleau-Ponty says, I do not have this experience of objectification when a *dog* looks at me. Secondly, the very possibility of formulating a philosophical doctrine like solipsism requires the existence of a language, and that in turn implies the existence of a community of language users, of other conscious beings like myself with whom I can communicate: in other words, the falsity of solipsism. To formulate a doctrine of solipsism (i.e. to present it as a communicable proposition) is self-defeating.

Taken strictly, then, solipsism is and must be false. But the fascination that the idea of solipsism holds comes from the fact that it expresses something true about human existence, if in a rather confused form. The element of truth in solipsism is that it expresses the necessary *otherness* of other selves, the impossibility of my genuinely sharing their experiences in the way they do (or vice versa of their genuinely sharing mine). We cannot doubt the existence of others, nor can we be without some knowledge of what they are thinking and feeling, since they can communicate their thoughts and feelings to us in a language we share with them. But since they are ultimately *other* selves, that knowledge can never be perfect.

This also illustrates the necessarily limited and derivative nature of objectivism. The possibility of communication with other selves allows us to speak of an objective, common world that we can all apprehend alike, and so to give sense to the idea of a "universal subject" that expresses what is common to all human experience. But the fact that there is a *plurality* of actual human subjects, each essentially distinct from every other, means that we cannot, in the manner of rationalist metaphysics, identify this universal subject with God, the Being who transcends the world and so views it from outside, from no particular point of view. Even at its most "objective", our view of the world is still a "view from somewhere", from a point *within* the world, namely, that point where we ourselves are. (The relevance of this for Merleau-Ponty's conception of philosophy itself will be discussed later in the chapter.)

The relation of one individual to other individuals has to take account of this paradoxical situation. Merleau-Ponty has some profound, but all too undeveloped, remarks in this connection about Christian ideas of love. If universal subjectivity could be identified with God, then in God I could be conscious of others as myself – that is (I take it), the distinction between myself and other selves would disappear in being subsumed into the divine subject. I could then truly "love others as myself" in God, since in God there would be no distinction between my love for myself and my love for another. However, as Merleau-Ponty points out, the problem is that we have to start from our finite and discrete selves in order to reach the concept of an infinite self, or God, in whom the distinction between selves disappears. My love for others *in God* would not truly be *my* love, but, as Merleau-Ponty says, quoting Spinoza, "the love which God has for himself through me".[18] It is unfortunate, to put it mildly, that Merleau-Ponty does not take this disturbing thought any further or explore its wide repercussions for religion, morality and metaphysics. Some of these repercussions, expressed in non-theological language, are, however, explored in his social and political thought.

The relation of one self to other selves is ultimately what we mean by "society". And what has been said about the relation of self to self implies that the relation of individual to society is a complex one. On the one hand, society is not an *object* external to individual selves; the social is an inescapable dimension of our very individuality, since our identity as individuals depends in part on our relations with others and on the concepts supplied by our culture in terms of which we identify ourselves. Even our relationship to physical nature is not purely individual, since it is necessarily mediated by the culture's conceptions of nature and of its meaning for us. On the other hand, individuality cannot simply be subsumed in the collective, since each individual is necessarily separate from every other individual. To use a term that Merleau-Ponty is fond of using, and whose meaning should become clearer in the next section, the relation between individual and society is "dialectical".

IV

The individual can understand their own life, as we have seen, only in relation to their past. But that past is in part a *collective* past: my life (whoever I am) has been lived at a certain period of history, and I am what I am in part because I have lived at this time in history rather than any other. Conversely, however, the character of this period of history is shaped, not by some impersonal forces, but by the actions, inactions and decisions of the individual human beings who live in it (as well as by those of individuals who have lived before). I define my own individual identity in terms of concepts derived from my culture; but the culture, and its concepts, are the expression of individuals thinking about and acting to change their world; once again, they are not external forces deterministically acting upon individuals. One sense in which the relation between individual and society is "dialectical", then, is that it is reciprocal: individuals shape culture, but culture also shapes individuals, and this reciprocity ultimately depends on the fact that neither individuals nor culture can be totally separated from each other. "History", as Marx says in *The Holy Family*, "does nothing"; "history" is not the name of some deterministic metaphysical force, but simply a way of referring to human beings acting in pursuit of their goals (or sometimes, although Marx does not say so, and would probably not have accepted it, acting *aimlessly*). But it does not follow that the concepts by which we characterize those goals ("nation", "class", for instance) are arbitrarily chosen individual values. The relation between individual consciousness and the direction of history is far more complex than that.

The quotation from Marx is appropriate because Merleau-Ponty's philosophy of history embodies a certain strand of Marxist thinking. But it is not the mechanistic or scientistic Marxism with which we are, perhaps, more familiar. That sort of Marxism is more characteristic of Marx's later thought, and was taken even further in the twentieth century when "scientific socialism" became the official ideology of the Soviet Union and its satellite states. The Marxism that influenced Merleau-Ponty, however, was the version that he had come to know from the lectures and writings of Alexandre Kojève in the 1930s (see Chapter 1), and from such "Western Marxists" as the Hungarian thinker Georg Lukács (about whom there will be further discussion in Chapter 6). This version was inspired in large part by the rediscovery of the writings of Marx's youth, in which he seemed to express a more "humanistic" view. Although influenced by humanistic or "Western" Marxism, however, Merleau-Ponty's philosophy of history is essentially the fruit of his own reflections on the nature of humanity and society. The full discussion of this philosophy of history and its bearing on politics will have to wait until Chapter 6, but something can be said in a preliminary way here, to relate Merleau-Ponty's view of collective history to the examination of his account of individuals and their past, which has been a major theme of this chapter.

The starting-point for Merleau-Ponty's reflections is the recognition that "man" or "humanity" is not so much the name of a biological species as of a "historical idea".[19] What we are, as individuals or as a species, is defined not by some predetermined essence, such as our biological characteristics, but by what we make of the situation in which we find ourselves; but we do not have absolute freedom to make what we wish of that situation.[20] Merleau-Ponty makes these remarks in the context of a discussion of sexuality and Freudianism, but he immediately goes on, in a footnote, to draw the analogy between his interpretation of psychoanalysis and his proposed interpretation of Marxist "historical materialism". In both cases, he argues, if we see human beings as actively making themselves by solving the problems of their existence – problems that are set for them, not by their choice, but by their situations as embodied beings – then the way is open for a method of understanding human history that is not "reductionist", but is nevertheless in a perfectly intelligible sense "materialist".

It is not "reductionist" because it does not treat history as the product of impersonal forces, operating in accordance with "laws" conceived on analogy with the causal laws of classical physics. Rather, it sees history as the outcome of the activities of human subjects, in which they try to give form to their lives, by their relationships of love or hate, their creation of works of art or their failure to do so, their decision to have or not to have a family.[21] Human beings coexist with each other in society, and in this coexistence they formulate conceptions of their lives and their purposes that give them reasons for acting as they do, and human history is what results. That much seems plain common sense, but how can such a view of history be described as "materialist"? The materialist part of "historical materialism" enters, in Merleau-Ponty's interpretation, in that the conceptions of our existence and the reasons for acting that we form cannot be understood without taking into account the objective situation in which we exist. It is fundamental to this situation that we are a species of living beings with certain biological needs that we must satisfy in order to exist (and in order to be able to formulate abstract conceptions of our existence). In that sense, economics, as the system by which we attempt to satisfy our needs, is basic to our existence, and so to the understanding of human history. A materialist theory of history is one that understands the "obvious" content of history, the official concepts of law and politics, in terms of the "latent" content, the actual concrete (economic) relations into which human beings must enter in order to satisfy the needs of their existence. But it does not need to see these concrete economic relations as external forces acting upon human beings; history is not reduced to economics, but rather economics becomes part of history. In other words, a "humanistic" version of historical materialism, such as Merleau-Ponty advocates, consists in emphasizing that economic activity is human purposive or intentional activity, even if the purposes or intentions are not explicitly conscious.

There is a more extended discussion of these themes in part three, chapter three of *Phenomenology of Perception* (the chapter on "Freedom"), which helps to shed further light, not only on Merleau-Ponty's philosophy of history, but also on his account of human freedom, both at the level of individuals and of humanity as a whole. The discussion there is largely concerned with Marxist conceptions of "class" and "class consciousness" and their role in the historical process. One of the most famous Marxist statements is that "the history of all hitherto existing societies is the history of class struggles",[22] and the notion of class struggle is central to any Marxist analysis of history. "Class" is defined in economic terms, that is, in terms of the relation of a particular class to the "means of production", the means by which a society satisfies its economic needs. But is a "class" in that sense an objectively existing entity that causally determines the course of history? Mechanistic or scientist versions of Marxism usually speak as if it were. Thus, if I have nothing to sell but my own labour, then I am *objectively* working class; that is a fact which determines my behaviour, and my role in the historical process, independently of my subjective recognition of it. Indeed, my subjective recognition will be one of the things determined by my objective position in the productive process; if I am a proletarian, I will necessarily come to see myself as such and adopt appropriate attitudes to society and to other classes. Full-blown idealism is the exact opposite of this: what makes me a "worker" or a "proletarian" is, for the idealist, nothing but my own conception of myself as such – there is no "objective fact of the matter". It would seem to follow that a successful businessman, for instance, who thought of himself as a "proletarian" would be one, even if he actually had much more to sell than his own labour.

Merleau-Ponty rejects both these extremes, of objectivism and idealism. People can clearly experience proletarian conditions of existence, including oppression, without thinking of themselves as proletarians or oppressed, and without therefore seeking to resist that oppression. I become a proletarian only when I come to see my conditions of existence as oppressive and so come to revolt against them. In short, contrary to the objectivist, people's *consciousness* of their situation is the prime determining factor in history; there is a class struggle only where people think of themselves as engaged in class struggle. But that is not a concession to the idealist. Our conceptions of our class position are not *caused* by the objective facts of our situation; but they do need to be *motivated* – they are not the result of a purely arbitrary "free choice" – and what motivates them are the objective facts of our situation. I am not made a proletarian, Merleau-Ponty argues, by the working of impersonal economic or social forces, but by the way in which I experience these forces within myself, the way in which I am "in-the-world" in this socioeconomic setting.[23]

Mention of being-in-the-world in that last quotation reminds us of the impossibility of separating Merleau-Ponty's thought about politics and history from his general philosophy of human experience (there will be more about this in Chapter 6). What is wrong with both objectivist and idealist interpretations of history, in Merleau-Ponty's view, is that both accept the falsely abstract distinction between the "for-itself" and the "in-itself", between "subject" and "object", as if either could exist except in relation to the other. But if human being is being-in-the-world, then human history, like the life of individual human beings, is the outcome of the *dialectical interaction* between our subjective conceptions of our situation and the objective facts of that situation. To speak of a dialectical interaction is precisely not to say that the objective *determines* the subjective, or *vice versa*: each influences the other, but in a way that allows for a certain amount of free play. It is like the way in which the different participants in a dialogue (a word that comes from the same root as "dialectic") influence each other but clearly do not causally determine each other's thoughts or utterances.

Take one of Merleau-Ponty's examples, that of a day-labourer, without a farm of his own, who makes a living as best he can by going from farm to farm at harvest time and hiring himself out. To a large extent, his existence is outside his own control, and he may well recognize this; he may have the feeling that he is the victim of some "anonymous power" that forces him to live this kind of existence. He certainly did not *choose* to follow this way of life; he was born into a world in which this, or something very like it, was the only option open to him. In this sense, his situation is an objective fact, which he must simply recognize. Because of factors equally beyond his control, he may find himself unable any longer to earn a livelihood. Here he does have a choice between different ways of understanding his situation. He may, for example, resent urban workers for being in regular employment, unlike him, and for forcing up the cost of living by striking for higher wages. In that case, he will not develop any sense of class solidarity or common cause with them; he will not see himself as a "proletarian". Indeed, he may well feel he has more in common with the bosses in opposing workers' power and the social disorder it brings about. On the other hand, he may come to see those elements in the lives of urban workers that give their situation something important in common with his. Then he will think of himself as a "proletarian" and see his own difficulties and the answer to them as part of the same struggle as the one in which the urban working class is engaged. Either "subjective" response to the same "objective" facts is possible, but neither can be understood as the product of an arbitrary decision, without reference to the objective situation.

"Class" comes into existence as a factor in history when different groups of people who share a common situation come to *see* their situation as common and to act together in defence of their common interests. A "revolutionary situation" emerges to the extent that these different people come to see the difficulties in existing that each one of them individually experiences as a *common* problem for them all.[24] But this does not imply that they necessarily form a conscious "representation" of their situation as revolutionary. Merleau-Ponty cites the example of the Russian peasants in 1917. It is very doubtful, he says, whether they saw that the end of the road on which they were travelling would be a revolutionary transfer of property, and, indeed, they might have been horrified if they had realized that that would be the outcome. This does not mean that history is the play of blind forces, or that the ways in which the historical actors express their (perhaps only half understood) intentions are mere epiphenomena on the surface of the activity of the real historical forces; rather the historical actors immediately understand certain descriptions of what they are doing – for example the slogans proposed to them by agitators – because they can recognize them as explicit statements of what is implicit in their experience.

The historian, in attempting to understand the movement of history, can likewise do so in terms of the purposes and intentions of the actors, without presupposing that these purposes and intentions are conscious or explicit. And in any complex historical situation, there will be more than one narrative available to make sense of the sequence of events, by relating it to different ways of conceiving of the purposes and goals of the protagonists. There is no single narrative for making sense either of history as a whole, or of an individual life within history, and hence neither history nor the individual life has any *single* meaning. The purposes of human beings have to take account, not only of the physical situation in which they find themselves, but also of a social and historical situation. The problems and constraints upon choice that the individual faces come not only from the necessity of satisfying biological needs, but also from the necessity to coexist with other beings in a human society sharing a common culture, with common values, concepts and institutions that will mediate even the ways in which we satisfy those biological needs. (How important, for instance, is eating in that society? What are its dietary requirements? What special types of cuisine does it favour? Does eating certain kinds of food express one's social status? And so on.) This culture in turn will have a history: it will embody the choices (not usually conscious decisions) of previous generations to do one thing rather than another.

These cultural and historical dimensions to our situation will be no more a matter of choice than the physical conditions in which we act; like them, they will set limits to what we are free to do. We cannot pretend to ourselves that the situation that faces us now is no different from that which confronted people before, for instance, the invention of the computer or of radio and television, or before the decline in organized religion or the rise of the mass media. Without that specific position in history, nothing in our social environment would have the meaning it does for us, or indeed any meaning at all. What meaning could we attach to, say, the family or private property if we did not occupy a particular position in human history? Equally, the way in which we see our own actions, even in dealing with the physical environment, cannot be separated from our sense of belonging to a particular society, and in particular from our position and role in that society. The freedom of individuals and societies is necessarily freedom within a situation, and freedom within a situation is freedom constrained by the nature of that situation. But freedom constrained, as we have seen, is not freedom destroyed. A choice between alternatives presented to us by nature, society or history is still a choice, and one kind of choice that the constraints of our situation cannot rule out is the choice to change those constraints themselves, provided only that that change is intelligibly related to the situation that we first find. We can still speak of making a choice, of course, even when we are not explicitly aware of the alternatives that confront us, and/or do not explicitly deliberate about what we shall do.

We shall have more to say about political freedom and the direction and interpretation of history in Chapter 6. In the meantime, I shall round off this chapter by discussing the implications of Merleau-Ponty's conception of history for his view of the nature of philosophy itself. If human being is being-in-the-world, and is therefore essentially in a situation that is defined ultimately by its place in history, then human being is necessarily historical. The human subject, whether of thought or action, is not an eternal being located outside time and history, but is always what it is in its relation to the historical situation in which it finds itself. The meanings that I can find in the objects of my experience, natural or social, and the reasons that I can formulate for making one choice rather than another, will thus depend on the way in which history has shaped my social, cultural and natural situation, although "meanings" and "reasons", by their very nature, are not external powers acting upon me but depend for their force on my acceptance of them and my willingness and ability to think them through.

The conceptions of rationality (of "good reasons" for thinking something true or for doing something) that prevail at any given time will thus not be eternal. (A possible exception to this might be the fundamental laws of logic, like the law of non-contradiction, which, because of their purely formal and basic character, may be regarded as universal principles to be accepted by any rational being anywhere and at any time.) The principles of what is to count as "rational" in thought and action will change in a historical fashion. That is not an expression of relativism, since to change in a *historical* fashion is, as suggested earlier in the chapter, to *develop* in such a way that the principles of rationality accepted at any given time are not arbitrarily chosen, but grow out of and go beyond those accepted previously. What does that mean? Only that, in so far as they are principles of *rationality*, they emerge from a continuing dialogue between the beliefs and the standards of action accepted in the past and the reasons for accepting them, and the beliefs and standards of action that we want to accept now as our paradigms of rationality. We are continually adjusting what Merleau-Ponty calls our "hold upon the world" in the light of our experience, and part of doing that is a continual revision of our standards of what counts as "rational", not in an arbitrary manner but in a direction dictated by our need to maintain our hold upon the world.

It is here that philosophy comes in. Philosophy's role, as Merleau-Ponty describes it, is to "make explicit" our hold upon the world, to enable us to see it more clearly, in order that we may communicate with the world better and have a better sense of who we are, what meaning we give to the idea of being human. In doing this, philosophy "destroys itself" as a separate activity.[25] Philosophy is not therefore a separate science, adding to our knowledge of ourselves and our world, but aims, by the phenomenological reduction, at loosening our hold on the world in order that we can understand it more clearly and so in the end strengthen it. In terms of rationality, philosophy's task is to make clearer the canons of what counts as a "good reason" for acting or believing that have emerged from the dialectic between ourselves and our world. In the author's preface to his collection of essays *Sense and Non-Sense*, Merleau-Ponty

107

rejects the twentieth-century revolt against reason by saying "As soon as we desire something or call others to witness, that is, as soon as we live, we imply that the world is, in principle, in harmony with itself and others with ourselves. *We are born into reason as into language* [my italics]."[26] Human beings, in short, cannot exist without an idea of reason and truth, since they cannot exist without cooperating and communicating with each other.

It is the primary aim of philosophy to understand that inescapable idea of reason and truth, but in understanding better, we are taking part in that dialogue in which the idea is formed, and so helping further to develop it. One of the gains in "existential" and phenomenological philosophy, although ultimately derived from Hegel, is in Merleau-Ponty's view the recognition that this makes philosophy, not an abstract reflection *about* human experience, but a part of that experience itself (in the sense, Merleau-Ponty says, that the word "experience" has in ordinary language "when a man speaks of what he has lived through"[27]). The task of twentieth-century philosophy was thus not to make a cult of unreason, but, as Hegel had done, "to explore the irrational and integrate it into an expanded reason":[28] for example, to take note of the allegedly non-rational aspects of human behaviour emphasized by Freud and Marx, and to develop a wider conception of reason that could give them a rational significance. The interpretations that Merleau-Ponty himself offers of psychoanalysis and of historical materialism, in *Phenomenology of Perception* and elsewhere, can be seen as part of such a project.

It is in this sense that Merleau-Ponty's philosophy is a form of "humanism". He is not a humanist in the sense derided by such later French thinkers as Foucault. That is, he does not accept the Enlightenment idea of an eternal essence of humanity or of reason that provides the model for social organization and the guarantee of scientific truth and which can be accessed by us in so far as we adopt the position of a "transcendental ego". If humanity for Merleau-Ponty is, as quoted earlier, the name of a "historical idea", rather than a biological species, then it follows that there is no predetermined essence of humanity; rather, it is up to us to *construct* the idea of humanity. And if humanity is always in process of construction, then it is never completed; what it means to be human is always still to be defined, and the direction of human history is not determined by some alien force. All that the philosopher can do is to make clearer the view of reason that we can see from the position in history that we occupy. Nor is there a transcendental ego, but only a self that is constructed in the course of a person's historical existence. This much could probably be accepted by Foucault. What he could almost certainly not accept is what follows from Merleau-Ponty's conception of human being as being-in-the-world. Because we are human beings, and so social beings who conceive and carry out their projects in combination with others, with whom they must communicate, there is an implicit universality in our projects and our ideas, at least a fragmentary idea of a common humanity which informs our projects and gives at least the outline of a meaning to human history. The problem of living in history is that we need to make sense of our lives by trying to discern that outline of meaning, while accepting that, since we cannot step outside history and contemplate it as a whole, the ultimate meaning of our lives remains "unfathomable".[29] The importance of this ambiguity of history for Merleau-Ponty's conception of the possibilities of political action will be considered in Chapter 6.

CHAPTER SIX

Politics in Theory and Practice

I

Even in his later years, when he had withdrawn from much of his former active involvement in political life, Merleau-Ponty continued to think about politics, in the sense both of general political theory and of the particular concrete problems of his day. Theory and practice were for him, as for many French intellectuals, ultimately inseparable: the position we take on particular practical problems (such as the relations of France and Europe as a whole with the USA) must be determined by a general theoretical view of the kind of society we want to create. In turn, his political theory can be understood only against the background of his general philosophical account of humanity and its nature, in particular his view of the inescapably social nature of human beings. But it is also true that the application of the general political theory to particular practical issues fills out our understanding of the theory itself, and of its foundation in general philosophy. Many of the concrete political issues that so preoccupied Merleau-Ponty and his contemporaries have by now become merely a part of history, but it is still worthwhile to examine his responses to them in order to increase our understanding of his social theory and general philosophy, and the ways in which they might be applied to the political dilemmas of our own time.

As has already been said in Chapter 1, Merleau-Ponty was reported by Sartre as saying in 1947 that "he had never recovered from an incomparable childhood".[1] He looked back upon his childhood as a golden age, from which adulthood had expelled him; and certainly it seems as if he had grown up in a comfortable middle-class environment as the cherished child of his widowed mother. Not surprisingly, in view of this, he seems to have been a somewhat conventional young man. Above all, perhaps, we can see the continuing influence of his childhood in his acceptance, in his student days and beyond, of the Catholic faith and practice in which he had been brought up. What is not so expected is that he gave his Catholicism a socially radical interpretation, and that when it came to the crunch he preferred to sacrifice the Catholicism rather than the social radicalism.

In his essay "Faith and Good Faith", reprinted in his collection *Sense and Non-Sense*, Merleau-Ponty tells us of a "young Catholic" (himself) who was "led 'to the Left'" by his faith. The occasion was the shelling in 1935 of working-class districts in Vienna by the Right-wing Austrian Chancellor, Dollfuss, and the protests against this action published in a Christian journal, with the support of one of the Catholic religious orders. When dining with members of this order, Merleau-Ponty was

> astonished to hear that, after all, the Dollfuss government was the established power, that it had the right to a police force since it was the proper government, and that the Catholics, as Catholics, had nothing against it, although as citizens they were free to censure it.

In Merleau-Ponty's eyes, "this justified the workers' opinion of the Catholics: in social questions they can never fully be counted on".[2] Christianity, he came to think, was ambiguous politically: as he expresses it in one of his post-war essays, if Christianity is considered as a religion of the Incarnation, it can be revolutionary, but when considered as a religion of the Father, it is thoroughly conservative.[3] What is most striking about this is that it was the crisis of faith provoked by this essentially political rejection of the Catholic Church as an institution that led to his final break with the Catholicism of his childhood.

This incident reveals also that Merleau-Ponty's fundamental political values were on the Left from the beginning, and they clearly remained so throughout his life, even if in his last years, disillusioned with Communism and above all with the Soviet Union, he may have expressed these values in his writings rather than in active political involvement. To say that they were on the Left means that he saw the main aim of political activity as being the attempt to create a more human and rational society, in which resources were used, not to provide profits for relatively few individuals, but to promote the well-being of as many people as possible. But an essential ingredient in human well-being was freedom, so that the pursuit of equality and social solidarity was not to undermine the freedom of individuals to live their own lives in their own way. In short, properly to understand what is involved in being human implies striving to realize that humanity more fully in our social arrangements and institutions; this implies a view of human history as having a goal, not in the sense of tending inevitably in a certain direction, but in the sense that we human beings can realize our own humanity only by working towards certain ends.

In the atmosphere of the 1930s, in which the triumph of Fascism and Nazism in Italy and Germany, and later in other countries, seemed to threaten a regression to barbarism rather than this kind of human advance, many young Left-inclined intellectuals were attracted to some variety of Marxism. Merleau-Ponty certainly seems to have made a close study of Marx's writings at that time, particularly after his break with Catholicism, and to have had some sympathy with the French Communist Party (PCF) as well as with some of the Trotskyite "heretics" from orthodox Communism. His interpretation of Marxism, as has been said earlier, was influenced above all by the lectures on Hegel's *Phenomenology of Spirit* given in Paris in the 1930s by Alexandre Kojève, which he attended along with many of his contemporaries. (The lectures were published in book form in 1947, with an English translation in 1969.[4]) Kojève was a Russian *émigré* who had left Russia in 1920, but who nevertheless retained considerable sympathy for the Soviet Union. His lectures offered a reading of Hegel that at the same time made him a kind of proto-Marxist and made Marx, at least in his younger days, a neo-Hegelian. This was achieved by interpreting Hegel's Absolute, not as a philosophical version of God, but as an expression of human self-transcendence; as in Marx, the primary mode in which human beings transcended themselves was by means of labour, in which, by mastering nature, they affirmed their own freedom. Central to Kojève's interpretation of Hegel was the account of the "Master–Slave dialectic", in which the slave eventually triumphs over the master because he stands in an *immediate* relation to nature, which he transforms by work, whereas the master's relationship to nature has to be mediated *via* the slave. There are clear echoes in this of the Marxist notion of the class struggle as the motive force of human history.

But, as said above, this reading of Hegel also implies an interpretation of Marxism that is significantly different from the "Stalinist" orthodoxy. Marxism is not, on this view, "scientific socialism", providing a set of "laws of history", modelled on the laws of natural science, which can explain in a causally deterministic fashion why the historical development of humanity has taken the course it has and can predict the inevitable next stage in human society. Rather, it is an account of human history that makes sense of the course it has taken in terms of the activities of human beings in pursuit of their purposes, and can predict only that human society will take a certain direction *if* human beings choose to act in certain ways. It is clear from what has already been said in previous chapters that such an interpretation of Marxism fits well with the view of human society and its history that Merleau-Ponty was himself developing on the basis of his reading of phenomenology, and so it is not surprising that he found Kojève's reading of Hegel and Marx congenial.

But it is also worth saying that his discovery of Hegelianized Marxism had an effect on his interpretation of phenomenology: Merleau-Ponty's subject, in *Phenomenology of Perception*, is not the "transcendental ego" of the earlier Husserl, and Merleau-Ponty goes even further than the later Husserl in insisting that the being of the subject is "in-the-world", and in a world that is social and historical as well as physical. Merleau-Ponty's phenomenology was historical, rather than transcendental. Merleau-Ponty himself explicitly connects Marx's critique of traditional philosophy with that of existential phenomenology in his essay "Marxism and Philosophy" (reprinted in *Sense and Non-Sense*), when he says "This concrete thinking, which Marx calls 'critique' to distinguish it from speculative philosophy, is what others propound under the name 'existential philosophy'."[5] Both are "concrete thinking", in that both take the human subject to be more than the subject *of knowledge*; the subject, "by means of a continual dialectic, thinks in terms of his situation, forms his categories in contact with his experience, and modifies this situation and this experience by the meaning he discovers in them".[6]

Merleau-Ponty's interest in Marxism in the 1930s was mainly philosophical. Apart from Sartre, those who knew him at that time saw no evidence of active political engagement, although of course, like most intellectuals of the time, he expressed anti-Fascist attitudes, and engaged in endless discussion of current politics with his friends. It was the outbreak of the Second World War and the subsequent fall of France and its occupation by the Nazis and their Vichy-French collaborators that led him into active political involvement. Merleau-Ponty, as was said in Chapter 1, was mobilized as an infantry officer in August 1939 and served in that capacity until the collapse of France in 1940, when he returned to Paris. He immediately joined a small resistance group, whose main occupation seems to have been printing and distributing pamphlets attacking the Occupation. In the following year, when Sartre returned from the prison camp in which he had been held since the French defeat, Merleau-Ponty's group became part of the network that Sartre helped to organize under the name *Socialisme et Liberté* (Socialism and Liberty). As its name suggests, this network was explicitly ideological in character, aiming to create a society that would be socialist, but would also respect individual freedom. Its membership included both Marxists and non-Marxists. Merleau-Ponty was responsible for drawing up the group's manifesto (on which that of the journal *Les Temps modernes* was later based – see below) and for a draft political constitution to which the group subscribed.

Socialism and Liberty, however, broke up within a few months, and Merleau-Ponty once again concentrated on more academic activity, teaching philosophy at the Lycée Carnot, where he continued the work of the Resistance by introducing his students to Marxism (in defiance of the school authorities). He also used his time during the war to deepen his understanding of Marxist theory by reading further in Marx himself and in the writings of Lenin and Trotsky. After the Liberation, he joined with Sartre and Simone de Beauvoir to found the journal *Les Temps modernes*, which, like Socialism and Liberty, aimed to support a socialist transformation of society without becoming subservient to or absorbed in the Communist Party or the Soviet Union. Merleau-Ponty, much more than Sartre, remained at first close to some highly placed members of the PCF, while also maintaining friendly relations with some Trotskyists, who were anathema to the PCF.

II

Thus, during and immediately after the Second World War, Merleau-Ponty and his colleagues, including Sartre, regarded themselves as on the non-Communist, but certainly not the anti-Communist, Left. In the author's preface to his work *Humanism and Terror*, published in 1947, Merleau-Ponty says, "It is impossible to be an anti-Communist and it is not possible to be a Communist."[7] He could not be a Communist in large part because it was becoming increasingly clear how distorted and repressive a society the Soviet Union was becoming under Stalin, and how the French Communists were prepared doggedly to defend those distortions and repressions. (One suspects also that no one as reflective and sceptical as Merleau-Ponty could have subordinated himself to an organization as dogmatic and as ruthlessly disciplined as the Communist Party, even if its aims had been nobler and closer to the ideal.) On the other hand, he could not simply do as some others were doing at the time and become a Cold War opponent of Communism and the Soviet bloc. Just before the sentence quoted above, he says, "The Marxist critique of capitalism is still valid and it is clear that anti-Sovietism today resembles the brutality, hybris, vertigo, and anguish that already found expression in fascism."

France and western Europe generally, it seemed to him, were caught between the two super-powers, the Soviet Union and the USA. Economically and politically weak after the devastation of the war, Europe had to find a role as a "third force", not taking sides in the competition between the two super-powers and developing a view about society that was neither that of Stalinist Communism nor that of the American untrammelled market system. In this way, Europe could hope to act as an intermediary between them and try at least to prevent the Cold War from heating up into an actual armed conflict. Underlying this view of the contemporary global situation is a complex and subtle theoretical position. As the passage cited at the end of the last paragraph clearly states, Marxism as a *critique of capitalism* is still accepted, which in turn implies that the values and institutions of capitalism that Marxists criticize are rejected by Merleau-Ponty too. His objections to the Soviet system and its French Communist defenders were therefore not objections to Marxism as such, or to those elements of Marxism that remained in the ideology and practice of the Communist Party. To put it differently, he did not criticize the Communist system from the point of view of a "bourgeois liberal".

For instance, he did not see the suppression of individual liberty of thought and expression in the Soviet bloc as an outcome of Marxist ideology or as an argument for Western liberal democracy. The claim by liberals to be defenders of freedom was seen by Merleau-Ponty at this time as a "false ensign", a defence of an idea rather than a reality: liberals "defend liberty instead of free men".[8] A "practical freedom", such as Marxism demands, would be an actual possession of everyone, since no one's freedom would be restricted by economic exploitation or other forms of oppression. The kind of Marxism that Merleau-Ponty espouses is not the mechanistic materialism that Western liberals criticize and Soviet Communists defend, in which "moral" or "spiritual" values like freedom are treated as merely "ideological" covers for the real economic motive power of historical development. For Merleau-Ponty,

> the dominant idea of Marxism is not, in the last analysis, the sacrifice of values to facts, of morality to realism. It is the idea of replacing the verbal morality which preceded the revolution with an effective morality, creating a society in which morality is truly moral, and destroying the morality that exists, dreamlike, outside the world, by realizing it in effective human relationships.[9]

The Marxist objection to capitalist society, in other words, was not that it was based on individual freedom, but that it wasn't: it talked a lot about the *idea* of freedom, but prevented most people from being *really* free. A genuinely Marxist society, if so, ought to be much freer than any capitalist society really was.

But then Soviet society could not be a genuinely Marxist society, since "The Marxist transition from formal liberty to actual liberty has not occurred and in the immediate future has no such chance."[10] Those who, like Merleau-Ponty, valued personal and intellectual freedom, did not therefore need to renounce their Marxism, but to keep the Soviet Union and its French followers at arm's length; as Marxists, however, they could not take that to mean that they should fall into the arms of capitalism, which by its very nature, according to the Marxist view, denied people real freedom. At least capitalism in France, and perhaps in most western European countries to a greater or lesser extent, was to some degree restrained by the existence of an organized socialist and labour movement in a way that American capitalism, especially after the McCarthyite persecutions of the early 1950s, was not. The conclusion seemed to be for Europe to follow a middle way between American capitalism and Soviet Communism, one that would be truer to the Marxist vision as Merleau-Ponty understood it.

The problems of internal French politics were connected with this international situation, but took on their particular character from the local context. The PCF had gained considerable prestige from the part that it had played in the resistance to the German occupation of France, and the mood of France after the Liberation was for radical social change: the first governments of the Fourth Republic, established after the end of the war, were broadly of the Left. One might have expected that the PCF, in line with its revolutionary rhetoric, would have played a full part in these governments, but the French Party was not an independent body: one of its major roles was to defend the interests of the Soviet Union, regarded as the homeland of socialism, and if there was a conflict between these interests and those of the French working class, then the PCF was required to give priority to the former.

In the France of the immediate post-war period, this led the Party to follow a confused and confusing course. On the one hand, the Communists had ministers in the democratically elected government and officially subscribed to the idea of a union of all Left-wing forces, and on the other, they voted against that same government, supported local strikes, and engaged in machinations against their alleged allies and open abuse against the non-Communist Left, especially against non-Communist intellectuals. Merleau-Ponty sought to make sense of this behaviour by seeing it as the result of the Communists' inability to free themselves from the habit of regarding politics as a form of war, at the very moment when they had in effect abandoned the notion of class struggle on which that habit was based. If they had been genuine Marxists, Merleau-Ponty thought, they would have seen their present actions in the light of French history, and in particular in the light of the attempt to free the French working class from oppression. They could then have seen the need for genuine union with any other groups in French society with whom they shared that aim, and could even have been willing to accept comradely discussion with and criticism from those groups. But their subservience to the Soviet Union had two consequences. First, it meant that they had inherited from the Russian Bolsheviks the idea of themselves as the sole true representatives of the proletariat, who must defend that position at all costs against other would-be claimants. Secondly, it meant that they were committed more to the defence of the interests of a Soviet system in which the revolutionary impetus had come to a halt than to promoting real revolution in France itself.

In view of the news that was increasingly coming out of the Soviet Union, it seemed clear to Merleau-Ponty that the Soviet Union was no longer a revolutionary society: it was increasingly hierarchical, with the proletariat as such having no real power; there was no public political debate; political dissent was punished as if it were a criminal offence; and Marxism itself was interpreted, not dialectically, as a living method of analysis, but dogmatically, as an alleged "science" of historical development. The French Communists simply took over these non-revolutionary attitudes and positions, and so rendered themselves incapable either of collaborating with other groupings on the Left or of proposing genuinely radical change in French society. But if the largest organized force on the French Left had thus effectively abandoned the revolutionary road, the prospects for anything that Merleau-Ponty would have regarded as a real advance in French society seemed bleak.

If so, then what could the good non-Communist Marxist do in a situation such as existed in France and the world in the late 1940s? Making a decision about what to do was not, for Merleau-Ponty, a matter of mechanically deducing a conclusion from a theory; we need to make a judgement, which will inevitably be imperfect because we are ourselves in the midst of history, not God-like figures able to observe the facts from the outside, in an "objective" or "scientific" fashion. "Marxist action presupposes . . . a certain reading of history in terms of what is likely – and with whatever errors such a reading may imply."[11] Nothing can guarantee the "correctness" of our decision; there is no logical difference, he says further down the same page, between "Marxist or dialectical contradictions" and "opportunistic compromises". We need a philosophy of history to provide a perspective in terms of which some facts can be ranked as "dominant" and others as "secondary", but such a philosophy of history must recognize that history would not exist if either everything that happened made sense or nothing that happened made any sense at all.

In view of that, what did Merleau-Ponty think ought to be done by intellectuals such as himself? First of all, there was obviously the important task of analysis of the current situation using the concepts of an undogmatic Marxism. What prospects were there of a future revival of the class struggle and the revolutionary activity of the proletariat, and how, if at all, could those prospects be enhanced? Secondly, at the very least the non-Communist Left must *refrain from* doing anything that might prevent or retard the possibility of future radical action. This meant, among other things, as Merleau-Ponty saw it, being a "fellow-traveller" of the Communist Party, that is, someone who was not a member, and reserved the right to engage in friendly criticism of particular policies, but at the same time refused to participate in the anti-Communist and anti-Soviet polemics that were initiated by the Right and by the American side in the Cold War. More positively, "fellow-travellers" would lend active support to certain Communist causes that embodied their own values, such as anti-colonialism or opposition to racism. Thirdly, non-Communist intellectuals could do what they could to work for international peace, to prevent the Cold War heating up into an actual armed conflict between the Soviet Union and the USA and their respective allies. Given the invention of atomic weapons, most people thought such a conflict would mean, not just the end of any possibility of socialism, but of human civilization itself. Fourthly, by marching side by side with the Communists, "bourgeois intellectuals" like himself could perhaps better defend their own humanist values – of respect for individual liberty, for unrestrained debate, and for artistic and cultural freedom – to all of which orthodox Communists were hostile (on the basis of what Merleau-Ponty saw as their scientistic distortion of Marxist "materialism").[12]

III

Sartre tells us that Merleau-Ponty remained on good terms personally with several Communists, but the Communist Party officially rejected his attempts, in editorials and articles in *Les Temps modernes* and, elsewhere, in the formation along with Sartre of the short-lived non-Communist Left-wing party *Rassemblement Démocratique Révolutionnaire* (RDR) and in other ways, to create a bridge between the non-Communist Left and the PCF. *Humanism and Terror* seemed to the Communists to be much too even-handed in its dealings with the conflict between the USA and the Soviet bloc. On the other side, some of his associates, such as Camus, saw his fellow-travelling as a willingness to *justify* the excesses of the Soviet regime, in the labour camps, the persecution of dissidents, and the show-trials. He was accused, as he tells us in the author's preface to *Humanism and Terror*, of claiming that the Party was infallible (even though he had denied that the notion of an infallible Party was genuinely Marxist); or of "adoring

History", when that quasi-religious attitude to the abstraction called "History" was precisely what he had been criticizing; and so on. In short, he suffered the usual fate of those who try to follow the middle way, of being attacked from both sides of the centre. But it is also true that, as the post-war period wore on, his own doubts about Communism, and the revolutionary idea in general, were increasing. Further and further details about the realities of the Soviet system were filtering through to the West, and the brutal Communist overthrow of the social-democratic government in Czechoslovakia in 1949 revealed even more clearly the unwillingness of Communists to be anything other than the dominant force on the Left, to cooperate with other parties in the interests of social progress. The final straw seems to have been the outbreak of the Korean War in 1950, in which Merleau-Ponty saw the Chinese and North Korean invasion of South Korea as part of a Soviet policy of imperial expansion. All this combined with Merleau-Ponty's temperamental scepticism (in *Humanism and Terror* he speaks of "a problem which has troubled Europe since the Greeks, namely, that the human condition may be such that it has no happy solution"[13]) to lead to a retreat from active involvement in politics. Perhaps the failings of the Soviet Union and the Communist Parties were not merely the result of a deviation from true Marxism but were inherent in Marxism itself.

The details of Merleau-Ponty's progressive disillusionment with fellow-travelling politics, leading to his estrangement from Sartre and his resignation from his position as editor of *Les Temps modernes*, have already been narrated in Chapter 1, and we do not need to repeat them here. What is more relevant in this chapter is the way in which these developments affected his theoretical thinking about politics and history. The major text for understanding Merleau-Ponty's political thought at this period is *Adventures of the Dialectic*, published in 1955. In this work, we see someone who is still instinctively on the Left, and who moreover retains the belief in a need for a historical perspective on current politics, and even some residual respect for Marxism, but whose natural scepticism and sense of the fragility of the human situation have been revived by the experiences of the decade after the liberation of France. *Adventures of the Dialectic* takes further some of the reservations that were already present in *Humanism and Terror*; there is no longer a suggestion of anything that could really be called "fellow-travelling" with Communism.

The book begins with a distinction made by the French philosopher Alain between a "politics of reason" and a "politics of the understanding". The politics of reason is based on a grand theory of history as a whole and aims to achieve the goal of history by enabling humanity to recreate itself in line with the idea of essential humanity that has always been inherent in human history. The politics of the understanding, on the other hand, has much more modest aims: it simply seeks to solve particular problems that confront human beings, accepting that the grand design of history is unknowable, but attempting as far as possible to achieve in the solutions to these problems an increase in the humanity of our social arrangements. But this, in Merleau-Ponty's view, is a false and excessively polarized distinction. He quotes approvingly from critics of Alain such as the leading French political theorist Raymond Aron, who said that what is needed is rather a politics of understanding *and* reason. Such a politics, while acknowledging the impossibility of knowing the total meaning of history, nevertheless seeks to achieve a (necessarily incomplete) view of the current period, or the current set of problems, as a whole and in relation to the movement of history as far as we can know it, and bases its prescriptions for action on that view.

Such a view of politics is in line, Merleau-Ponty says, with some aspects of the thought of Marx himself, who did not speak of an "end of history", but of an "end of *pre*-history" and who "well understood that universal history is not to be contemplated but to be made".[14] Whether or not this is true of Marx, it is certainly a characteristic expression of Merleau-Ponty's own conception of the relation between theory and practice in politics. History is something we have to *make* by our own actions: the meaning of history is not an object to be contemplated or studied in a quasi-scientific fashion, but is the image of our humanity that we create by the solutions we find to the problems created for us by past human activity. But those solutions will themselves be based on a sense, however dim, of what it means to be human, which we derive from our interpretation of the course of history up to now; in this sense, human history follows a "dialectical" path, in which the "dialogue" between the present and the past creates the future. The book as a whole is an examination of the limitations of both the politics of reason and the politics of understanding, taken on their own, and of the ways in which a synthesis of the two may perhaps be achieved. The method adopted is to try to develop a clearer understanding of the concept of "dialectic" by following the vicissitudes of that concept in a number of thinkers of the twentieth century. Most of the thinkers considered are Communists of different stripes, together with Sartre, who was at that time broadly sympathetic to Communism, but the book begins with a study of Max Weber, the great liberal sociologist and social theorist.

IV

As a liberal, Weber had a natural affinity with the politics of understanding, but he was, according to Merleau-Ponty, beginning to recognize its limitations. Political action cannot be, as Weber came to realize, merely a matter of "pragmatic" solutions to particular isolated problems, if only because human action, including politics, takes place in a historical context: what we think about the present situation is necessarily affected by our understanding of the past. His view that history, and human social action, necessarily have a "meaning" for the agents concerned, which must first be "understood" as such before an adequate causal explanation is possible, did not imply, according to Merleau-Ponty, that those "meanings" were a special kind of observable *object*. Rather, we can see meaning in the actions of others because they are human beings like ourselves, and because we can relate the meaning that they attributed to their own actions to concepts that we can understand ourselves. As far as history is concerned, we can understand its meaning only because we are ourselves part of history: we define ourselves in terms of it.

The main reason why a purely pragmatic "politics of the under-standing" is impossible, then, is that we cannot even begin to *understand* the problems which confront us now, let alone to find solutions for them, in isolation from each other. They are related to each other as part of a total configuration that is the present situation, and which can itself be understood only against the background of history. This is because we ourselves, the would-be solvers, and the ways in which we conceive of the problems, cannot be separated from our place in history. Weber's own account of the origins of the "spirit of capitalism" in certain kinds of Protestant theology, in particular Calvinism, is a good illustration of this. It presupposes a certain conception of what the "spirit" or essence of capitalism is, namely, a tendency towards "rationalization" of society and the economy, in the sense of an ordering of life based, not on the satisfaction of certain personal desires, but on the indefinite postponement of such satisfaction in the interests of a kind of impersonal efficiency.

On this interpretation, then, modern capitalism was not seen simply as a set of purely economic arrangements, but as part of a whole system of attitudes and values that linked together religion and the economy (and also, for reasons that there is not space to go into here, law, science, civil administration and government, and many other aspects of life). There are in this account of modern Western history hints of a dialectical approach, although it is not recognized by Weber as such, and is in some ways inconsistent with his own explicit views. The idea of dialectic is present, for instance, in the idea that human action needs to be *understood* in terms of the meaning that the agents themselves attribute to their action, rather than (or, as Weber holds, as well as) *causally explained* in terms of general laws of a scientific kind. It is also to be found in Weber's conclusion from this that there is no possibility of finding a meaning for human history as a whole, since such a meaning could be accessed only by the impossible means of stepping outside history and viewing it *sub specie aeternitatis*. Where Weber remains undialectical is in his invalid inference from this that our choice of conceptions by which to interpret history is ultimately arbitrary and irrational, and that the only rationality possible in human social action is of the instrumental kind, of choosing the most efficient means to achieve a given end.

The best Marxists, Merleau-Ponty argues, have learned the lesson of Weber's efforts to produce a "serious" dialectic of history. The next three chapters of *Adventures of the Dialectic* consider some of these Marxists, starting with so-called Western Marxism, as expressed particularly in the work of the Hungarian social philosopher and literary critic Georg Lukács. Lukács was taught by Weber, and many of his ideas were formed in reaction to those of his teacher. In particular, according to Merleau-Ponty, he was dissatisfied with Weber because he had not been relativistic *enough*. Weber's view that the meanings we attribute to history are ultimately arbitrary was the result, in Lukács's eyes, of an implicit belief that there *were* absolute meanings, but that they were ultimately not accessible to us. This amounted to a failure to relativize the notions of subject and object themselves: to treat history not as an "in-itself" existing independently of our knowledge of it, but as equivalent to "the totality of observed facts".[15] Then our inability to know the meaning of history as a whole can be seen as due, not to any limitation on our capacity to achieve absolute knowledge, but to the fact that the idea of "absolute knowledge" is devoid of content. What we can do is to discover the meaning of history as it relates to us now and the decisions we have to take about the advances that may be made in the future. Relativism is itself relativized, and the meanings we find in history become rational by our own standards; in the absence of any higher standards, that means they become simply "rational".

The other main way in which Lukács differed from Weber was, of course, in being a Marxist, and also in the way in which he understood Marxist materialism. Weber, in line with many interpreters, took Marx to be saying that cultural phenomena like philosophy, religion, law and literature were merely derivative expressions of an underlying reality that consisted in purely economic relationships. Lukács, by contrast, interpreted Marxist materialism as the doctrine that all human relationships have to be mediated by things – that our personal life has to be "objectified" in roles and institutions before it can play a real part in the world. This does not imply that some particular factor (such as economics or technology) is somehow ontologically or explanatorily fundamental in history, but that all aspects of human life are equally expressions of this phenomenon of objectification. Human history is the record of human thoughts and purposes being embodied in institutions, an embodiment that then creates an "inertia" which can only be overcome by further human action.

On Lukács's interpretation of Marxism, then, as reported by Merleau-Ponty, human history is "rational", but not, as in most interpretations of Hegel, because it proceeds according to a kind of predetermined logical necessity. The rationality of human history consists in the fact that human beings can (but need not) *make* it rational by progressively overcoming the inertia of the objectified form of the decisions of past human beings by reintegrating it into their own subjective conceptions (which must themselves be expressed in the objective form of new institutions and social arrangements). These new subjective conceptions are themselves responses to the problems thrown up by the existing arrangements, and in this sense cannot be fully understood except in relation to the past. So we see a further way in which history is dialectical; it can be seen as a metaphorical dialogue between the present and the past, in which, as in any conversation, the outcome may be a position that is not already contained in those from which either participant started. "Historical accumulation or 'sedimentation' is not", Merleau-Ponty says, "a deposit or a residue. The very fact that an advance has occurred changes the situation; and to remain equal to itself, progress has to face the changes that it instigated."[16]

It is not hard to see the similarities between Lukács's interpretation of Marxism, as here described, and the philosophy of history that Merleau-Ponty himself presents in *Phenomenology of Perception*, and which has been outlined in Chapter 5. The natural inference is that, in discussing Western Marxism here, Merleau-Ponty is describing his own views at the time of writing that earlier work. The Marxism with which he then sympathized did not guarantee social progress, but it did seem to offer a way of reading the present in the light of the past that would make it clear how an advance was possible, and what the direction of advance should be, in the present situation. In particular, it implied that in modern capitalism, the basis for any possible advance to a better, more human, society must lie in the proletariat and its position. The proletariat in capitalist society is, by the Marxist definition, the class that is most thoroughly "alienated" from institutions of that society: the products of its labour are utilized for the profit of the capitalist class, and proletarians are themselves simply objects, part of the machinery of production. The only way in which an advance to a more human society is possible, therefore, on the Marxist reading, is by the proletariat's overcoming its own alienation by taking over that machinery from its oppressors, in order that it should be used to satisfy the needs of all rather than the profits of a few.

The proletariat, however, according to the very view of history that has just been sketched, will not *inevitably* recognize its own oppression or seek to overcome it in this way. It needs to become *conscious* of its own existence as a class, and as an oppressed class, before it can fulfil its progressive role. If it is not inevitable that it will become conscious in this way, then clearly there is a need for those who will help to raise consciousness, an "advance-guard" of the proletariat, perhaps armed with a knowledge of Marxist theory, who can help others to understand their wretched situation in existing society and the ways in which they can escape from it. Thus the notion of a revolutionary "Party" enters Marxist thought. In Lukács's conception, the Party is not seen as separate from the proletariat, directing it from the outside in the "right" direction. The Party and the proletariat must rather be in a relation of dialogue: the Party is simply the means by which the meaning of the present situation becomes clear to the proletariat.

This modest view of the Party's role did not, however, appeal to Marxist orthodoxy, as accepted by Lenin's Bolsheviks in the Russia of the early twentieth century. Lenin, in his book *Materialism and Empirio-criticism*, which became the defining text of Soviet Marxist philosophy, emphatically rejected this sort of interpretation of Marxism as a whole, reaffirming the interpretation of Marxist materialism that Lukács was to oppose. The reason for this rejection on Lenin's part was, Merleau-Ponty suggests, not entirely philosophical; in large part it must have been a matter of political tactics, since Lenin himself in later writings put forward subtler interpretations of Marxism. "What he [Lenin] wanted to do in this earlier work was, therefore, to furnish a simple and efficacious ideology to a country which had not gone through all the historical phases of Western capitalism."[17] Nevertheless, Lenin's authority, together with the situation of the Party in the Soviet Union, helped to establish an essentially undialectical version of Marxism, as a quasi-natural science that could view history as a whole from a position outside history. The Party then became the scientific experts who could direct the proletariat on the basis of their expertise, rather than a group who could engage in dialogue with the proletariat to work out together what might be the next step to take.

Merleau-Ponty accepts, however, that this conflict between Leninism and Western Marxism is already to be found in Marx himself, who wavered between a truly dialectical account of history and notions of "scientific socialism". Western Marxism corresponds to the views of Marx's youth; but Leninism is truer to the version that Marx adopted in his mature years, after 1850, in which we cannot "understand" our situation in human terms as the outcome of meaningful human relations, but can only causally "explain" it as the product of impersonal economic forces. Revolution on this view is akin to social engineering: the "technicians" (the professional revolutionaries, the Party) have to use their knowledge of the mechanisms of history in order to manipulate them in the required direction. Reference to the dialectic is retained, in order to distinguish Marxism from "bourgeois" or positivistic social science, but the dialectic is itself interpreted naturalistically, as a certain kind of reciprocal causality, so that the result is an "unstable mixture of Hegelianism and scientism".[18]

The irony is that Marxism by this process has become, not something that might qualify as knowledge, but an "ideology" that justifies the status and power of a new ruling class: the Soviet Communist Party. The "history" of which it talks is not the actual activity of human beings in pursuit of their ends, which we can all understand just in virtue of being human ourselves, but some kind of metaphysical object proceeding according to laws of its own, which can be understood only by those scientifically qualified. "Socialism" comes to mean, not a system in which human relations are no longer alienated in their objective expression in things, but the kind of system of industrialization and centralized planning that existed in the Soviet Union, and which inevitably created new class divisions between the bureaucrats who planned and the workers whose activity was planned by the bureaucrats. Even Trotsky, despite being expelled from the Soviet Union by Stalin and his followers, did not ultimately diverge from this view, Merleau-Ponty argues. He saw the establishment of the Soviet system as a genuine socialist revolution, and the Stalinist takeover as a "counter-revolution"; but Stalin and his supporters achieved power through the very processes of the Soviet system, which Trotsky did not seriously question.

Merleau-Ponty offers a dialectical account of this abandonment of dialectical thought. As soon as a Party that claims to have the absolute knowledge of the inner workings of history achieves power, it needs to sustain itself in power in order to continue with the application of its knowledge in engineering the society of the future. Because it is necessarily distinct from the proletariat, which is merely its instrument in achieving that engineering, the society of the future will not be one in which the proletariat transcends itself to create a classless system, but one in which a new ruling class, the bureaucracy, takes over from the old. Perhaps this is even a necessary feature of any revolution: in its success it ceases to be revolutionary. Merleau-Ponty's account of the "adventures of the dialectic" is thus not merely a critique of Soviet-style Communism, but of Marxism itself. All that remains of Marxism, if he is right, is his own minimalist version, the doctrine that human beings make their own history, but in conditions that they do not themselves choose: a claim that implies nothing about a "final stage" of history in which a fully human and fully rational society will be established.

The last, and by far the longest, main chapter in *Adventures of the Dialectic* is devoted to analysing what Merleau-Ponty sees as the logic, if not necessarily the intentions, of Sartre's position at that time, under the title "Sartre and Ultrabolshevism". As suggested in Chapter 1, it is tempting to regard this critique of Sartre (which Sartre and Simone de Beauvoir indignantly rejected as a travesty of his real views) as the, or at least a, major motive for writing the book at all: part of the philosophical and personal quarrel between the two men. But the chapter's philosophical significance can be understood only in relation to the chapters that precede it. The account of Sartre's views is based on articles that he wrote for *Les Temps modernes*, "Les Communistes et la paix" ("The Communists and Peace"), which appeared in three parts between July 1952 and April 1954, and "Réponse à Claude Lefort" ("Reply to Claude Lefort'), which appeared in the issue for April 1953. In them, according to Merleau-Ponty, Sartre attempts to defend Communism without recourse to the ideology by which Communists usually defend themselves: as Sartre says, "by reasoning from *my* principles and not from *theirs*".[19]

Sartre's principles are, of course, those of his own philosophical position, which, Merleau-Ponty argues, effectively denies the possibility of a dialectical understanding of human action. The relation between subject and object in Sartre is purely external: meaning is found only in the subject, and the object is meaningless matter. Such a view, Merleau-Ponty argues, can no more allow for genuine historicity than the kind of objectivism that is found in the Bolshevik version of Marxism, of which, indeed, Sartre's philosophy is the mere mirror image, for historical action requires a dialectical relationship between the subjective and the objective, in which the subjective responds to an objective situation, which is already the expression of previous subjectivity, by expressing itself in a new objective situation, and so on *ad infinitum*. Sartrean subjectivism can only present history as a series of unmotivated acts, without any reference to what came before them, so that the present is the mere negation of the past. Bolshevik objectivism, on the other hand, reduces history to a series of causal relationships, so that the present is only externally related to the past. Thus Bolsheviks can at least treat the present state of the Soviet Union as the necessary causal outcome of what happened in the past; for Sartre, however, history has no relevance for understanding the present state of the Soviet Union.

Any justification that he offers of Communist practice will therefore take no account of history; the Party will not be able to justify itself as the instrument by which a historically oppressed class, the proletariat, seeks to shake off its oppression. The proletariat is not the outcome of a real historical process, but is the *creation* of the Party: there was no proletariat until the Party created the concept of such a class (and hence the creation of that concept was itself an arbitrary act of will, since Sartre's philosophy implies the impossibility of any objective reasons or criteria). The solidarity of the proletariat with the Party comes about, according to Merleau-Ponty's reading of Sartre, from this very fact that it is the Party's creation. It follows that the Communist Party and its actions on behalf of the proletariat are removed from rational criticism. The Communist Party does what it does as a matter of pure arbitrary choice; it is pure action.

Not only is this a rejection of the central insight of Marxism, Merleau-Ponty argues, but, perhaps more important, it involves a denial of any possibility of finding a rational meaning in history, and so of seeing any policies as the rational next step to take in the development of humanity. Revolution, for example, can be recommended only as an arbitrary act of will, a simple *decision* to create socialism rather than Fascism. But as soon as one turns from abstract philosophizing to the real world in which political action must take place, a world of probabilities and compromises, it can reasonably be asked, Merleau-Ponty says, "whether revolution in the Marxist sense is still the order of the day".[20] In this way Sartre's analysis may have performed a useful service. He has stripped away all ideology from Communism, and so removed all its pretensions to express the underlying movement of History, or to be the necessary expression of the interests of the historically existing working class. Even if Sartre himself is unwilling or unable to submit the Party to any kind of rational evaluation, he has thus enabled us to judge it by a humbler kind of rational standard, that of what practical value, in promoting the interests of the working class, or furthering the cause of world peace, there may be in supporting the Party's line.

What is the outcome of this discussion for Merleau-Ponty's original question, about whether a "third way" is possible between the "politics of reason" and the "politics of the understanding"? In the epilogue to the book, Merleau-Ponty sums up what has emerged about the notion of "dialectic". "There is dialectic", he says,

> only in that type of being in which a junction of subjects occurs, being which is not only a spectacle that each subject presents to itself for its own benefit but which is rather their common residence, the place of their exchange and of their reciprocal interpretation.[21]

128

Human history is "dialectical" therefore, as we have seen, because human beings are essentially social beings, who communicate with each other, and who therefore share a common world; they communicate with each other *about* this shared world, and in so doing cooperatively shape this world, give it a human or rational form. But the world that they share has already been shaped by human beings, and the shape that they themselves give this world will be the background to the shaping performed by future generations; in this sense their dialogue is not just among those who presently exist, but between past, present and future. Above all, a dialectical conception of history is one that insists that historical action has to be *understood*, as we understand the meaning of what someone says, rather than *causally explained*, in the way we explain the behaviour of physical objects on the basis of the laws of natural science. And it is one in which no artificial barriers are erected between different areas of our common social life: no social problem is seen as isolated, since all arise in the context of our continuing relation with each other as members of a society and of the history that we have in common.

Orthodox Marxism is an example of the "politics of reason". It has a philosophy of history that claims to understand the whole course of human history up until now and to predict on that basis the next, and final, stage in which humanity will at last come into its own. This philosophy of history is said to be "dialectical", but this, in Merleau-Ponty's eyes, is a misuse of the term: a truly dialectical view of history would not pretend to predict the end of history, since we can understand history only from within, and so cannot have a vision of "history as a whole". Orthodox Marxism has such pretensions because it is an attempt to be "scientific" about history, to offer causal explanations of the historical process, and so distorts the dialectic into a peculiar type of causality. But at least it retains from the notion of dialectic the idea that the present can be understood only in the light of the past, and that society and its problems must be considered as a whole.

Conventional "pragmatic" liberalism, on the other hand, is completely undialectical. A phrase of Popper's, almost certainly unknown to Merleau-Ponty, is useful here: liberalism is concerned with "piecemeal social engineering", in which problems are considered and solutions to them are proposed in isolation, on the basis of a positivistic social science which aims to offer causal explanations on the lines of the natural sciences. But at least this kind of liberalism, for that very reason, does not propose the kind of total social upheaval that orthodox Marxism envisages, in which the freedom, and the lives and well-being, of actual human beings of the present generation are threatened in the name of some distant goal of a fully human society.

129

A vice common to both orthodox Marxism and conventional liberalism is their "scientism", the belief that human actions and the human situation are to be causally explained in the manner of the natural sciences, and consequently that the solutions to human problems are essentially technical. If so, then achieving these solutions is work for technicians, for "social engineers": the Party in the case of Marxism, the political élite in the liberal case. Both therefore are marked by a technocratic élitism (although at least in the liberal case, the technocrats may be accountable to the population at large through parliamentary democracy).

The third way must obviously try to combine as far as possible the virtues of the other two, while minimizing their vices. It will be based on a dialectical understanding of history, in a truer sense than the politics of reason; that is, it will understand the present situation as a whole, and in the light of history, but without attempting to relate it to some final goal of history as a whole. The lack of a need for such a grand vision of history will be its similarity with the politics of the understanding, but it will differ in its acceptance of the need for a global and historical understanding of the present situation as the basis for worthwhile solutions to present problems. And because it aims at a humanistic "understanding", in terms of the purposes of the human beings involved, rather than a positivistic causal "explanation", which treats human agents simply as a particular sort of objects to be manipulated by those who know how to do so, it will avoid the technocratic conception of political action that is common to both the politics of reason and the politics of understanding.

In practice, in the France of Merleau-Ponty's time, what this meant was, on the one hand, a form of liberalism that recognized the necessity of parliamentary institutions. For that was, in his view, the only way that "guarantees a minimum of opposition and of truth",[22] despite the many defects in existing parliamentary procedure, which could anyway be reformed within the parliamentary institution itself. On the other, it would take over from Marxism the recognition that existing society was not the harmoniously functioning system of idealized liberal conceptions, with disagreements only at the level of political ideas, but that, for historical reasons, there was a class struggle in which some are oppressed by others. In that situation, anyone of progressive sympathies must of course side with the oppressed against their oppressors. Merleau-Ponty had serious doubts by this stage about the ability of the Communists to defend the interests of the oppressed, and still more about whether the installation of a Communist regime, even if it did advance proletarian interests to some degree, would be worth the cost, even in the eyes of the proletariat themselves. The interests of world peace, as well as the need to defend the interests of the working class, might still, however, require us to avoid the rabid *anti*-Communism of much Right-wing thinking at that time.

Much has changed since Merleau-Ponty's day, especially since the fall of the Berlin Wall, so that the details of his political programme are now of merely historical interest. There is little point in speculating about what he would have thought about the present political situation, about the universal dominance of the market, the political and economic integration of Europe or the competition between European welfare capitalism and the more *laissez-faire* American version. What is of more permanent value, however, as was said at the beginning of this chapter, is the underlying view of politics and history, rooted in his philosophical conceptions of human being as being-in-the-world and of the need to understand the human situation dialectically. The discussion of *Adventures of the Dialectic* reinforces Merleau-Ponty's central theme that "humanity" is not just the name of a biological species but stands for an "idea" that we have to create in the course of our history. We do not and cannot have any conception of where this process of creation of ourselves is ultimately going, but it does not follow that we can avoid reflecting on where we are now in the light of our history so far and seeking to glean from those reflections some notion of what the nature of humanity is and what can be done to advance it. That such a notion must be possible seems to follow from the very fact that we live together with other human beings in society and have bonds with them; and if it is possible, nothing can excuse us from the responsibility to act on it. "In morality as in art", Merleau-Ponty says in the author's preface to *Sense and Non-Sense*,

> there is no solution for the man who will not make a move without knowing where he is going and who wants to be accurate and in control at every moment. Our only resort is the spontaneous movement which binds us to others for good or ill, out of selfishness or generosity.[23]

Political or moral action necessarily proceeds from where we are, and is guided by our inevitably limited perspectives, but it does not follow that it is nothing more than a leap in the dark.

CHAPTER SEVEN

The Arts

I

Phenomenological philosophy, in Merleau-Ponty's conception, consists as we have seen in "re-learning to look at the world", attempting to get behind the theoretical constructions that we erect on the basis of our immediate experience of the world in order to describe that experience itself. In so doing, he says, we do not simply reflect a pre-existing truth: philosophy is, "like art, the act of bringing truth into being".[1] The analogy between phenomenology and art, especially the visual arts, runs through Merleau-Ponty's writings, sometimes as asides to a general philosophical discussion, and sometimes in the form of extended essays on particular arts. His comments on the arts illuminate and are illuminated by his account of phenomenology as philosophy. As we shall see later, in the direction that his thought took in the last years of his life, as reflected in the two uncompleted books that were published only posthumously (*The Prose of the World* and *The Visible and the Invisible*) and in the last paper published before his death ("Eye and Mind"), the visual arts in particular and their relation to philosophy seem to become more central in his thinking. This development will be considered in the last section of this chapter and in Chapter 8. First, however, we should consider the relation of art and philosophy in his earlier works.

Phenomenology rests on our *pre-objective* engagement with the world: as embodied beings-in-the-world we perceive the world not as something that is "presented" to us, as a mere object of thought, but as the milieu in which we exist. If we adopt a phenomenological approach, Merleau-Ponty says, we discover that vision is not "thinking about seeing", as Descartes described it, but is direct contact with the visible world. Perception is not a matter of intellectual contemplation, but of active involvement with things. Because of this, vision is charged with the meanings that we find in the objects of perception because of our active involvement with them. Philosophy, in the form of phenomenology, attempts to describe in words the way in which these "lived" meanings emerge, as the basis for the meanings that we may attribute to the world in more abstract accounts, such as that given in the sciences. But art can do more than simply *describe* that pre-objective world of perception: it can directly *present* it in the works which it creates. The painter that Merleau-Ponty refers to most of all in his writings is Cézanne, who, he says, had tried in his work to capture "the physiognomy of things and faces" by reproducing the way in which it was configured.[2] Cézanne, he says, had first of all tried, in portraits, to start by capturing the facial expression of his subject, in the sense of the familiar way in which we come to see each other in our social lives; but he soon learned that that was impossible. A face can express something only because it is physically configured in certain ways, and the painter's task is first of all to capture that configuration from which the meaningful expression emerges.

In much the same way, Merleau-Ponty says, again referring to Cézanne, "By remaining faithful to the phenomena in his investigations of perspective, Cézanne discovered what recent psychologists have come to formulate: the lived perspective, that which we actually perceive, is not a geometric or photographic one."[3] Merleau-Ponty's language here (he uses similar language elsewhere) is interesting: he speaks of Cézanne as engaged in a kind of phenomenological research ("remaining faithful to the phenomena in his investigations of perspective") in his attempt to depict perspective adequately in his painting. By means of this research, he corrects the errors of a more "objectivist" philosophy and the science based on it. In "Eye and Mind", for instance, Merleau-Ponty considers Descartes's account of perspective in his *Dioptrics*, which did treat perspective in geometric terms, as if it were merely a matter of relations in an objective space, detached from all human points of view. This geometric conception of perspective is also "photographic", in that it treats our relation to the things we see as like that of a camera, which receives light passively through its lens. But that account of perspective is not based on attention to the phenomena of lived experience, in which we do not passively contemplate the world but are actively involved with it; it depends on a priori metaphysical reasoning concerning what matter and its perception *must* be like if an objective science is to be possible.[4]

It is not only paintings that are seen as contributions to phenomenological research, however, but also other types of art. Movies, for example, are said to directly present to us such things as the "special way of being in the world ... which clearly defines each person we know". They can do this because they are not thought, but perceived. And the relation between movies and phenomenology is then made explicit: phenomenology differs from classical philosophy because it sees the self as "inhering in a world", and is an "expression of surprise" at this inherence of self in world, in which the aim is to "make us *see* the bond between subject and world rather than *explain* it in the manner of classical philosophies".[5] The movies, by their very nature as depictions of human beings in action in the world, are peculiarly suited to make this inherence manifest – in other words, again simply to present the phenomena to us directly without an attempt at a theoretical explanation of them.

Even literature, especially novels and plays, can be related to phenomenological philosophy (I say "even" simply because in literature the presentation of phenomena is, of course, mediated by words rather than direct). Literature could not have the same relationship with classical rationalist philosophy, which sought, in a quasi-scientific fashion, to construct grand explanatory theories, which by their nature were concerned with generalities and abstractions, rather than the concrete world of actual human existence, with which the novelist in particular deals. A "philosophical novel", in the context of classical philosophy, could only mean an allegorical fable like Plato's myths or Voltaire's *Candide*. The literary form in such cases amounts to little more than an embellishment of philosophical ideas that could be expressed equally adequately, if less entertainingly, in a philosophical treatise. But, Merleau-Ponty argues, "Everything changes when a phenomenological or existential philosophy assigns itself the task ... of formulating an experience of the world, a contact with the world which precedes all thought *about* the world."[6] The task of that kind of philosophy cannot be distinguished from that of the novel, and novels and plays can become "philosophical" in their very being, in that the writing of a novel may be regarded as a form of phenomenological research.

We do not normally think of paintings, movies, novels and so on in this way, as pieces of philosophical research, but as works created by artists in which we take aesthetic pleasure. So what is it that works of art are supposed to do over and above giving pleasure? At one point, Merleau-Ponty suggests that the experience of a work of art leads to a change (presumably for the better) in our aesthetic experience in general. Taking the paintings of van Gogh as an example, he says that, even if he cannot recall individual pictures, the fact that he has become acquainted with them will affect the whole of his later aesthetic experience.[7] What is not clear here is what is meant by "aesthetic experience". Does Merleau-Ponty simply mean that when I look at other paintings subsequently, my experience of them will be significantly different from that of someone who has never seen a van Gogh? If so, then this is an important point on the nature of human experience in general and the way in which the past influences the present, but it does not seem in itself any particular reason for attributing philosophical significance to the painter's work. On the other hand, he may mean that my whole experience of the world is transformed by having seen van Gogh's paintings: that, for instance, how I see trees will be affected by his depiction of them as vibrantly alive and as it were pushing themselves upwards. Learning to see the world differently in this way is, after all, as was said earlier, the aim of phenomenology; seeing the world in a new way could be regarded, furthermore, as "bringing into being a truth" about the world that was not simply a reflection of what was there anyway, which Merleau-Ponty sees as a common feature of art and phenomenology.

Some other examples of ways in which art may lead us to see the world or aspects of it differently may help to make this point clearer. In *Phenomenology of Perception*,[8] for instance, Merleau-Ponty discusses experiments on the viewing of colours in different lighting. This leads him in turn to ask what exactly lighting *is*. The answer to his question, he says, may be found in certain visual arts, notably painting, photography and film. These arts, in which lighting of course plays an important role, can in his view help us to see what is peculiar about it as a feature of our perceptual experience. They show that the part played by lighting is to direct our gaze towards the object and so see it. Lighting is one of the elements that Merleau-Ponty lists in "Eye and Mind" (along with light, shadows, reflections and colour) as the "means" by which an object such as a mountain makes itself what it is before our eyes. Not everyone sees them; it is the painter's task, he there says, to "unveil" them, to ask them "what they do to suddenly cause something to be and to be *this* thing".[9]

Another feature of perception that art can draw to our attention is the way in which the different sensory properties are integrated with each other. Merleau-Ponty again cites Cézanne, who said that part of the content of a painted landscape is the very smell of the countryside that it depicts, by which he meant that the colour that something has is not independent of its shape, its tactile properties, its resonance or its smell.[10] In attempting to paint the landscape, the artist has to recognize this essential unity created by the interaction of different properties (even belonging to different senses) and in embodying this recognition in the painting makes it manifest to the rest of us. This "synaesthesia", the working together of different senses, is of the essence of perception as we actually live it, although it is very hard to explain in the objectivist terms of science, in which lived experience is set aside in favour of a physical explanation of the causal relations between organized bodies and objects. If we start from the conception of ourselves as body-subjects, and of our bodies as a "synergic system" functioning as a whole in our active involvement with the world, however, then synaesthesia becomes only what we should expect. It is expressed artistically, for example, in the fact that adding sound to a silent movie, or dubbing a foreign-language film, changes the whole nature of the experience. The presence or absence of sound of a particular kind, whether in the form of dialogue, sound effects, or music, works together with the purely visual elements to produce the film as we experience it.[11]

In ways like this, the arts can perform a similar role to a phenomenological philosophy, that of making us more aware of the way in which we "inhere" in a world as embodied, perceiving subjects. In *The Structure of Behaviour*, Merleau-Ponty says that the arts especially raise perception from immediate experience to a more universal level, to a "knowledge of truth", in which we perceive a "universe", of which our immediate experience and its objects are but a part.[12] In saying that art can achieve a knowledge of truth in this way, however, Merleau-Ponty is certainly not assimilating art to science or to traditional philosophy. He says quite firmly that it is not the task of the novelist, the poet, the painter or the musician to "expound ideas" but to create a certain kind of object that *depicts* events. The work exists in its own right as an individual object, and all its meaning is contained in the way it is expressed. But this also implies that the "truth" that we know by means of it is not truth in the conventional sense, of correspondence between a proposition, with a meaning determined by general rules independent of the person uttering it, and a "fact" identified by reference to that same proposition and its accepted meaning. The artistic representation, having its own, non-conventional, meaning, is able to give "knowledge of truth" in a sense that seems to be something more like a *fresh* or *unconventional understanding* of the event depicted.

The medium of expression in the case of the novelist or poet, unlike those of the painter, musician or dancer, is, of course, words, but the words are used, not to refer to objects in the world, but to create the literary object, just in the way that pigments are used by the painter or notes by the composer. The *literary* meaning of the novelist's or poet's words is no more separable from the created object than is what is expressed artistically or musically in the other cases. In this sense, none of the arts, even literature, is concerned simply to *describe* the world as we conventionally experience it. A prime characteristic of the descriptive use of language is that, in it, thought seems to become detached from its changing material embodiments and to become something eternal.[13] The meanings of words in their non-fictional use are relatively impersonal: what the word "perception" means, for instance, is not what *I* mean by it, but what the shared rules of the language (in this case, English) determine it as meaning. In using language in this non-creative way, therefore, we can do more than present, say, "what perception is like for me"; we can talk about the idea of perception in an abstract, general and timeless way. But the meaning of the brush strokes in a painting, or the notes in a piece of music, or the events narrated in a novel cannot be isolated in this way from the structures to which they belong, and so cannot be expressed except in that form.

The positive side to that is that the work of art can achieve something that prosaic philosophy can't, and in that way perhaps show us what a truly phenomenological philosophy might be capable of. Referential language is based on rules; it works as a medium of communication only because both speaker and hearer *already* understand the conventional meanings of the words used, and they do this because they share a common, established world, in which these words have their reference and in which there are shared standards of what is "reasonable". But the artist, communicating in a way that is independent of these meaning-rules and of a shared world of culture and reason, can recall us from our ordinary commitment to the rules and the shared standards of rationality. In so doing, the artist may reveal to us new standards of rationality, rooted not in a historical culture, but in the nature of our being-in-the-world. "The meaning of what the artist is going to say . . . summons one away from the already constituted reason in which 'cultured men' are content to shut themselves, toward a reason which contains its own origins." The artist, unlike the traditional philosopher, calls human beings to get away from conventional and narrow conceptions of rationality, embedded, say, in the practice of science; but does so not by the plausibility of his or her arguments, but by awakening "the experience which will make their idea take root in the consciousness of others".[14]

II

Art can achieve this because of its own special nature, and it is this question of the character of art as Merleau-Ponty sees it that I want to address in this section. One way in which art clearly differs from a straightforward presentation of what we perceive has just been mentioned. The artist, by definition, is a *creator*; he or she *makes* some object – a painting, a poem, a dance, a movie, a novel, a piece of music, and so on – which then exists independently of its creator. Even the photographer, in so far as he or she is an artist, does not just *record* what is in front of his or her eyes; does not, for instance, simply put the camera down at random and click the shutter.

Rather, the photographer, at the very minimum, points the lens in a certain direction, chosen by himself or herself, and selects in the viewfinder a shot that is attractively composed, or interesting, or startling, or in some other way has some artistic value. Photographers also, of course, manipulate the processes of developing and printing, or nowadays use their computers in certain ways, to produce a picture that may be very different from the scene "as it actually was".

Because the medium of the resulting work is not conventionally referring language, whatever meaning it has will not be expressible in any other terms than those of the work itself. It is not an *arbitrary* meaning: because we cannot give a "correct" translation into some other medium, it does not follow that we can give the work any meaning we care to. A poem's meaning, for instance, is, Merleau-Ponty says, given entirely in the words printed on the page.[15] One consequence of the inseparability of the expression and what is expressed is that the artist cannot know the meaning of the work before creating it, and may not *ever* be in a position to know its meaning in full: "the artist launches his work just as a man once launched the first word, not knowing whether it will be more than a shout".

Art is the *expression of a meaning*, which originates in "the flow of [the artist's] individual life".[16] But does that mean that artists are doing no more than expressing *themselves* in the work which they produce? What is the relation between artists' personality and their work?

Merleau-Ponty considers this issue using the example of Cézanne, who had a personality that many people might classify as schizophrenic. He had difficulties with ordinary human relationships, and one could, Merleau-Ponty suggests, see his extremely close attention to inanimate nature and the impersonal character of his paintings (Merleau-Ponty quotes his remark that a face should be painted as an object) as indicative of an alienation from the human world. In this sense, knowledge of his personality is relevant to understanding his paintings, but does it follow that his paintings are nothing more than expressions of the kind of person he was (which would imply that they have nothing to say to those who have different sorts of personality)? There is, Merleau-Ponty goes on, another possible way of thinking of the relation between the artist and his work. Perhaps it is his problems which give him a particular insight, denied to others with a less disturbed personality, which enables him to communicate something of value to everyone. In Cézanne's case, for example, his particular way of seeing may have led to his ability to depict objects that are not, as was the case with the Impressionists, almost dissolved in their relationships to the atmosphere and other objects, and so have more solidity and substance. In general, his painting, Merleau-Ponty says, suspends our usual habit of seeing things only through their human use and "reveals the base of inhuman nature upon which man has installed himself".[17]

The artist thus starts from where he or she is, from his or her individual personality, and creates a work that expresses a meaning that he or she is probably not fully aware of. The meaning is entirely contained within the work created, so that the artist *could not* formulate it in any other way beforehand and then simply embody a fully explicit meaning in the material form of a painting, sculpture, film, novel, poem or whatever. The artist's individuality is expressed in the work, but the work transcends the artist as an individual. In much the same way, Merleau-Ponty contends, a work of art (like a philosophy, he here says) certainly expresses the time when it was created, with all its special circumstances, but necessarily goes beyond being a *merely* historical product. In his discussion of Marxism as he interprets it, Merleau-Ponty emphasizes the essentially historical nature of human existence, with its consequences both that everything we do and are belongs to a particular time and that it points beyond that time. If this is so in general, then plainly it is true of our creation of works of art and philosophy. "A philosophy, like an art or poetry, belongs to a time, but there is nothing to prevent it from capturing – precisely through that time – truths which are acquired once for all, just as Greek art discovered the secret of an 'eternal charm' (Marx)."[18] The parenthesis in this sentence is important: we "capture" permanent truths "precisely through that time": the artist, poet or philosopher arrives at permanent truths not by trying (impossibly) to occupy a position outside history, but from where he or she actually is. This is why both the individual psychology of the artist and the history or sociology of the artist's society are relevant to understanding and appreciating the work, even though the significance of the work cannot be reduced to an expression of its psychological or sociological origins.

III

So far, we have been considering "the arts" collectively and what different forms of art have in common. But Merleau-Ponty certainly did not think there were no significant differences between one art and another, between painting, literature, music and film, for instance. Given that he holds that what a work expresses cannot be separated from its physical form, it obviously follows that he must hold that differences in that physical form constitute differences in what can be expressed. In this section, therefore, we shall examine what he has to say about the specific features of two individual art forms, film and the novel, about which relatively little specific has been said so far.

We shall begin with the cinema, with which Merleau-Ponty was as fascinated as many other French intellectuals. Films have a number of distinguishing features. First, they are a type of visual art, but differ in an obvious way from other types, such as paintings, drawings, sculptures and still photographs, namely, that they present *moving* visual images. If a film depicts human beings, for example, it can depict them *in action*, not simply as static objects. Secondly, a film is not simply a sequence of random shots of people or things in motion, but *tells a story*, a connected series of events that relates what happens to certain people, or what those people do, over a period of time. This story need not be fictional; even a documentary film can be said to tell a story, in that the sequence of shots is not random but connected by a linking theme. Thus films are like novels, in that they have a narrative structure, but like paintings in that they are a form of visual art. Theatre plays too, of course, are visual in the sense that we go to *see* the play, and follow the narrative by observing the events going on on the stage. But film differs from theatre in that the story is told, not just by the movements and actions of the performers, but by the director's and editor's selection of shots, from different angles and distances, and the sequence in which those shots are shown.

Merleau-Ponty expresses the narrative character of films by saying that a film, as a perceptual object, "is not a sum-total of images but a temporal *gestalt*".[19] The word *gestalt* here is derived from the terminology of the Gestalt school of psychology; he means that the film is a structured whole, in which the meaning of any part has to be understood in terms of its relation to the whole. It is a "temporal" gestalt, in that the whole is not capable of being taken in in a momentary perception, but has to be grasped as it develops over time. We come to understand the meaning of any given shot by relating it to what has preceded; the sequence of shots has a "rhythm" to it, and through following the sequence of shots in this way we follow the story, which is the "meaning" of the film as a whole. The full meaning of the film, and so of the individual shots within it, is grasped only once the whole, and the relation of the parts to it, have been seen. Film is a visual art, but since the invention of the "talkies" it is much more: music, dialogue, sound effects and even silence all contribute to the structured whole. The way sight and sound are combined in a film constitutes part of the medium by which the meaning of the film is expressed.

In a sense, of course, the story of the film can be narrated independently of the film itself, as it is in the screenplay, but a screenplay is clearly not a film, and the film does more than illustrate the screenplay: it is a self-standing object to the creation of which the screenplay merely contributes, and whose meaning is much richer than that of the screenplay on its own. A film may also in some cases have an "idea", which can be expressed independently: for example, it may be an "anti-war film". But it is not its function as a film to communicate that idea to us: "the idea is presented in a nascent state and emerges from the temporal structure of the film".[20] If someone simply wanted to say that war was wrong, they could say it in so many words; to embody this idea in the narrative of a film is to give it a richness that comes from the very nature of its embodiment.

The nature of film gives it an affinity with what Merleau-Ponty calls "the new psychology", by which he means the Gestalt psychology referred to just above. The characteristic of Gestalt psychology is that it rejects the atomistic account of perception found in classical psychology (and classical philosophy). According to the latter our awareness of the world as a whole is built up from the perception of individual, isolated and in that sense "meaningless" elements; the linking up of these isolated elements is the work not of "sensation", but of "judgement" or intellect. Gestalt psychology, on the other hand, Merleau-Ponty says, rejects this distinction between sensation and judgement; perception is a combination of the two. Finally, the new psychology denies the classical version of our knowledge of our own and others' minds. On the classical view, I know my own mind by introspection, and that of others by interpreting their outward behaviour. For the new psychology, however, we understand our own and others' minds in the same way, by grasping what function, say, an emotion like anger serves in human life and how it is expressed in behaviour, gesture, facial expression, words and so on. In all these ways, Gestalt psychology, in Merleau-Ponty's view, is part of the same movement of thought found in existential phenomenology, in which mind is not set over against the world, but is simply an aspect of someone's being-in-the-world.

The movies are, he thinks, also part of this movement of modern thought. They present human life and behaviour, as has been said, in a "temporal *gestalt*", in which the different senses, notably sight and hearing, combine, and in which we directly understand the behaviour of others through their gestures and expressions, just as we do in actual life, and so can "read" the meaning of the film in exactly the same way as we grasp the meaning of real events. Movies, for that reason, have a "basic realism", although it is a realism filtered through the movie-maker's own way of expression; a movie is not (except in special cases like some of Andy Warhol's films) the outcome of simply putting the camera in front of a scene and letting the light fall through the lens. The realism of movies, Merleau-Ponty says, "does not mean . . . that the movies are fated to let us see and hear what we would see and hear if we were present at the events being related".[21] The movies, as was said earlier in the chapter, are particularly good ways of making manifest what is meant by "the inherence of the self in the world", and so are natural parts of the same cultural mood in the post-war generation, which had produced the new psychology and the phenomenological philosophy that were its basis.

If we turn now from cinema to literature, we must recognize to begin with the obvious differences between different literary forms. We shall here concentrate on the novel. What is common to all forms of literature, of course, and what distinguishes them from other arts, such as painting, film and music, is that the medium out of which they are constructed is words. Unlike brush strokes, camera shots or notes, words belong to a language whose rules determine their conventional reference. In straightforward literal prose, as in scientific papers, this rule-governed meaning is of primary importance (although Merleau-Ponty came to think that there were special reasons for this in science, and that ordinary conversational and other non-literary uses of language could not be accounted for *simply* in terms of this factual reference). But in literature, as in other arts, we use words in order to create structures that have a meaning in themselves, independent of any reference to external things. In the novel, these structures take the form of stories, narratives, just as in films, but expressed in words rather than moving pictures. The novel is also a temporal *gestalt*, in which the meaning of the individual episodes is determined by their relation to the total structure of the plot, and in which we can follow the plot in virtue of the same abilities by which we follow events in the "real world".

The fact that the world of the novel, unlike that of the film, is not directly presented to perception, but mediated through words, makes a significant difference. Novels are inevitably more reflective than works of visual art, and their philosophical role is therefore not simply to make us more aware of our being-in-the-world and of our ties with objects, but to be a means of reflection on ourselves and our place in the world, our relations with others, in short, on metaphysics in its bearing on *moral* questions. As examples of this, let us consider two passages from Merleau-Ponty, one in which he analyses an episode from Proust's novel sequence *À la recherche du temps perdu* (a title that Scott Moncrieff translated into English as *Remembrance of Things Past*) and one in which he considers Simone de Beauvoir's novel *L'Invitée* (*She Came to Stay*).

The discussion of Proust can be found in *Phenomenology of Perception*, part three, chapter 2. The passage of the novel in question concerns the love of one of the main characters, Swann, for another, a woman called Odette, and the jealousy that he feels at the thought of possible rivals for her affection. Proust, like many other novelists, Merleau-Ponty claims, wrongly sees Swann's love, his jealousy and so on, as distinct facts that stand to each other in merely external or causal relations. "Proust shows how Swann's love for Odette *causes* the jealousy which, in turn, *modifies* his love, since Swann, always anxious to win her from any possible rival, has no time really to look at Odette."[22] But this, Merleau-Ponty says, is based on a mistaken view of human consciousness as a collection of unrelated and lifeless "psychic facts", each of which is the effect of some external cause. Swann's love, he says, is not the *cause* of his jealousy; his feeling jealous is already a part of what it is for him to love. The potentiality for jealousy was inherent in Swann's whole way of being towards Odette, because the pleasure that he felt in looking at her, for example, was derived from the fact that he was the only one to do so.

It is worth considering what is going on in this passage. On the one hand, Merleau-Ponty is using this episode from Proust's novel simply to illustrate a philosophical point he is making about the relation of the self to time, and the nature of consciousness, but at the same time, he seems to be saying that Proust's handling of this episode in his novel reveals an inadequate grasp of the phenomenology of human consciousness; the philosophical point about self, time and consciousness is being used to make a literary criticism. In particular, Proust's treatment of Swann's love for Odette is unsatisfactory because it is based on an inadequate psychological and philosophical account of the nature and workings of human emotions. In other words, the passage from the novel is more than a mere *illustration* of an independently arrived-at philosophical view; it is by reflecting on its literary adequacy or otherwise that one is led to the philosophical conclusion. In this sense, Proust too can be described as engaged in a kind of phenomenological research (although Merleau-Ponty is disagreeing with the *results* that Proust derived from this "research").

The other example, the discussion of de Beauvoir's *L'Invitée*, is to be found in the essay "Metaphysics and the Novel", reprinted in *Sense and Non-Sense*. Merleau-Ponty uses the novel in this case explicitly as an illustration of the way in which novels can become philosophical when philosophy, as in the case of existential phenomenology, becomes "literary", in the sense described in section I. To formulate what is involved in someone's being-in-the-world, he suggests, necessarily has a *moral* significance, and this is what is illustrated by de Beauvoir's novel. The particular aspect of our experience that is central to the novel is our sense of the world, and particularly other people, as radically Other than ourselves. We may seek to "sublimate" the discomfort of this experience of Otherness by trying to treat the world and other people as our own creation, but to do this is, paradoxically, to deny our own selfhood also, since it is to place ourselves outside the world. But it is only the contrast between ourselves and the rest of the world, especially other selves, that defines us as the individuals we are. Françoise, a main character in *L'Invitée*, attempts to surmount the experience of the Other in this way, regarding herself as "impersonal and free". She loves another character, Pierre, but does not treat him as a fully separate person, thinking of the world as shared between them. Even the other women in Pierre's life are accepted, as part of this shared world, at least as long as Pierre does not become seriously involved with any of them. Thus she seeks to make the love between herself and Pierre invulnerable by making it part of the world that she herself ultimately controls, of which indeed she is ultimately the creator.

All this is undermined when Xavière comes on the scene. Xavière flirts with Pierre, and Pierre responds. Pierre, as Merleau-Ponty says, is for once involved in a *real* love affair, which is not and cannot be part of Françoise's controlled world. All her illusions about being able to be bound to Pierre and yet to leave him free are shattered. These illusions were based, in Merleau-Ponty's reading of the novel, on a conception of herself and Pierre as two Kantian pure egos, whose wills as such were in a necessary harmony with each other. The arrival of Xavière on the scene would then make it plain that such harmony is unattainable, that all three of them (and by implication others too) are more like Hegelian selves, which can affirm themselves only by seeking the death of the other. And this metaphysical conclusion has moral consequences. It shows, for example, that "All action is a response to a factual situation which we have not completely chosen and for which, in this sense, we are not absolutely responsible."[23] In an absurd world, our actions change their meaning because of changes in the circumstances around us that are beyond our control, so that there is no absolute guilt or innocence. But what an existentialist philosophy like de Beauvoir's fails to explain is that "language and behaviour do have meaning for those who speak and act" and that, "after all, love does exist".[24] The general moral conclusion we should draw from *L'Invitée*, Merleau-Ponty thinks, should be based more on the characters' good faith, loyalty to promises, respect for others, generosity and seriousness. The lesson of the novel is that value "consists in actively being what we are by chance, establishing that communication with others and with ourselves for which our temporal structure gives us the opportunity and of which our liberty is only the rough outline".[25]

What does this example tell us about Merleau-Ponty's view of the novel in general? It is clear in this case that he does not want to treat *L'Invitée* simply, in classical fashion, as a parable illustrating in an entertaining form some preconceived philosophical or moral ideas that could equally well have been expressed in an essay. On the other hand, his own analysis of the novel and its themes consists in applying certain philosophical ideas to the particular case of the characters and situation in the novel. Is there an inconsistency here? The appearance of inconsistency can be removed, at least to some extent, if we take into account Merleau-Ponty's own insistence, earlier in the paper, that something changes in philosophy itself when it becomes "existential" or "phenomenological", concerned not with discovering the "conditions of possibility" of human experience but with formulating what it is like to be human. But there is still a problem, and it is a fundamental one not only for Merleau-Ponty's view of literature but for his conception of philosophy itself. It is this – if a novel also formulates an experience of the world, why do we need phenomenology? Merleau-Ponty still seems, at this stage, to think that something is added by philosophy to the mere formulation of experience, namely, reflection at a more general or conceptual level. But this reveals an uncertainty about his account of the nature of phenomenology, which was supposed to differ from classical philosophy in that it simply described experience, without attempting to explain it. By making reflection, as something distinct from mere description, the differentiating feature of a philosophical, as opposed to a purely literary, approach, is he not betraying the original motivation of phenomenology itself? This uncertainty about the very nature of philosophy seems to have been coming more and more to the fore in Merleau-Ponty's thinking in the last years of his life, as we shall see in the remainder of this book.

IV

There have been several references earlier in the chapter to the last paper that Merleau-Ponty saw published before his death, "Eye and Mind". This was published first in the inaugural issue of the journal *Art de France* in January 1961. Merleau-Ponty died on 3 May 1961, and after his death the paper was reprinted along with some articles devoted to him, including Sartre's "Merleau-Ponty *vivant*", in *Les Temps modernes*, no. 184–5. It was published in book form in French in 1964, edited by Claude Lefort, and in an English translation by Carleton Dallery in the collection *The Primacy of Perception and Other Essays*, edited by James M. Edie and published by Northwestern University Press, also in 1964. The references to it given here will be to the English version. Its peculiar interest lies in the fact that it is a statement, in a form that Merleau-Ponty himself had prepared for publication, of ideas about art, language and philosophy that he was working on in the last years of his life. These ideas are also to be found in the books that he left unfinished at the time of his death, and that were only published in their incomplete form posthumously. The posthumous works will form the subject matter of Chapter 8, so the discussion in this section will introduce some of the themes that are to be more closely examined there.

One of the central themes of "Eye and Mind" is the contrast between science, at least as conceived of in post-Cartesian European thought, and the arts, especially painting. Our science, like our classical modern philosophy, is a consequence of Cartesianism; modern science and modern philosophy are "two monsters born from its dismemberment".[26] Their view of reality (or of "Being", to use the Heideggerian term, which, significantly, Merleau-Ponty frequently uses in this paper) is of something external to us, not of something in which we live. Our vision of that reality is thus an indirect process: what we perceive are "representations" that are caused in us by the effect of the "external world". But these representations are not supposed to be purely private to a given individual; any object that we perceive is treated in this science and this philosophy as an "object-in-general", something that is equally available to any perceiver, and is detached from any human meaning.

If we conceive of "objective reality" in this way, as something independent of human beings, then even our own bodies become, in a way that is by now familiar to us from discussion of Merleau-Ponty's earlier writings, one other kind of object in the world, acted upon by other objects, including the bodies of other people, to produce "representations". Our bodies, in other words, are not the means by which we engage with objects, but simply objects themselves; our selves are reduced to a disembodied "mind". And the language that we use to think about the world derives its meaning not from the character of our bodily engagement with things, but from its purely representative relation to objects. The world and our minds are distinct, and language (ideally at least) bridges the gap by correlating words, in accordance with general rules, with distinct types of object. Essentially, on this view, sense-perception is a form of thought, since both involve the self-same indirect relation to their objects. But sense-perception is a *confused* form of thought, since it represents the world as it appears from a particular point of view; reason or intellect represents it *clearly* and *distinctly*, by thinking in terms of the abstract concepts of a properly formed language.

The development of art, at least in recent times, has, as Merleau-Ponty sees it, taken a different direction. By "art" here, he means, almost exclusively, *painting*. Music, for example, is more or less irrelevant to this discussion, since by its very nature it makes no claim to depict reality. A piece of music is a constructed object, made of notes, which is "too far beyond the world" to be able to depict "anything but certain outlines of Being".[27] Films are referred to only briefly in this paper; perhaps the view is that, to the extent that, as argued earlier in this chapter, they are a visual art like painting, what is said about painting can more or less apply to them. Prose literature, presumably in virtue of the fact that it uses language, is assimilated to philosophy rather than painting.[28] Poetry, which, of course, also uses language, is nevertheless by contrast assimilated to painting,[29] on the grounds that, in it as in painting, we find things "coming to be"; the poet Apollinaire is cited in support, in his dictum that "in a poem there are phrases which do not appear to have been *created*, which seem to have *formed themselves*". Painting is central to Merleau-Ponty's discussion, then, in that it is the paradigm case of a relation to Being which is different from that of Cartesian science and philosophy.

What is this difference? Of crucial importance is that painting is an activity of the *body*, not of the (disembodied Cartesian) *mind*: "we cannot imagine", Merleau-Ponty says, "how a *mind* could paint".[30] The painter, as embodied, is *part* of Being, not *apart from* it, contemplating it from on high. The painter's vision is thus not a form of (abstract or conceptual) thought, and paintings are not mere indirect *representations* of Being. But paintings are equally not themselves "things"; we don't so much "see" them as "see according to them".[31] A painting is not something produced as the passive effect of Being on the painter; the painter needs skill and practice if he or she is to earn "the gift of the visible". All painting, in all civilizations, figurative or "abstract", "celebrates no other enigma but that of visibility".[32] Although it is not a form of conceptual thought, it is nevertheless a form of thinking, in which the painter interrogates Being, or a particular element of Being, such as a mountain, in order to "unveil" what makes it a mountain.

The painter's way of seeing is, Merleau-Ponty says, in some ways "prehuman"; there is a sense in which things "look at" painters, rather than the other way round. That is, as I interpret Merleau-Ponty, the painter looks at the world not in a human way in which we are concerned with the meaning of things *for us*, but in order to uncover our own being as inhering in a Being that provides the given context in which we necessarily exist before we begin to attribute meaning to things. "It is the mountain itself which from out there makes itself seen by the painter" and what the painter asks of it is "to unveil the means, visible and not otherwise, by which it makes itself a mountain before our eyes".[33] And the painter does this, not by discursive *talk about* the mountain, but by *creating* a picture; the truth of the painter's work does not consist in its correspondence with a pre-existing fact, but is something that comes into being in the process of expressing the inherence of our humanity in this wider Being.

In Chapter 8, we shall consider Merleau-Ponty's further development of these reflections on truth and Being in his posthumously published works. Before we do so, however, we should, as a way of concluding the present chapter, briefly consider a possible general objection to Merleau-Ponty's whole account of the arts, namely, that in his preoccupation with the ways in which art can be of use to philosophy, he neglects to consider art *in its own right*. One aspect of this, it might be said, is that he seems to ignore art that does not aim to present the perceived world: abstract painting, for example, or icon painting, which seeks rather to open a window on to a spiritual or supra-sensible realm. In part, the answer to this objection is that this neglect is only a defect if Merleau-Ponty had professed to be offering a general aesthetics, which he did not claim to do. But, in the course of pursuing his own interest, he does (and this is the other part of the answer) manage to illuminate in passing a number of features of the particular arts that are relevant to critical reflection: about the role of artistic language, the relation of morality to literature, the sense in which a painting may be "true", and so on.

CHAPTER EIGHT

The Later Thought

In 1952, Merleau-Ponty was appointed to a chair at the Collège de France in Paris, one of the pinnacles of academic life in France, and continued in that post until his death in 1961. His inaugural lecture, "In Praise of Philosophy", in which he examines the function of philosophy, first through considering particular past philosophers (Lavelle, Bergson, Socrates) and then by discussing in more general terms the relation between philosophy's past and its present, was published in book form in 1953.[1] Summaries of his lecture courses at the Collège de France were published in book form after his death, in 1968,[2] and he published a number of articles, both on philosophy and on current political issues, in journals and periodicals. But he did not publish any further philosophical monographs in his lifetime. He was, however, working in these last years on two book-length projects, which reveal interesting new developments in his thinking. One, *The Prose of the World*, seems to have been abandoned without completion; he was still working on the other, *The Visible and the Invisible*, at the time of his death, so that it is incomplete for different reasons. Both were published in their incomplete form, with some editing by his friend Claude Lefort, after his death. In this chapter, I want to examine each of these works in turn before attempting to draw some general conclusions, from them and from the earlier writings, about Merleau-Ponty's work as a whole.

I

As part of his candidacy for the chair at the Collège de France, Merleau-Ponty produced a "prospectus" of his future programme of work. In it, he speaks of "works in preparation" that "aim to show how communication with others, and thought, take up and go beyond the realm of perception which initiated us to the truth".[3] He saw this work as both "fixing the philosophical significance" of his earlier works and at the same time developing that significance in new directions. His earlier work, as we have seen, had focused on perception as the fundamental relationship in which we stand to the world in which we have our being. But of course we seek to go beyond perception in order to achieve *knowledge* of the world and to *communicate* about it to others. Knowledge and communication are not separable from each other, since knowledge presupposes communication; knowledge is expressed above all in the *language* by which we communicate with others, because it embodies a *shared* or *shareable* view of our common world. And the standard correspondence notion of truth is of truth as a relation between a proposition in language and a "fact" in the world. "Going beyond" perception in this sense does not imply getting away from it, but rather preserving it while transforming it. Meaning in the linguistic sense is possible because we are embodied subjects, whose movements about and interaction with the world necessarily bring meaning into being. But in expressing meaning in language we are led

> to a thought which is no longer ours alone, to a thought which is presumptively universal, though this is never the universality of a pure concept which would be identical for every mind. It is rather the call which a situated thought addresses to other thoughts, equally situated . . .[4]

Merleau-Ponty intended to confront the problem of truth in a projected work to be called *L'Origine de la vérité* (*The Origin of Truth*), but first to approach it in a more indirect fashion in a book on which he had already begun to work, on literary language. (In part, he seems to have been motivated by a wish to offer an alternative to the book that Sartre had recently published on writing, *What is Literature?*[5]) By considering literary language, he hoped to get away from the idea that words are just the "clothing" of thought, and to show that the choice of expression and the thought to be expressed could not be separated. The book was to be called *Introduction to the Prose of the* World, and it is this work, in its unfinished form, that was published posthumously in 1969 as *The Prose of the World*. The editor, Claude Lefort, says in his preface that "There is good reason to believe that the author deliberately abandoned it and that, had he lived, he would not have completed it, at least in the form that he first outlined."[6] However, there is considerable overlap between *The Prose of the World* and a paper that Merleau-Ponty did publish in his lifetime, "Indirect Language and the Voices of Silence",[7] and that paper can therefore be used to help in interpreting *The Prose of the World*. I shall return a little later to the significance of this abandonment, but first I want to consider the actual content of the book as we now have it.

Merleau-Ponty begins by challenging the widely shared (and natural) notion that the paradigm of language is to be found in those expressions and statements which, as it were, point us directly towards the objects they refer to and in which the meaning of what is being said can be precisely determined. He talks of examples like "a rose", which seems unequivocally to refer to a particular kind of flower, and "It is raining", which appears to say something absolutely precise about the weather.[8] This kind of use of language for making statements is taken to be primary, and other uses, for making promises or puns, for telling stories or making eloquent speeches, are treated as somehow secondary and derivative. (This almost sounds like J. L. Austin or the later Wittgenstein.) If we take this view, then the meaningfulness of language comes about by means of rule-governed, but ultimately arbitrary, correlations between words and the objects they refer to. An ideal language of this sort would effectively be like a transparent pane of glass between us and things. Such an ideal language would be perfectly suited to science (again, we may think of Frege, Russell and the early Wittgenstein), since it would directly reveal the facts, free of human "subjective" interference, and would be perfectly "algorithmic": that is, would make the truth-conditions of any statement absolutely perspicuous. The algorithm, Merleau-Ponty says, is an attempt "to redefine it [language] to match the divine mind" and "to tear speech out of history".[9] It is as if we thought that, if we could construct such an ideal language, we could see objective reality plain and unadorned, as God can, rather than seeing it through spectacles distorted by our own history.

Even in literature, this notion of a language that would perfectly embody thought is influential, in part because of an experience that all writers have, of struggling to say what one wants to say and then, if one is lucky, suddenly finding the right words to express it. The feeling is of having rediscovered the thought that one had had all along but had forgotten until then. It is as if language already contained the possibility of all the thoughts anyone might want to express. But that would mean, Merleau-Ponty argues, that *real* communication was impossible, because no one could tell us anything new, anything that we did not already know. As long as we "live" language, he says, that is, as long as we simply *use* language as part of our lives, we know full well that things are not like that: that new things can be said. But when we stop living language and start to reflect on it, we seem unable to see how that could be possible. How could language function successfully unless words were correlated by rules with things?

153

Perhaps this apparent conflict can be resolved, Merleau-Ponty argues, if we recognize that there are *two* "languages". One is *language as an institution*, language as a set of established rules, which we all learn in learning to speak our own, and later perhaps other, languages. Language in this sense tends to "efface itself", so that we are hardly aware, when we are reading, say, that these are *words* and *sentences* that we are reading; we pass right through them to their meaning. This is the kind of language that gives rise to the idea of an "ideal" language especially suited for the purposes of science and philosophy. The other kind of language is that "which creates itself in its expressive acts, which sweeps me on from the signs toward meaning".[10] The archetype of this second, creative, kind of language is obviously the literary use of language, in which authors find ways of expressing *new* thoughts, adding to the conventional meaning of sentences. But this is a matter of *addition*, rather than replacement. The literary author depends on the common meanings of words in the language that he or she shares with the readers in order to come to "dwell in" the readers' world. But by varying the conventional meaning of words, the author carries readers toward a new meaning, which may transform the way in which they see the world. Merleau-Ponty cites the example of the way in which the ordinary meaning of the word "rogue" (or its French equivalent) is extended by Stendhal in one of his novels by applying it to a particular character, Rossi the revenue man. By seeing the way in which the character so described behaves in the novel, the reader comes to grasp the new meaning that Stendhal wanted to give to this common word and so to dwell within Stendhal's "imaginary self". "I create Stendhal; I am Stendhal while reading him. But that is because first he knew how to bring me to dwell within him."[11]

But of course, once Stendhal has extended the language in this way, his innovations themselves become part of the language as an institution. We may then think that Stendhal has not in fact thought anything new at all, that the thought was already in our minds before we or anyone else had even read Stendhal. But this literary use of language is not something apart from language in general; it manifests something that has to be taken account of in any consideration of language, even in science. To think otherwise is to imagine that we could extract ourselves from language and contemplate the relations between "language" and "the world" from the outside. That is what gives rise to the idealized, algorithmic, conception of language discussed earlier, but even to understand the notion of such an ideal language, we need to have a non-ideal language first, in which we can talk about and give meaning to the symbols of the idealized language. Hence it cannot be the job of philosophy to use such a language as the standard by which to judge the imperfections and obscurities of ordinary language. Rather, philosophy must differ from ordinary language in much the same way that literary language does; it must be creative, using language as "the gesture of renewal and recovery which unites me with myself and others".[12] Language of all kinds – everyday, literary, scientific – functions within a society, with a history; it gets its meaning from that society's way of being-in-the-world. Individuals on their own would never develop a language: the meanings that words and other expressions acquire come from the communication between one individual and another. In using language, we are therefore necessarily brought up against the fact that we are in the presence of *other selves*, and it is our shared history that makes communication between us possible. Philosophy is therefore not the search for some timeless rationality, but an effort to extract the rationality that is implicit in our present communication.

At this point, Merleau-Ponty introduces some of the key ideas of the Swiss pioneer of modern linguistics, Ferdinand de Saussure. Saussure and his linguistics were much discussed among French intellectuals at that time, and, partly through their transmutation in the writings of Merleau-Ponty's friend, the anthropologist Claude Lévi-Strauss, they were to have a profound influence on the development of French philosophy away from transcendental phenomenology and the philosophy of the subject after Merleau-Ponty's death. We can perhaps see the beginnings of some of these developments in these late writings of Merleau-Ponty (although, as I shall argue later, *only* the beginnings at most).

What is crucial from the present point of view is Saussure's rejection, or at least downgrading, of a *historical* linguistics: of, for example, any attempt to explain the present meaning of an expression in terms of its etymology, its historical development. The very fact that words change their meaning over time shows that we can't explain a word's present meaning in terms of its history. We manage to communicate with each other successfully without (in most cases) any knowledge of the etymology of the words we are using. All this suggests a distinction between "language" (*le langage parlé*), the historically developed institution, in which there is no clear connection between the meaning of one word and that of another, and "speech" (*le langage parlant*), in which order is introduced into this chaos by the needs of current communication. Speech is an integrated whole, in which each expression has an unequivocal meaning because of its relation to all other expressions. What makes for clarity in language, therefore, is not that the terms have an established reference to the things that they denote, nor that speaker and hearer already share the same thought because they share the same rules, but "the way it [the sign in question] functions in living language".[13]

Again, for someone familiar with analytical philosophy, the resemblances to the later Wittgenstein are striking, although that is not meant to suggest any influence in one direction or the other. This gives a particular slant to one of the most familiar doctrines of Saussurean linguistics – that signs are not "the representations of certain significations" but "the means of differentiation in the verbal chain".[14] We see here the notion of "difference", which has assumed such central importance in late twentieth-century French philosophy: the doctrine that the meaning of any sign is given only by its *difference* from other signs, so that the meaning of any sign cannot be given apart from the whole system of signs to which it belongs. (We should not forget that Derrida, in whose thought *difference* features most prominently, was a doctoral student under Merleau-Ponty's supervision.)

We might object (as some have objected to Saussure) that this is contrary to common sense. If no sign has any meaning in itself, how can one sign get meaning from its differentiation from others? Obvious though this objection sounds, however, it misses the point. What gives meaning to signs is their *use* in speech, and the use of one sign cannot be considered apart from that of other signs. In "Indirect Language and the Voices of Silence", Merleau-Ponty explains the point like this:

> To understand [speech], we do not have to consult some inner lexicon which gives us the pure thoughts covered up by the words or forms we are perceiving; we only have to lend ourselves to its life, to its movement of differentiation and articulation, and to its eloquent gestures.[15]

It follows from this that talk of a "complete" language, or a "complete" inventory of all the meanings in a language, is strictly nonsensical. For if the meaning of any sign in the language depends on its relation to all the others, then the chain can never in principle be completed. For the same reason, we cannot speak of a completely clear expression of any meaning: "all language is indirect or allusive – . . . if you wish, silence".[16]

There is and could be no "ideal language", if that means a language that perspicuously reveals the world as it really is by unambiguously picking out for each of its signs one of the types of object that actually exist in the world. Signs express what they do, not because they denote objects, but in virtue of their place in a system of relations to other signs, and the system as a whole is expressive because of its use by human beings. For the same reason, there cannot be an abstractly "universal" language, a language of eternal reason inherent in human nature as such. What there can be is a *concretely* universal language: that is, in speaking one language which gains its meaning from its use by human beings, I necessarily have the capacity to learn other human languages. I begin by thinking of the other language as a variant of my own, and then, eventually, if I immerse myself in the other language, I come to think of my native language as a variant of it. Each language can thus be distinct from every other, with its own grammatical and idiomatic characteristics, but still inter-translatable into the others.

How then did language originate? It could not, Merleau-Ponty argues, have come into being in a world without communication – the point being, presumably, that the very concept of communication can be understood only when there is some communicative activity, however minimal, already in existence. The pre-linguistic communicative activity in which human beings engage comes about through the expressiveness of their bodies: by facial expressions, gestures, "body-language" and styles of behaviour, tones of voice and the like, we were able to communicate before there was verbal language and can still communicate wordlessly. Since we are body-subjects rather than Cartesian subjects, our subjectivity necessarily participates in a public world, is necessarily expressive and communicative. In using signs of any kind, we start from ourselves, and address ourselves to others, but in the process what began as something individual becomes universal.

It is an essential part of being a human being that we can go beyond signs toward their meaning:[17] that is, can use existing signs in new ways, to express new thoughts. To express a meaning is not, after all, to copy something that already exists, but to make use of the relations between signs to create something new. Expression is a "transformation" rather than a "representation". We are thus not imprisoned in language as it is, but can make use of the multiple interconnections between signs in order to change the whole nature of the system and create a new meaning. Other forms of communication, like painting (also, as we saw in Chapter 7, a product of our embodiment), are like language in this way. It used to be part of the conventional way of thinking of the history of art that classical painting aimed to reproduce "nature": indeed, that was the way in which classical painters thought of themselves. On this view, the difference between classical and modern art is that the moderns seek "creative expression" of their own individuality. But if we look, as Merleau-Ponty, following André Malraux, suggests, at what was supposed by classical artists to be their greatest discovery as a means of "pure representation", namely, perspective, we shall see that the difference between classical and modern is not so great, for classical perspective is not "a law of perceptual behaviour", but "one of the ways man has invented for projecting before himself the perceived world".[18] We do not actually see the world in the manner of classical perspective, although the latter is one possible interpretation of our natural ways of seeing.

As in painting, so in linguistic or literary expression, we do not simply reproduce what is in the world, but transform it into a thought. But this does not mean that our "minds" somehow "impose" a meaning on a meaningless substratum of "matter"; meaning *emerges* from the contact between the subject and a world of which, after all, the subject themself is a part. Perception is already a "stylization" or "patterning" of the world, and pictorial expression transcends that initial patterning. Perception is already "primordial expression", "the primary operation which first constitutes signs as signs".[19] Treating painting as a language thus helps us to understand something about language in the ordinary or narrow sense, namely, that beneath the ready-made or institutionalized language of rules is "an operant or speaking language, whose words have a silent life like the animals at the bottom of the ocean".[20] Just as language (whether verbal or pictorial) gets its meaning from its roots in this "indirect" or "silent" language of perception and gesture, and then institutionalizes it in the form of rules, so the literary artist starts from this inherited and institutionalized language and both destroys it and fulfils it at the same time. "Ready-made" language with its "half-dead" meanings cannot convey the life of what he wants to say, so the writer creates new significations for the expressions of his inherited language (which are then in turn incorporated into the rules). This is one way in which the literary artist differs from the painter: the writer cannot exist except in an established language, whereas each painter creates his or her language anew.

One important consequence of this is that what is expressed in language implies a concept of truth that is simply not applicable to painting (and here we see a different view from that expressed in "Eye and Mind" and discussed in Chapter 7). To express something in language, as in literature, philosophy and science, is necessarily to aim at something potentially shareable with everyone, something that is in that sense *universally* true, true before any individual discovers it or states it. Because of this, what is expressed in words has a different relation to time than what is expressed pictorially. What is expressed pictorially, because its language is fashioned by the painter rather than being part of a continuing historically developed institution, belongs to a "dreaming eternity";[21] the content of a painting (e.g. the styles of clothing worn by the people in it) may belong to a particular historical epoch, but that is irrelevant to it as a work of art. Writing on the other hand necessarily belongs to a time, but can "transcend" its time in ways that are impossible to a painting: it can appeal to a meaning (and so a truth) that goes beyond the time in which it was created. But it can do this only by starting from that time, so that we cannot understand what the writer is saying to us except against the background of the historical period in which the work was created. Philosophy is, says Merleau-Ponty, the "inventory of this dimension":

> With respect to language, philosophy can only point out how, by the "coherent deformation" of gestures and sounds, man manages to speak an anonymous language and, through the "coherent deformation" of this language, to express what existed only for him.[22]

But if philosophy is reflection about language, as this implies, there seems to be a difficulty. If reflection about language means trying to explain the clarity and meaningfulness of language by *deducing* it from something else, then that is a "dead end": there will always be something more to language than we can include in our view of it (because we who are reflecting are also *using* language in doing so). But fortunately, Merleau-Ponty says, there is another sort of philosophical reflection, which consists in going back to the simple fact that we *do* use language and can *understand* what others say. "All that is needed – and this is the whole of philosophy – is to cash in on this evidence, to confront it with the ready-made ideas we have of language and of the plurality of spirits."[23] Once again, this sounds remarkably like the later Wittgenstein's attempt to free us of the "pictures which hold us captive" by taking us back to the language-games in which our expressions have their natural home. What Merleau-Ponty adds, however, which is at least not obvious in Wittgenstein, is a sense of the sheer *mystery* of language, which is implicit in this basic, unanalysable experience of meaning.

The Prose of the World is, as said earlier, incomplete and not in a form ready for publication. There is a fair amount of repetition in it, of going over again themes which have already been touched upon, perhaps from a slightly different point of view; no doubt, if there had been further work on it, much tidying up would have been done. But Merleau-Ponty does not seem to have left it in this incomplete and disorganized state merely through lack of time and energy; if Claude Lefort is to be believed, he had *abandoned* the work, that is, had taken a deliberate decision not to proceed further with it. We can only speculate about his reasons for this, but it seems likely that, as Lefort says, it was because his thought in these years was beginning to move away from his earlier understanding of phenomenology. There are, in *The Prose of the World*, one or two new elements in his thinking; there is, for example, the interest in Saussurean linguistics and the idea that meaning depends not on reference to the world but on the difference between one expression and others, both of which were, as said earlier, to dominate much of French philosophy after

Merleau-Ponty's death. And there is a subtle but important change beginning to emerge in his conception of philosophy as such. He was coming to see it, not as a presuppositionless description of the world as perceived, but as a creative redescription of the experience itself, in which we better understand meaning and our place in being; the interest in the arts as a model from this point of view is also beginning to appear. But for the most part, *The Prose of the World* is, as his prospectus of work in progress (referred to earlier) states, continuous in doctrine with the earlier writings. His other posthumously published work, *The Visible and the Invisible*, moves further away in style from *Phenomenology of Perception*. Whether this change is as radical as is thought by some commentators will be explored in the next section.

II

It is impossible to give a simple account of *The Visible and the Invisible* for a number of reasons, the most significant of which is that it is not a finished work, either quantitatively or qualitatively. It is incomplete quantitatively, in that the text simply runs out; but more importantly it is incomplete qualitatively, in the sense that the whole character of the text as we have it reveals it to be "work in progress" rather than a polished presentation of ideas that Merleau-Ponty had worked through to his own satisfaction. Because of this, it is not possible to describe anything that might be called "the doctrines" of *The Visible and the Invisible*, only to attempt to disentangle what seem to be some of Merleau-Ponty's central concerns in the work. Moreover, the style of the posthumously published text is very different from that of the works published in Merleau-Ponty's lifetime: it is written for the most part in an intense and almost impenetrable prose, frequently coming back to a number of recurrent themes. In the first of the "Working Notes" that appear in the published version at the end of the continuous text, Merleau-Ponty speaks of "Our state of non-philosophy – Never has the crisis been so radical",[24] and it is evident that he was experiencing a crisis in his own philosophical development that he was attempting to resolve in writing this book. What is important is to try to understand the *nature* of that crisis.

As he says in the same note, what was needed to resolve this crisis was to return to "ontology", in particular to "the subject–object question, the question of intersubjectivity, the question of Nature". The return to ontology was a move to a position prior to that of phenomenology, the position that he (at least officially) had occupied in virtually all his earlier writings. He speaks critically of Husserl at a number of points in *The Visible and the Invisible*, and also of his own earlier work; for instance, in another "Working Note", he says that "The problems posed in *Phenomenology of Perception* are insoluble because I start there from the 'consciousness'–'object' distinction."[25] The increasing influence of Heidegger rather than Husserl is apparent: Heidegger's name occurs at a number of points, and there is frequent use of Heideggerian terms like "Being" (sometimes spelled with a small "b" and sometimes with a capital in the text). Heidegger too had started from Husserlian phenomenology but had gone beyond it, although much further than Merleau-Ponty did. In the latter's case, it is not so much what Husserl was *doing*, particularly in his late period, that Merleau-Ponty criticized, as the theoretical framework in which Husserl often *presented* what he was doing, and of which Merleau-Ponty himself had in his earlier work been insufficiently critical.

The framework in question was of philosophy as a "transcendental" activity, in which a "transcendental subject" "suspended the existence of the world".[26] This was the *epoché* referred to in Chapter 1, in which the subject was supposed to "put the world in brackets", to treat it as if it did not exist, or at least not to raise the question of its existence. The objectionable thing about this was that it implied a distinction between the subject, or consciousness, and its object, which, as Merleau-Ponty had now come to believe, made the problems of *Phenomenology of Perception* insoluble. To have a chance of solving them, and at the same time fully to realize the potential of Husserl's later concept of the "*Lebenswelt*" or "life-world", a different concept of the relation of consciousness to Being was needed; in effect, we had to take more seriously the concept of human being as "being-in-the-world", which was itself, as was said in earlier chapters, an originally Heideggerian concept. It is the conception, as has been explained, that we are not spectators of our world, contemplating it from a point outside it, but are actively involved in our world. The "transcendental subject" is a spectator; indeed, even to speak of "subject" and "object" at all implies a gap between them, such that the relation between them can only be that of contemplation. Talk of "being-in-the-world", by contrast, is not talk of a *relation* (or at least not an *external* relation) between ourselves and our world at all, since our own being cannot be separated from that of the world we inhabit.

The necessity of a return to ontology is the requirement to think what we *mean* by "ourselves" and "world" if we are properly to grasp the manner of our belonging to the world. The "meaning" in question, Merleau-Ponty is at pains to point out, is not that of the *words* "consciousness" and "world", at least if that is taken to be equivalent to the lexical meaning of these words in what he called, in *The Prose of the*

World, an "institutionalized" language. Philosophy, he insists, is not "linguistic analysis" in that sense: "It is the things themselves, from the depths of their silence, that it wishes to bring to expression."[27] Ontology is the exploration of the meaning in this sense of "subject–object", "intersubjectivity" and "Nature", all in the context of their place in Being (since ontology is the study of Being as such). The philosophical problem, like all philosophical problems, arises from the same feature of human experience that St Augustine referred to when he said that each of us knows perfectly well what time is until we begin to try to explain it. In the same way, Merleau-Ponty argues, we all share the "perceptual faith" that "the world is what we see":[28] that is, all of us, philosopher and non-philosopher alike, share a conviction (although to call it that is misleading, since it suggests a set of propositions of which we are convinced by evidence) that there is a real world and that when we open our eyes, in normal circumstances, we see it. But as soon as the philosopher tries to explain this faith, we seem to enter "a labyrinth of difficulties and contradictions".

In the course of the first part of the published version of *The Visible and the Invisible*, Merleau-Ponty considers three more traditional philosophical attempts at such an explanation, which he calls "the philosophy of reflection", "the philosophy of the negative" and the "philosophy of intuition". The philosophy of reflection seems to correspond roughly to the mainstream tradition of philosophy descending from Descartes (and in that sense including at least the earlier Husserl). This starts from something that seems self-evident as soon as we begin to think about our experience: that my experience is *my* experience, and hence that where we have to start from is not how things are "in themselves", but how they appear to me. But once we grant that, our simple perceptual faith that we are in direct touch with the world is thrown into confusion. We are separated not only from the world, but from any community with other subjects, for the world that I experience is how it appears *to me*, and how can I have any access to the world as it appears *to others*? So we seem to have, as the only secure part of our experience, those purely private "appearances"; and what seems impossible to explain is how the perceptual faith in a world beyond these private appearances can be justified. Our ordinary "'openness to the world" seems to be subject to doubt.

The philosophy of reflection thus leads to "methodological doubt", as in Descartes, or to the kind of "reduction" that Husserl advocated in his phenomenology. In this process, we try to "detach" ourselves from our engagement with the world, and to consider the world not as something we see, but as something "intelligible", something we intellectually understand. What distinguishes the set of appearances we call the "real world" from those that are imaginary can then only be the greater *coherence* of the former. Thus, what we share with other subjects is not our common opening on to the visible world, but our common intellectual or conceptual structures by which we give coherence to our experience. But what is "fallacious" (to use Merleau-Ponty's word) about this is that it is the reality of the perceived world that gives coherence to our experience rather than the other way round. The philosophy of reflection makes the perceptual faith which it sets out to explain into a set of propositional beliefs, based on evidence, whereas it is only our perceptual faith in the reality of the world we perceive that makes it possible to found hypotheses on evidence (and moreover that perceptual faith is presupposed in the idea of the method of doubt or of the phenomenological reduction). The philosophy of reflection is essentially viciously circular: its method of doubt makes sense only if we already have an awareness of an independent reality (since to doubt one thing, we must take the truth of other propositions to be beyond doubt), but the application of doubt or reduction undermines that same awareness.

Furthermore, the doubt or the reduction makes all *objects* things external to the mind, so that the mind or subject cannot itself be a thing or an object. In this way, the philosophy of reflection leads on naturally to the philosophy of the negative, by which Merleau-Ponty clearly means primarily (as he often makes explicit) the kind of philosophy expounded by Sartre in *Being and Nothingness*. In this philosophy, the existence of a world "in-itself" is accepted, and the possibility of our access to that world, which, as being-in-itself, is not in any sense a construction of our minds. That must mean that it conceives of our own subjectivity as having nothing in common with being-in-itself, as being a pure opening on to Being which is therefore itself *non*-Being, or "nothingness". But to conceive of the relation of subject to object as one of nothingness to Being, of the "for-itself" to the "in-itself", is to deny any possibility of real interaction between the two. In fact, as Merleau-Ponty says, this is to deny that there is a "subject" of experience at all, since that would be a being which was yet at the same time a non-being, which is plainly a contradiction.

Once again, however, we are faced with the problem of "other" consciousnesses. If all consciousnesses are nothingnesses, "How would one discern one 'nothing' from another?"[29] But to ask this question is, Sartre would say, to ignore the fact that each nothingness is particularized because it is a *determinate* nothingness, the nothingness that opens on to a *specific* situation, the situation in which an individual finds themself and which they exist by negating. The philosophy of the negative thus marks an advance over the philosophy of reflection in that it allows two essential elements of the perceptual faith: the acceptance of a real world existing independently of our subjectivity, and the existence of other subjectivities. All these other subjectivities open on to Being in the same way that mine does. Thus there is a sense in which the philosophy of the negative "provides us with what we were searching for, terminates our research, brings philosophy to a standstill",[30] for it makes our contact with reality direct and pre-reflective: reality becomes, not a set of propositions, but that which is in-itself and is what it is independently of anything we may think about it. If my self is a Nothingness, then in returning to myself and to my own thoughts, I am returning to Nothingness, and hence I am immediately thrown out again into Being.

Nevertheless, the philosophy of the negative is ultimately unsatisfactory. The very notion of a pure Nothingness, confronted with pure Being, is completely abstract. Neither pure Nothingness nor pure Being can actually be found anywhere: the actual self (the "for-itself") is, as Merleau-Ponty says, "encumbered with a body, which is not outside if it is not inside",[31] which does not, in other words, fit into the neat dichotomy of "for-itself" and "in-itself". Pure Nothingness and pure Being *could* not be united with each other in order to constitute an experienced world, since to experience the world it is necessary to have being as part of it. And the nature of our experience is such that it must be embodied, since we do not perceive the whole of Being in one go, but only what is perceptible from the place in Being where our bodies are located. We have to think of ourselves, not as a wholly transparent "for-itself" confronted with a world of being-in-itself that wholly transcends our consciousness of it, but rather as embodied beings within the world. This implies that our position is ambiguous. On the one hand, we ourselves do not have being *purely* for ourselves; there is a level of our being deeper than that of the Cartesian *cogito*, the level of the "pre-reflective *cogito*", without which reflection and hence negation would be impossible. On the other, the "transcendence" of our consciousness by Being cannot mean that it is absolutely beyond that consciousness, since consciousness, as embodied, is necessarily part of Being: it must rather mean that we "hold it at arm's length by a sort of abnegation".[32] The philosophy of the negative does not *explain* our perceptual faith, but undermines it.

The philosophy of intuition is the least discussed by Merleau-Ponty, although what little he has to say about it is important for his own argument. He associates the idea of intuition primarily with Bergson, although much of what he says about it might equally well fit some aspects of Husserlian phenomenology. The aim of the philosopher of intuition is to withdraw from "naive cognition" into the depths of one's self, into a realm in which there is a "coincidence" between experiencer and experienced, in order there to discover "the secret of Being". The problem with this, as Merleau-Ponty points out, is that, in order to make such a discovery, one has to use *language*: one has to *say* what the secret of Being is. But to use language is to introduce a division between ourselves and what we experience, since language speaks *about* objects that are distinct from itself. A thoroughgoing philosophy of intuition would therefore need to remain silent, but a silent philosophy is an absurdity. "He [the philosopher] wrote in order to state his contact with Being; he did not state it, and could not state it, since it is silence."[33] It might be, as Bergson himself thought, that we could overcome this problem by using, not "ready-made" language, with meaning determined by rules correlating signs with the independent objects they signify, but a more creative language, which itself coincided with what it expressed, and so "made the things speak". Merleau-Ponty, as he shows in *The Prose of the World*, is not hostile to the idea of such a language, but to accept that possibility is in effect to undermine the central assumption of the philosophy of intuition, namely, that there is a "deep self" to which we can return as the source of metaphysical truth. That implies that the deep self is separate from the self that is directed towards the world, so that "retiring into oneself" is not identical with "leaving oneself"; but if what one finds deep within oneself has to be expressed in a language that makes the things speak, then in retiring into oneself one is necessarily also leaving it to rejoin the world of things.

What all three of these philosophical approaches have in common, then, is the assumption of a radical distinction between the experiencing self and the experienced world. But once one makes that assumption, it becomes impossible to explain the perceptual faith, for without a point of contact between self and world, we cannot explain how we can be so confident that when we open our eyes we see the world. Moreover, these philosophies get things the wrong way round: it is only if we start from the notion of our experience as an unreflective opening on to the world that we can explain the notions of reflection, of consciousness as negating, and of a withdrawal from naive cognition into ourselves. Our being-in-the-world is prior to any distinction we may draw between ourselves as subjects and the world of objects. What is wrong with the three philosophies, in a sense, is their whole conception of philosophy itself; philosophy has to begin again,

> reject the instruments reflection and intuition had provided themselves, and install itself in a locus where they have not yet been distinguished, in experiences that have not yet been "worked

over", that offer us all at once, pell-mell, both "subject" and "object".[34]

Philosophy needs to start from the perceptual faith itself, not in order to *explain* it, but in order to clarify what it involves. This is not simply to describe it, but to attempt to understand it, above all, to understand how it is possible to reconcile the two apparently incompatible elements of the perceptual faith, that my vision is both "in me" and "at the thing itself".

This will involve reflection, although perhaps not the kind of reflection we were considering earlier. It will be a reflection that concerns itself only with what the "crude" conviction that we are in direct contact with things themselves means. ("Crude" is the translator's version of Merleau-Ponty's word "*barbare*", literally, "barbarian".) But this philosophical question will not be answered simply by being given some pre-existing "meaning" or "essence". A philosophical question is characteristically many-layered: it returns upon itself, asks itself also "what to question is and what to respond is".[35] Because it arises, not from some intellectual desire for cognition, but from the nature of our own existence and our desire to understand it, it must necessarily ask, not just what Being is, but what we mean by asking that question, and what kind of response would be appropriate. We are reflecting on ourselves as well as on Being (just as, in reflecting on ourselves, we are questioning Being also).

If we try to reflect on our existence in the world in this way and to discover what Being is in terms of our own involvement with it, we have to reject the idea of a Being that is something absolutely exterior, and turn towards a Being "that is meaning, and meaning of meaning".[36] We discover also that we have an ambiguous relation to Being, because we are both part of it and yet not part in the way that objects are. The essential role of our bodies in our experience of the world is crucial here, for our bodies are both objects in the world, which can be perceived like other objects, and at the same time the means by which we perceive things. Merleau-Ponty frequently points to the way in which our bodies can be both touched and touching, or seen and seeing, as when one hand touches another, or when we shake hands with someone, so that we are both being touched and touching. This illustrates the dual status of the body, as both the means by which we make a world (by for instance arranging things in a way we find coherent) and the way in which we are passively affected by the world. The body, as our intermediary with the world, is not a thing, but, as Merleau-Ponty puts it, a "sensible for itself",[37] something that is both perceived by the senses and has being-for-itself in the way that the other philosophies mentioned above reserve for consciousness. Merleau-Ponty frequently speaks of the "flesh of the visible", explaining that what he means is "that carnal being, as a being of depths . . . is a prototype of Being, of which our body, the sensible sentient, is a very remarkable variant".[38] Flesh is later described as "the coiling over of the visible upon the seeing body, of the tangible upon the touching body",[39] and on the next page as "the concrete emblem of a general manner of being". The body's possibility of being touched as well as touching expresses the general way in which we are in the world as embodied beings, acting upon things and at the same time being acted upon by them.

The notion of dialectic seems peculiarly appropriate to describe our relations to our world, for dialectical thought spurns sharp dichotomies (between the for-itself and the in-itself, for example) and aims to show how the truth of one term of the dichotomy can be fully grasped only when seen as forming a whole with the other term, even if the formation of such a whole seems to be precluded by the incompatibility of the two terms. Dialectical thought, Merleau-Ponty says, "is that which admits that each term is itself only by proceeding toward the opposite term, becomes what it is through the movement".[40] We can have being-for-ourselves only through being conscious of a world of the in-itself; but at the same time, there can be a *world* of the in-itself only because that is the meaning that beings have for our consciousness and our action. The for-itself becomes what it is by "moving towards" the in-itself, and vice versa for the in-itself.

In the same way, we can consider our relations with other subjects in dialectical fashion. Non-dialectical thought makes a sharp dichotomy between ourselves and others, between our immediate access to ourselves and our lack of access to the inner lives of others. But if I am unable to be aware of others as other *subjects*, then I can regard them only as objects in my world. To say that, however, is to say that my world is the only world, since what distinguishes my world from "the" world is that the latter is open to the gaze of subjects other than me. I myself am not therefore open to the world, and I cannot distinguish myself as a "for-itself" from a world of objects in-themselves. Once again, non-dialectical thought fails to explain the perceptual faith, and once again the fault lies with the assumption that we can simply "withdraw into" ourselves, as if our consciousness were an inner realm quite separate from the outer realm. We have rather to start again from the understanding that any for-itself becomes what it is by moving towards a world, and hence towards a world that it shares with other subjects. In becoming aware of myself as a conscious being, I am necessarily aware of other selves with whom I share the world.

The problem with such dialectical thought in the history of philosophy has been that it can never formulate what it is saying into definite theses without ceasing to be dialectical, for definite theses reinstate the very dichotomies that it was seeking to avoid. It is a "bad dialectic" that works in the manner of the textbook descriptions of Hegel's philosophy, proceeding through "thesis" and "antithesis", which are then reconciled in the form of a "synthesis". A "good" dialectic, indeed a good philosophy, will not attempt in this way to offer *solutions*, to resolve the contradictions. Philosophy will be one of the "artefacts [Merleau-Ponty uses the English word here] of culture", involving a creative use of language (here we can again see similarities with some of the remarks in "Eye and Mind", discussed in Chapter 7, on which he was working at the same time). Philosophy is "the perceptual faith questioning itself about itself";[41] it is part of the very nature of human existence that we are perpetually interrogating ourselves about that existence, taking our bearings in our situation in the world, but not aiming at *knowledge* of any new facts or *answers* to any cognitive problems. Philosophy is that self-questioning at its most fundamental level. Our situation in the world is not purely cognitive; we are not what Merleau-Ponty sometimes calls by the Greek word "*kosmotheoros*" ("world-spectator"). Our situation is one of active involvement with things and so with other human beings, and "taking our bearings" is therefore not simply a matter of formulating propositions. The question remains, however – and it is one to which Merleau-Ponty does not seem to have given an answer in this last work – what this philosophical taking of bearings *is*, and so how philosophical reflection upon the perceptual faith differs from a mere presentation of it.

III

Much of what Merleau-Ponty says in *The Visible and the Invisible* does not seem all that different from what he had been saying throughout his philosophical career. He emphasizes that human being is being-in-the-world, and that it is therefore necessarily embodied. The body is again described as playing an ambiguous role in our experience, both subject and object, both acting upon objects and being acted upon by them. Our experience as embodied is once more presented as perspectival; we survey the world, or Being, necessarily from where we are, and in the light of our own projects. Things appear to us, for example, as behind each other, as more or less distant from ourselves, and so on; and things appear to us as having a *meaning*, related to our bodily dealings with them. Merleau-Ponty makes the interesting point at one place that "Only at very great distances are the things it [vision] gives us pure things, identical to themselves and wholly positive, like the stars",[42] which I take to mean that things only become things in the full sense, have being in-themselves, when they are far enough removed from our bodies to have no practical meaning for us.

Being-in-the-world also implies, in *The Visible and the Invisible* as in earlier works, being in a *common* world, a world that I share with other similar beings. I could not, Merleau-Ponty argues, have an opening on to the world at all if I were a pure being-for-myself, an enclosed Cartesian consciousness. Because my opening on to the world depends on my embodiment, it follows that, first, I am not a pure, self-transparent subject, so that part of my own being is opaque to me; and, secondly, that I am necessarily aware of other similarly embodied subjects as sharing the world with me (otherwise, it would not be a *world*). As embodied beings, he also repeats in this last work, we are in time and space, we are historical beings, with a past, a present and a future that cannot be understood except in relation to each other. And, as we have seen in the last section, he reiterates that philosophy's task is not to *explain* what he here calls the "perceptual faith" that all our experience is rooted in a direct and pre-reflective contact with Being, but to elucidate it and explore its meaning.

If there is so much in common between Merleau-Ponty's last work and his earlier writings, however, what becomes of the claim that in his later thought he was developing in a new direction? It is still possible to make that claim, but we need to understand precisely what the novelty consisted in. What is new, in my view at least, is not so much the detailed content of what Merleau-Ponty had to say – that, as I have tried to show, had not significantly changed – but rather the way in which that content is presented, but this is not a mere trivial difference of style, since the way in which a philosophy is presented makes a significant difference to the philosophy itself. What Merleau-Ponty was dissatisfied with in his earlier works was that the framework in which the doctrine was presented in his view reduced the radicalism of the doctrine itself, and even in some ways distorted that doctrine. That framework was that of phenomenology, as modified in the later work of Husserl, but nevertheless still conceived as a science of essences, arrived at by the study of "phenomena", the appearances of things to consciousness.

We can recall the passage from the "Working Notes" cited earlier in which he ascribed the insolubility of the problems of *Phenomenology of Perception* to the fact that he had started in that work from the "consciousness"–"object" distinction (for reference, see note 24). That conception of philosophy itself now seemed, as I read him, to cut across his own aim of reinstating direct, pre-reflective perception of the world as the necessary foundation of any account of our relation to our world. By distinguishing between consciousness and its objects, it made it seem that our being was not, as Merleau-Ponty himself wanted to say, being-in-the-world, in which consciousness came to itself only by reaching out to objects, and so could not exist independently of objects. And then all the other characteristic things that Merleau-Ponty wanted to say, and which have been briefly summarized at the beginning of this section, seemed to be undermined. What was needed, therefore, was to abandon the description of what he was doing as "phenomenology", and to start from a new point, from what Merleau-Ponty refers to as "ontology". By this, he seems to have meant, as said above, the attempt to set out the nature of subjectivity and objectivity, the manner of being of subjects and objects, the aim of doing so being to put these same characteristic doctrines on a sounder footing in a better account of our situation in the world.

Part of the interest in understanding the nature of Merleau-Ponty's new direction in his last works comes from the need to "place" his thought in relation to the development of philosophy in France after his death. The better-known later French philosophers also abandoned transcendental phenomenology and the conception of philosophy as studying the contents of human consciousness (although, like Merleau-Ponty himself or the later Husserl, they may have remained "phenomenologists" in a looser sense, as philosophers of concrete lived experience). They lost interest in human subjectivity, and turned their attention to language, which they interpreted in a Saussurean way: meaning was determined not by a relation of signs to the world, but by the difference between one sign and another within a system of signs (with the consequence, as some would say, that meaning was perpetually "deferred", since the system could never be completed). Merleau-Ponty too, as we have seen, was much taken in his last years by Saussurean linguistics, by the notion of "difference", and by the rejection of the idea that the rule-governed semantics of institutionalized language, which gives each sign a precise meaning, was the only or the most interesting model for understanding language-meaning. His doctrine of the "body-subject", and rejection of the notion of the fully transparent subject, moreover, meant that, throughout his career, and not just in his final years, he shifted attention away from the human subject as central to philosophical understanding, in the way it had been thought to be since Descartes and the Enlightenment.

Does this mean that Merleau-Ponty in his last works was shifting to a position closer to that of the "structuralists" and "post-structuralists" of later French philosophy? The answer to that question is not straightforward. There is a sense in which Merleau-Ponty had *never* been a fully fledged phenomenologist, no matter what he himself thought. Or perhaps it would be better to say that he had always been pushing against the limits of phenomenology; he had found in the later works of Husserl the idea of the life-world, which attracted him because it seemed to correspond with much that he wanted to say about the nature of human existence and our place in the world. Because Husserl presented this as a development within phenomenology, Merleau-Ponty took over a phenomenological language in which to express his own thoughts. But by the end of his life he had come to realize the inadequacy of phenomenology, at least as Husserl had originally understood it, to encompass what he wanted to say, and was seeking (without ultimate success, as I suggested above) for an alternative. In one sense, then, he had not shifted his position, since his fundamental views were unchanged; in another, he had, since, as he himself would say, the way in which a philosophical view is expressed affects the character of the view itself. His views had never been "humanist", in the sense in which that became a dirty word in later French philosophy; that is, he had never placed the contents of explicit consciousness at the centre of philosophy, or thought of "reason" as timeless truths accessible to that pure consciousness. But he always remained a "humanist" in the more important sense that he saw the problems of philosophy as arising from the very structure of human existence, from the need to "get our bearings" in a world that we shall never fully understand. His reflections on those problems remain a permanently valuable contribution to philosophy.

Notes

Chapter One: Merleau-Ponty in Context

1. J.-P. Sartre, "Merleau-Ponty *vivant*", reprinted in J. Stewart (ed.), *The Debate Between Sartre and Merleau-Ponty* (Evanston, Ill.: Northwestern University Press, 1998), p. 566.
2. *Ibid.*, p. 565.
3. E. Husserl, *The Crisis of European Sciences and Transcendental Phenomenology*, D. Carr (trans.) (Evanston, Ill.: Northwestern University Press, 1970).
4. Merleau-Ponty, *In Praise of Philosophy and Other Essays*, J. Wild, J. M. Edie and J. O'Neill (trans.) (Evanston, Ill.: Northwestern University Press, 1988).
5. Merleau-Ponty, *In Praise of Philosophy*, p. 30.
6. Merleau-Ponty, *The Structure of Behaviour*, A. L. Fisher (trans.) (London: Methuen, 1965), p. 3.
7. Sartre, "Merleau-Ponty *vivant*", p. 567.
8. *Ibid.*, p. 568.
9. Cf. e.g. Merleau-Ponty, *Phenomenology of Perception*, C. Smith (trans.), with revisions by F. Williams and D. Gurrière (London: Routledge, 1989), pp. 52–3.
10. K. Marx, *Eighteenth Brumaire of Louis Bonaparte*, quoted from L. S. Feuer (ed.), *Marx and Engels: Basic Writings on Politics and Philosophy* (Glasgow: Collins, The Fontana Library, 1969), p. 360.
11. Cf. Sartre, "Merleau-Ponty *vivant*", p. 578.
12. Reprinted in his collection *Signs*, R. C. McCleary (trans.) (Evanston, Ill.: Northwestern University Press, 1964), pp. 263–73.
13. Sartre, "Merleau-Ponty *vivant*", p. 594.
14. *Ibid.*, p. 601.
15. *Ibid.*, p. 599.
16. Merleau-Ponty, *The Adventures of the Dialectic*, J. Bien (trans.) (Evanston, Ill.: Northwestern University Press, 1973).
17. *Ibid.*, p. 29.
18. *Ibid.*
19. *Ibid.*, pp. 97–8.
20. *Ibid.*, p. 98.
21. *Ibid.*, p. 100.
22. J.-P. Sartre, *Being and Nothingness*, H. E. Barnes (trans.) (London: Routledge, 1989; previously published by Methuen), p. 58.
23. *Ibid.*, p. 489.

24. Merleau-Ponty, *The Adventures of the Dialectic*, p. 198.
25. See note 4 above.
26. Merleau-Ponty, *Sense and Non-Sense*, H. L. Dreyfus and P. Allen Dreyfus (trans.) (Evanston, Ill.: Northwestern University Press, 1964); and Merleau-Ponty, *Signs*.
27. Merleau-Ponty, *Sense and Non-Sense*, p. 4.
28. Summarized in *Themes from the Lectures at the Collège de France, 1952–1960*, first published in French in 1968 and in an English translation by John O'Neill in 1970; the English translation is now included in Merleau-Ponty, *In Praise of Philosophy*.
29. Merleau-Ponty, *Signs*, p. 3.
30. "Editor's Preface", in Merleau-Ponty, *The Prose of the World*, J. O'Neill (trans.) (Evanston, Ill.: Northwestern University Press, 1973), p. xi.
31. See "An Unpublished Text by Maurice Merleau-Ponty: *A Prospectus of His Work*", A. B. Dallery (trans.), in *The Primacy of Perception and Other Essays*, J. M. Edie (ed.) (Evanston, Ill.: Northwestern University Press, 1964), pp. 3–11.
32. "An Unpublished Text", pp.8–9.
33. See Merleau-Ponty, *Signs*, pp. 39–83.
34. "An Unpublished Text", pp. 8–9.
35. *Ibid.*, p. 3.
36. Merleau-Ponty, *The Prose of the World*, p. 31.
37. *Ibid.*, p. 103.
38. *Ibid.*
39. Merleau-Ponty, *The Visible and the Invisible*, A. Lingis (trans.) (Evanston, Ill.: Northwestern University Press, 1968), p. 274.
40. Cf. Merleau-Ponty, *Phenomenology of Perception*, p. ix.
41. Paul Ricoeur, "Hommage à Merleau-Ponty", *Esprit* **29**, June 1961, 6.

Chapter Two: Phenomenology

1. M. Heidegger, *Being and Time*, J. Macquarrie and E. Robinson (trans.) (New York: Harper and Row, 1962), p. 58.
2. E. Husserl, *The Crisis of European Sciences and Transcendental Phenomenology*, D. Carr (trans.) (Evanston, Ill.: Northwestern University Press, 1970), p. xxv.
3. Cf. Husserl, *The Crisis of European Sciences*, p. 50.
4. Cf. *ibid.*, p. 79.
5. Cf. *ibid.*, p. 80.
6. Merleau-Ponty, *Phenomenology of Perception*, p. xv.
7. *Ibid.*, p. vii.
8. *Ibid.*, p. viii.
9. *Ibid.*, p. ix.
10. Cf. *ibid.*, p. xiii (quoting Husserl).
11. *Ibid.*
12. *Ibid.*, p. xiv.
13. *Ibid.*
14. *Ibid.*, p. xv.
15. *Ibid.*
16. *Ibid.*
17. *Ibid.*, p.xvii.
18. *Ibid.*, pp.xvi–xvii.
19. *Ibid.*, p. xviii.
20. *Ibid.*, p. xx.

21. *Ibid.*
22. *Ibid.*, p. viii.
23. A. de Waelhens, "A Philosophy of the Ambiguous", in Merleau-Ponty, *The Structure of Behaviour*, pp. xviii–xxvii.

Chapter Three: Being-in-the-world

1. Merleau-Ponty, *Phenomenology of Perception*, p. xx.
2. See T. Nagel, *The View from Nowhere* (Oxford and New York: Oxford University Press, 1986).
3. See B. Williams, *Descartes: The Project of Pure Enquiry* (Harmondsworth: Penguin, 1978), esp. pp. 64–6.
4. "The Primacy of Perception and Its Philosophical Consequences", in *The Primacy of Perception*, pp. 12–42.
5. Merleau-Ponty, "The Primacy of Perception", p. 13.
6. For arguments along these lines, cf. John Searle's criticism of the phenomenology of Heidegger and Hubert Dreyfus in his paper "The Limits of Phenomenology", in M. Wrathall and J. Malpas (eds), *Heidegger and Cognitive Science, Essays in Honor of Hubert L. Dreyfus, Vol. 2* (Cambridge, Mass. and London: MIT Press, 2000), pp. 71–92, esp. Section III.
7. Merleau-Ponty, *Phenomenology of Perception*, p. 57.
8. *Ibid.*, p. 58.
9. Merleau-Ponty, "The Primacy of Perception", p. 12.
10. Cf. J. Locke:

> The mind ... takes notice also, that a certain number of these simple ideas go constantly together; which being presumed to belong to one thing ... are called, so united in one subject, by one name; which, *by inadvertency* [my italics], we are apt afterward to talk of, and consider as one simple idea ...: because, as I have said, not imagining how these simple ideas can subsist by themselves, we *accustom ourselves* [my italics], to suppose some *substratum*, wherein they do subsist ... which therefore we call *substance*.
>
> (*Essay concerning Human Understanding*, II.XXIII. 1)

11. Merleau-Ponty, *Phenomenology of Perception*, p. 4.
12. *Ibid.*
13. *Ibid.*, p. 15.
14. M. Heidegger, "Letter on Humanism", in Heidegger, *Basic Writings*, D. Farrell Krell (ed.) (London: Routledge and Kegan Paul, 1978), p. 197.
15. Heidegger, "Letter on Humanism", p. 199.
16. Cf. T. Nagel who, in his *The View from Nowhere* (see above, note 2), p. 40, moves from a tenable view that "The brain, but not the rest of the animal, is essential to the self" (i.e. is a necessary condition for having a self) to the unjustified conclusion that "I am my brain" (although he does at least accept that the latter statement is a "mild exaggeration").
17. R. Descartes, *Sixth Meditation*, in *René Descartes: Meditations on First Philosophy, With Selections from the Objections and Replies*, J. Cottingham (trans.) (Cambridge: Cambridge University Press, 1986), p. 54.
18. Descartes, *Second Meditation*, in *René Descartes: Meditations*, pp. 22–3.
19. Merleau-Ponty, *Phenomenology of Perception*, p. 50.
20. *Ibid.*, p. 55.
21. *Ibid.*, p. 57.

22. See *ibid.*, p. 34.
23. *Ibid.*, p. 53.
24. *Ibid.*, p. 52.
25. *Ibid.*, pp. xvi–xvii.
26. *Ibid.*, p. xx.
27. Cf. *ibid.*, p. ix.
28. *Ibid.*, p. 52.
29. *Ibid.*, p. 62.
30. *Ibid.*, p. 5.

Chapter Four: Embodiment and Human Action

1. Merleau-Ponty, *Phenomenology of Perception*, p. 203.
2. Compare the programme of such recent philosophers as the Churchlands to replace what they call "folk psychology" (which uses such concepts as "motive", "desire", "intention", etc.) with a more scientific psychology using only such neurological concepts as "neurone-firing", "neurotransmitters" and the like. See for example P. M. Churchland's paper "Eliminative Materialism and the Propositional Attitudes", *Journal of Philosophy*, **LXXVIII(2)** (February 1981), pp. 67–90.
3. Merleau-Ponty, *The Structure of Behaviour*.
4. *Ibid.*, p. 3.
5. *Ibid.*, p. 4.
6. *Ibid.*
7. *Ibid.*, p. 3.
8. *Ibid.*, p. 4.
9. Cf. *ibid.*, p. 4.
10. *Ibid.*, p. 9.
11. *Ibid.*, p. 13.
12. *Ibid.*, p. 40.
13. See *ibid.*
14. P. Guillaume, *La Formation des habitudes* (Paris: Alcan, 1936), p. 69, quoted in Merleau-Ponty, *Structure of Behaviour*, p. 100.
15. Merleau-Ponty, *Structure of Behaviour*, p. 122.
16. *Ibid.*, p. 20.
17. Merleau-Ponty, *Phenomenology of Perception*, p. 76.
18. *Ibid.*
19. See *ibid.*, pp. 77–8.
20. *Ibid.*, p. 79.
21. *Ibid.*, p. 108.
22. *Ibid.*
23. *Ibid.*, p. 106.
24. Gelb and Goldstein, *Zur Psychologie des optischen Wahrnehmungs-und-Erkennungsvorganges* (Leipzig: Barth, 1920), p. 77, quoted in Merleau-Ponty, *Phenomenology of Perception*, p. 113 n. 2.
25. Merleau-Ponty, *Phenomenology of Perception*, p. 108.
26. *Ibid.*, p. 156.
27. *Ibid.*, p. 137.
28. See *ibid.*, p. 168.
29. *Ibid.*, p. 167.
30. Merleau-Ponty, *The Structure of Behaviour*, p. 177.
31. See *ibid.*, p. 178.

32. There are similarities between Merleau-Ponty's interpretation of Freudianism and that of Paul Ricoeur: see Ricoeur, *Freud and Philosophy: An Essay on Interpretation*, D. Savage (trans.) (New Haven and London: Yale University Press, 1970).

Chapter Five: Self and Others

1. See Merleau-Ponty, *Phenomenology of Perception*, p. 378.
2. *Ibid.*, p. 376.
3. *Ibid.*, p. 381.
4. *Ibid.*, p. 379.
5. *Ibid.*, p. 405.
6. *Ibid.*, p. 349.
7. *Ibid.*, p. 238.
8. *Ibid.*, p. 410.
9. *Ibid.*, p. 415.
10. Cf. the heading of part 3, chapter 2 of Merleau-Ponty, *Phenomenology of Perception*, p. 410: the French word "*sens*" in the Claudel quotation, which I have translated as "direction", is ambiguous: it can also mean "meaning" or "sense". Claudel indicates in the continuation of the quotation that he is exploiting this ambiguity.
11. See D. Parfit, *Reasons and Persons* (Oxford: Oxford University Press, 1984), and elsewhere.
12. Merleau-Ponty, *Sense and Non-Sense*, p. 25.
13. See Sartre, *Being and Nothingness*, p. 489.
14. Merleau-Ponty, *Phenomenology of Perception*, pp. 436–7.
15. Sartre, *Being and Nothingness*, p. 3.
16. Merleau-Ponty, *Phenomenology of Perception*, p. 442.
17. *Ibid.*, p. 356.
18. *Ibid.*, p. 359.
19. Cf. Merleau-Ponty, *Phenomenology of Perception*, p. 170.
20. *Ibid.*, pp. 170–71.
21. *Ibid.*, p. 171 n.
22. K. Marx and F. Engels, *The Communist Manifesto*, S. Moore (trans.), with a preface by A. J. P. Taylor (Harmondsworth: Penguin, 1967), p. 79.
23. Merleau-Ponty, *Phenomenology of Perception*, p. 443.
24. *Ibid.*, p. 445.
25. See *ibid.*, p. 456.
26. Merleau-Ponty, *Sense and Non-Sense*, p. 3.
27. *Ibid.*, p. 65.
28. *Ibid.*, p. 63.
29. Cf. *ibid.*, p. 164.

Chapter Six: Politics in Theory and Practice

1. Sartre, "Merleau-Ponty *vivant*", p. 566.
2. Merleau-Ponty, *Sense and Non-Sense*, p. 172.
3. Cf. Merleau-Ponty, "Faith and Good Faith", reprinted in *Sense and Non-Sense*, p. 177.
4. A. Kojève, *Introduction à la Lecture de Hegel*, assembled by Raymond Queneau (Paris: Gallimard, 1947); published in English as *Introduction to the Reading of Hegel*, J. H. Nichols, Jr. (trans.) (New York: Basic Books, 1969).
5. Merleau-Ponty, *Sense and Non-Sense*, p. 133.

6. *Ibid.*, p. 134.
7. Merleau-Ponty, *Humanism and Terror: The Communist Problem*, J. O'Neill (trans.) (New Brunswick, NJ and London: Transaction Publishers, 2000), p. xxi (original publication of the English translation, New York: Beacon Press, 1969).
8. *Ibid.*, p. xxiv.
9. Merleau-Ponty, "For the Sake of Truth", in *Sense and Non-Sense*, p. 162.
10. Merleau-Ponty, *Humanism and Terror*, p. xxiii.
11. Merleau-Ponty, "For the Sake of Truth", p. 165.
12. On this see Sartre, "Merleau-Ponty *vivant*", p. 583.
13. Merleau-Ponty, *Humanism and Terror*, p. xxxviii.
14. Merleau-Ponty, *Adventures of the Dialectic*, p. 5.
15. Lukács, quoted in *ibid.*, p. 31.
16. *Ibid.*, p. 39.
17. *Ibid.*, p. 61.
18. *Ibid.*, p. 65.
19. Quoted in *ibid.*, p. 97.
20. *Ibid.*, p. 165.
21. *Ibid.*, p. 204.
22. *Ibid.*, p. 226.
23. Merleau-Ponty, *Sense and Non-Sense*, p. 4.

Chapter 7: The Arts

1. Merleau-Ponty, *Phenomenology of Perception*, p. xx.
2. *Ibid.*, p. 322.
3. Merleau-Ponty, "Cézanne's Doubt", in *Sense and Non-Sense*, p. 14.
4. Cf. Merleau-Ponty, "Eye and Mind", reprinted in *The Primacy of Perception*, pp. 171ff.
5. Merleau-Ponty, "The Film and the New Psychology", in *Sense and Non-Sense*, p. 58.
6. Merleau-Ponty, "Metaphysics and the Novel", in *Sense and Non-Sense*, pp. 27–8.
7. Merleau-Ponty, *Phenomenology of Perception*, p. 393.
8. See *ibid.*, pp. 307ff.
9. Merleau-Ponty, "Eye and Mind", p. 166.
10. Merleau-Ponty, *Phenomenology of Perception*, pp. 318–19.
11. *Ibid.*, pp. 233–4.
12. Merleau-Ponty, *The Structure of Behaviour*, p. 176.
13. Merleau-Ponty, *Phenomenology of Perception*, p. 391.
14. Merleau-Ponty, "Cézanne's Doubt", p. 19.
15. Merleau-Ponty, *Phenomenology of Perception*, p. 151.
16. Merleau-Ponty, "Cézanne's Doubt", p. 19.
17. *Ibid.*, p.16.
18. Merleau-Ponty, "Marxism and Philosophy", in *Sense and Non-Sense*, p. 132.
19. Merleau-Ponty, "The Film and the New Psychology", p. 54.
20. *Ibid.*, p. 57.
21. *Ibid.*, p. 57.
22. Merleau-Ponty, *Phenomenology of Perception*, p. 425.
23. Merleau-Ponty, "Metaphysics and the Novel", p. 32.
24. *Ibid.*, p.39.
25. *Ibid.*, p.40.
26. Merleau-Ponty, "Eye and Mind", p. 177.
27. *Ibid.*, p. 161.
28. *Ibid.*, p. 189.

29. *Ibid.*, p. 181.
30. *Ibid.*, p. 162.
31. Cf. Merleau-Ponty, *The Primacy of Perception*, p. 164.
32. Merleau-Ponty, "Eye and Mind", p. 166.
33. *Ibid.*

Chapter Eight: The Later Thought

1. Merleau-Ponty, *Éloge de la Philosophie* (Paris: Gallimard, 1953); published in English as *In Praise of Philosophy*, J. Wild and J. Edie (trans.) (Evanston, Ill.: Northwestern University Press, 1963).
2. Merleau-Ponty, *Résumés de cours, Collège de France, 1952–1960* (Paris: Gallimard, 1968); published in English as *Themes from the Lectures at the Collège de France, 1952–1960*, J. O'Neill (trans.) (Evanston, Ill.: Northwestern University Press, 1970). *In Praise of Philosophy* and *Themes from the Lectures* have now been published together in a single volume, by the same publisher, 1988.
3. Merleau-Ponty, "An Unpublished Text by Maurice Merleau-Ponty", p. 3.
4. *Ibid.*, p. 8.
5. J.-P. Sartre, *What is Literature?*, B. Frechtman (trans.) (London and New York: Routledge, 1993).
6. "Editor's Preface" to Merleau-Ponty, *The Prose of the World*, C. Lefort (ed.), J. O'Neill (trans.) (Evanston, Ill.: Northwestern University Press, 1973), p. xi.
7. Merleau-Ponty, "Indirect Language and the Voices of Silence", in *Signs*, pp. 39–83.
8. Merleau-Ponty, *The Prose of the World*, p. 5.
9. *Ibid.*
10. *Ibid.*, p. 10.
11. *Ibid.*, p. 12.
12. *Ibid.*, p. 17.
13. *Ibid.*, p. 30.
14. *Ibid.*, p. 31.
15. Merleau-Ponty, "Indirect Language and the Voices of Silence", p. 42.
16. *Ibid.*, p. 43.
17. See Merleau-Ponty, *The Prose of the World*, p. 103.
18. *Ibid.*, p. 51.
19. *Ibid.*, p. 78.
20. *Ibid.*, p. 87.
21. *Ibid.*, p. 101.
22. *Ibid.*, p. 113.
23. *Ibid.*, p. 117.
24. Merleau-Ponty, *The Visible and the Invisible*, C. Lefort (ed.), A. Lingis (trans.) (Evanston, Ill.: Northwestern University Press, 1968), p. 165.
25. *Ibid.*, p. 200.
26. Cf. *ibid.*, p. 171 (note of February, 1959).
27. *Ibid.*, p. 4.
28. *Ibid.*, p. 3.
29. *Ibid.*, p. 59.
30. *Ibid.*, pp. 64–5.
31. *Ibid.*, p. 68.
32. *Ibid.*
33. *Ibid.*, p. 125.
34. *Ibid.*, p. 130.

35. *Ibid.*, p. 120.
36. *Ibid.*, p. 107.
37. *Ibid.*, p. 135.
38. *Ibid.*, p. 136.
39. *Ibid.*, p. 146.
40. *Ibid.*, pp. 90–91.
41. *Ibid.*, p. 103.
42. *Ibid.*, p. 83.

Bibliography

Works by Merleau-Ponty (in English translation)

Works are given in alphabetical order of their English titles.

Adventures of the Dialectic, J. Bien (trans.). Evanston, Ill.: Northwestern University Press, 1973.

Consciousness and the Acquisition of Language, H. Silverman (trans.). Evanston, Ill.: Northwestern University Press, 1973.

Humanism and Terror: An Essay on the Communist Problem, John O'Neill (trans.). Boston: Beacon Press, 1985.

Phenomenology of Perception, C. Smith (trans.), with revisions by F. Williams and D. Gurrière. London: Routledge, 1989.

In Praise of Philosophy and Other Essays, J. Wild, J. Edie and J. O'Neill (trans.). Evanston, Ill.: Northwestern University Press, 1988.

The Primacy of Perception and Other Essays, J. M. Edie (ed.). Evanston, Ill.: Northwestern University Press, 1964.

The Prose of the World, John O'Neill (trans.). Evanston, Ill.: Northwestern University Press, 1973.

Sense and Non-Sense, H. L. Dreyfus and P. A. Dreyfus (trans.). Evanston, Ill.: Northwestern University Press, 1964.

Signs, R. C. McCleary (trans.). Evanston, Ill.: Northwestern University Press, 1964.

The Structure of Behaviour, A. L. Fisher (trans.). Boston, Mass.: Beacon Press, 1963 and London: Methuen, 1965.

Texts and Dialogues on Philosophy, Politics and Culture, H. J. Silverman and J. Barry Jr. (eds). Amherst, NY: Humanity Books, 1992.

The Visible and the Invisible, A. Lingis (trans.). Evanston, Ill.: Northwestern University Press, 1968.

A useful work containing material by and about Merleau-Ponty is *The Debate between Sartre and Merleau-Ponty*, J. Stewart (ed.). Evanston, Ill.: Northwestern University Press, 1998.

Useful background reading

Bannan, J. F. 1967. *The Philosophy of Merleau-Ponty*. New York: Harcourt, Brace and World.

Dillon, M. C. 1997. *Merleau-Ponty's Ontology*, 2nd edn. Evanston, Ill.: Northwestern University Press.

Gutting, G. 2001. *French Philosophy in the Twentieth Century*. Cambridge: Cambridge University Press.

Langan, T. 1966. *Merleau-Ponty's Critique of Reason*. New Haven, Conn.: Yale University Press.

Langer, M. 1989. *Merleau-Ponty's Phenomenology of Perception: A Guide and Commentary*. Basingstoke: Macmillan.

Madison, G. B. 1981. *The Phenomenology of Merleau-Ponty*. Athens, Ohio: Ohio University Press.

Mallin, S. B. 1979. *Merleau-Ponty's Philosophy*. New Haven, Conn.: Yale University Press.

Matthews, E. 1996. *Twentieth Century French Philosophy*. Oxford: Oxford University Press.

Moran, D. 2000. *Introduction to Phenomenology*. London: Routledge.

O'Neill, J. 1970. *Perception, Expression and History: The Social Phenomenology of Maurice Merleau-Ponty*. Evanston, Ill.: Northwestern University Press.

Priest, S. 1988. *Merleau-Ponty*. London: Routledge.

Rabil, A. 1967. *Merleau-Ponty: Existentialist of the Social World*. New York: Columbia University Press.

Whiteside, K. H. 1988. *Merleau-Ponty and the Foundations of an Existential Politics*. Princeton, NJ: Princeton University Press.

Index